Liberating Education

Zelda F. Gamson
and Associates

Nancy B. Black
Jamie Beth Catlin
Patrick J. Hill
Michael R. Mills
John Nichols
Terry Heitz Rogers

Afterword by David Riesman

Liberating Education

 Jossey-Bass Publishers

San Francisco • Washington • London • 1984

LIBERATING EDUCATION
by Zelda F. Gamson and Associates

Copyright © 1984 by: Jossey-Bass Inc., Publishers
433 California Street
San Francisco, California 94104
&
Jossey-Bass Limited
28 Banner Street
London EC1Y 8QE

Library of Congress Cataloging in Publication Data

Gamson, Zelda F.
     Liberating education.

     Includes bibliographical references and index.
     1. Educational innovations—United States—Addresses,
essays, lectures. 2. Education, Higher—United States—
Addresses, essays, lectures. 3. Education, Humanistic—
United States—Addresses, essays, lectures. 4. Academic
freedom—United States—Addresses, essays, lectures.
I. Black, Nancy B.
LB1027.G286   1984   378.73   83-49260
ISBN 0-87589-603-0

Manufactured in the United States of America

The paper in this book meets the guidelines for
permanence and durability of the Committee on
Production Guidelines for Book Longevity of the
Council on Library Resources.

JACKET DESIGN BY WILLI BAUM

FIRST EDITION

Code 8405

The Jossey-Bass
Higher Education Series

In memory of
Albert Mullen and Anita Mishler—
loving teachers, inspired friends

Contents

Preface

A twenty-eight-year-old shipping clerk from Queens, New York: "You become more active, more aware of people. You can change. You become sensitive and objective. You can take a stand. You become positive about life. If something goes wrong, you don't blame yourself."

A nineteen-year-old male from Long Island: "There's a line in an old Stevie Wonder song that says if you believe things you don't understand, you will suffer. Well, here you have a chance to understand. I don't take things at face value anymore. I go and I question."

A twenty-one-year-old woman from Winnetka, Illinois: "I can dispute facts with my friends. I realize that the men I know take too much for granted—assuming that housekeeping is for women, for instance. I am also beginning to understand the speech patterns of women: the coy young thing, being manipulative, acting dumb and naive."

These testimonials are not about the latest therapy. They are about something more modest—education. How could such feeling lie behind thinking? How could going to school be so full of life?

To answer these questions, we must experience education as these students do, along with the teachers and administrators in the schools that are the subject of this book. Although
we can visit only a small fraction of the 3,000 colleges and universities in this country, we can turn to many books and articles
on higher education. And what do they tell us? Higher education is an industry in decline, general education is a disaster
area, and faculty members are bored and unmotivated.

This gloomy picture may apply to some colleges and universities, but it does not hold for the ones in this book. On the
contrary, my own experience as an observer and participant on
the higher education scene leads me to a more optimistic view.
In travels to colleges and universities across the country, I have
encountered faculty members who are getting a new lease on
life by teaching undergraduates and planning new curricula
(Grant and others, 1979). I have come to know people in fourteen schools particularly well over the past few years, as a result
of a project on liberal education initiated by the Fund for the
Improvement of Postsecondary Education, a small agency in the
U.S. Department of Education that has provided support to different kinds of innovations in postsecondary education since
the early 1970s (Hendrix and Stoel, 1982). National Project IV,
as it was called, examined a wide variety of programs in liberal
education. First, it provided small grants to participants from
fourteen institutions for self-assessments. Second, it brought the
participants together regularly for discussions about what they
believed liberal education to be, for consultation about what
they were learning from the self-assessments, and for collaboration on questions of common interest. Third, it supplied them
with sympathetic but detached participants from a fifteenth
school who visited their campuses, brought them together periodically, gave them advice about how to do their self-assessments, asked difficult questions, and synthesized what they
learned.

I am one of the sympathetic but detached participants.
This book is the result of what I learned, as I worked collaboratively with four staff members and twenty participants in National Project IV. Most of the fourteen participating programs

are parts of larger institutions. (We, therefore, follow the convention throughout the book of referring to them as "programs" unless otherwise indicated). A diverse lot, as a group it represents students who are young and old, black and white, rich and poor, superbly prepared and abysmally prepared. We will come to know some of them well as the book proceeds. Resource A gives basic information about all the programs listed here:

- Brooklyn College: New School of Liberal Arts
- Hampshire College
- Hofstra University: Labor Institute of Applied Social Science
- Johnson State College: External Degree Program
- University of Nebraska at Lincoln: University Studies Program
- New York City Technical College: Institute of Study for Older Adults
- Northern Virginia Community College at Manassas: Project Intertwine
- Northwestern University: Program on Women, Certificate in Women's Studies
- University of Oklahoma: College of Liberal Studies
- Radcliffe College: Radcliffe Seminars
- Saint Joseph's College: Core
- State University of New York, College at Old Westbury: African-American Music Program
- State University of New York at Stony Brook: Federated Learning Communities
- Talladega College

As we learn more about these programs, we will see how necessary it is to get underneath what often appear at first to be nothing more than pieties. We will have to penetrate pinched and lifeless educational jargon to find the real people involved in the programs. While it is unabashedly narrative, this book is not simply descriptive. It presents analyses that apply and integrate works from several streams in the higher education literature. By bringing attention to the realities of a variety of institutions and programs, we range over a number of topics that are typically treated more abstractly and separately. Thus, for example, much has been written lately about the undergraduate curriculum (The Carnegie Foundation for the Advancement of Teaching, 1977; Rudolph, 1977; Levine, 1978), about liberal education (Conrad and Wyer, 1980; Wegener, 1978; Brann, 1979; Schwab, 1978), and about general education (Gaff, 1983; Boyer and Levine, 1981). Teaching practices, faculty rewards, and faculty renewal have been topics of concern in the past decade (Shor, 1980; Eble, 1972; McKeachie, 1980). More attention lately is being given to institutional character and politics as they determine the undergraduate curriculum (Gaff, 1983; Gamson, 1979; Grant and Riesman, 1978). Student development and ways of measuring the impact of college have been the subject of intense concern over the past twenty years (Chickering, 1981; Bowen, 1977; Winter, McClelland, and Stewart, 1981; Perry, 1970; Astin, 1977; Feldman and Newcomb, 1969). Related are efforts to evaluate educational programs imaginatively (Forrest, 1981; Parlett and Dearden, 1977; Whitla, 1977). Our task here is at once more general and more concrete than most of these works. It encompasses curriculum, teaching, students, evaluation, institutional politics, and educational philosophy as they are experienced by the students, faculty members, and administrators in the programs we will get to know in this book.

Part One begins with the specter of Orwell's *1984,* the year of publication for this book. It asks whether higher education—liberal education in particular—can stand against the kind of world *1984* depicts. Chapter One, in a review of what has happened to the undergraduate curriculum in the past thirty years, suggests that a liberal education has lost its meaning. In words actually used in discussions and interviews in National Project IV, a "commission" composed of several participants and students explores how liberal education can be reformulated for the 1980s and beyond. The "commissioners" arrive at a conception of liberal education they call "liberating." A liberating education has three central aspects. First, it leads students to a broad critical awareness. Second, it helps them apply what they learn to everyday life. Third, it increases their sense of power. Chapters Two, Three, and Four illustrate each of these three aspects of liberating education with examples from National Project IV. These examples, like those throughout the book, draw freely from field notes staff members and I made on site visits to the various campuses, as well as from transcripts and tapes of conversations among the participants in National Project IV. (These excerpts are not footnoted in the text; all quotes that do not have specific citations are from these sources.)

Part Two turns to an analysis of how a liberating education can be constructed. By referring to the examples in Part One, as well as to others, it grounds teaching and curriculum in the philosophical and institutional contexts of several of the programs. In Chapter Five, we see that, despite their many differences, these programs have managed to create lively intellectual communities that include undergraduates as well as faculty members. They have done so because they recognize that education with real power is based on structures as well as philosophies. Structures constrain and direct what is taught and how. Chapter Six shows that teaching in a liberating program of study is demanding and requires high levels of active involvement and articulation from students. Chapter Seven argues that a curriculum in such a program will include many different subjects, including some that are not traditionally thought to be part of the liberal arts. It will try to maximize certain principles, however. It will try to be diverse in its scope, integrative in its structure, experiential in its basis, and critical in its attitude.

The creation and survival of such programs in difficult times opens Part Three on how to change. Chapter Eight, a review of several different programs in National Project IV, points to the danger inherent in an "enclave" approach. Ways of integrating programs for liberating education into their institutions must be pursued with tenacity. In addition, open-minded and regular evaluation is critical to their survival as well as to what and how they teach. Chapter Nine argues that liberating education needs evaluations that are cumulative, collaborative, contextual, and critical. The concluding chapter draws the implications of a liberating education for the reform of the undergraduate curriculum and for higher education in general. The book then returns to the preoccupation with which it began: the meaning of liberal education in social perspective.

Several resources are available to the reader at the end of the book. Resource A provides basic information about the fourteen programs and institutions. Resource B summarizes the approaches to self-assessment used by National Project IV participants. Resource C contains the protocol my staff and I followed in visits to the fourteen campuses.

Pudd'nhead Wilson tells us that few things are harder to put up with than the annoyance of a good example. I take his warning seriously and do not claim that the fourteen programs are paragons—far from it. They have made many mistakes and will make more in the future. But they do have a certain claim on our attention by virtue of the students they work with, the aims they hold up, and the successes they have achieved. Taken together, they represent a variety of approaches to extending higher education to new kinds of students and to deepening the impact of college on traditional kinds. On the whole, they have done so without compromising the quality of what and how they teach or the standards they use to judge student performance. They labor in the name of the most noble, idealistic traditions of higher education. Their work, like that of many others, may help to revitalize our institutions at a time when they are in dangerous decline.

We hope that the examples in this book will inspire teachers and administrators in all kinds of colleges and universities to examine what they do and to take heart, at a time when many of them feel disheartened about their own work and the future of higher education. We offer some encouragement and useful ideas to faculty members and administrators who must find ways of reaching new kinds of students or who may feel they are not doing the best they can with the old kinds. Schools in the process of examining their curriculums—and there are hundreds doing so right now—may find some support in this book for an expanded and renewed faith in education. Those who are suspicious of newfangled "innovations" and "open admissions" will be surprised to find that it is possible to have quality with equity. We hope, especially, that legislators and other policy makers, as well as teachers, other professionals, and members of the public, will see yet again that a democracy depends on a citizenry educated in the very best ways.

"Liberating education" can be read two ways. Put the stress on "liberating" and it means the kind of education that frees students. Put the stress on "education" and it means freeing educational institutions and the people who work in them.

Acknowledgments

While I take the final responsibility for this book and any errors it may contain, many people have shaped this book. For close to two years, the participants in National Project IV struggled with me and with each other about the meaning of what they were doing. They spent countless hours conducting their self-assessments, writing working papers, filling out questionnaires, attending meetings and conferences, arranging site visits, and writing reports. They are at once the subjects and the authors of this book, and I am deeply grateful to them for their perseverance. While I cannot name all the faculty members, administrators, and students on the fourteen campuses who were drawn into the orbit of National Project IV at one time or another, I can indulge myself in the small pleasure of naming the colleagues who officially represented them: from Brooklyn College, Kenneth Hey at the beginning, Arthur Margon through the first year, and Nancy Black throughout; Black is coauthor of Chapter Six and has remained an astute critic of other chapters in this volume; at Hampshire College, Robert von der Lippe and Nancy Lowry, a wry commentator on teaching and women in science; at Hofstra University, Bertram Silverman and Raymond Franklin, passionate spokesmen for equality; at Johnson State, Laurent Daloz, chronicler of the lives of ordinary people; at the University of Nebraska, Leslie Duley in the first year and Donal Burns in the second, witty critics of educational jargon; from New York City Community College, Maria Burgio, teacher and researcher among the elderly poor; at Northern Virginia Community College, Elizabeth Grizzard, protector of programs for the academically disenfranchised; at Northwestern University, Bari Watkins, historian, administrator, researcher, and teacher of women in higher education; from the University of Oklahoma, Elizabeth Bertinot the first year and Phyllis Colyer in the second, women with a broad understanding of education for adults; at Radcliffe College, Susan Bailey in the first year and Norma Ware in the second, quietly struggling for the equality of women; from Saint Joseph's College, John Nichols, coauthor of Chapter Seven and a master of synthesis; at the State University of New York at Old Westbury, Charlotte Lawrence and Kenneth McIntyre, graceful and tough minded; at the State University of New York at Stony Brook, Patrick Hill, another coauthor (Chapter Five) and a major influence on all aspects of the project and this book; from Talladega, Roland Braithwaite and Michael Floyd, a team that combined wisdom with technical proficiency.

Members of the advisory panel to National Project IV may have felt like fifth wheels at times, but their backing at certain moments was critical: William Perry, Jr., brought the project together emotionally at a critical moment in its history with his plain-speaking Yankee style and understanding of how people think. Herman Blake and Harriet Sheridan's tactful counsel redirected energies at several points. Eva Brann's close reading of several papers and participation in a meeting sharpened the focus of the project at a significant stage. Robert Blackburn, my colleague in the Center for the Study of Higher Education at the University of Michigan, acted as a project adviser and wrote an essay on the history of liberal education that informs Chapter Seven.

Richard Hendrix, the staff member from the Fund for the Improvement of Postsecondary Education responsible for National Project IV, began as a distant figure and ended a close colleague. Alison Bernstein at the beginning and Carol Stoel throughout were continuing, patient supporters at the fund. Richard Johnson at the Exxon Education Foundation helped make additional funding available for a national conference on liberal education; Jamie Beth Catlin organized the conference with the unfailing help of Marina Buhler-Miko, Jerry Gaff, Rich-

ard Hendrix, Mildred Henry, Joseph Katz, Betty McNair, and
Arturo Madrid.

Others have read chapters in various drafts: Nancy Black,
Robert Blackburn, Roland Braithwaite, Jamie Beth Catlin,
Laurent Daloz, Peter Elbow, Beverly Kowalski Firestone, Ray-
mond Franklin, William Gamson, Elizabeth Grizzard, Richard
Hendrix, Sigrid Hutcheson, Helen Isaacson, Alice Adelman
Lowenstein, Nancy Lowry, William Maehl, Michael Mills, Anita
Mishler, John Nichols, Nancy Pierce, Victoria Steinitz, Clark
Taylor, Norma Ware, and Bari Watkins. I owe a special debt to
JB Lon Hefferlin, who encouraged me to take the risk of writ-
ing a book with strong convictions.

Beverly Kowalski Firestone worked on earlier versions of
Chapter One, contributing her broad knowledge of higher education to the first part and her sense of theater to the second
part. Barbara Carr, Sherylanne Lawrence, Lisa Pearson, LaRue
Cochran, and Marion Graham helped in the preparation of the
manuscript at different points.

I owe a special thanks to my colleagues at the Center for
the Study of Higher Education and the Residential College at
the University of Michigan for their forbearance during the
leave of absence demanded by this book. The College of Public
and Community Service at the University of Massachusetts in
Boston provided me a haven and inspiration during the final
writing.

Sincerest appreciation is extended to David Riesman for
agreeing to contribute his reflections on the book in an Afterword.

Finally, my deepest gratitude goes to the people in Ann
Arbor who worked with me as staff to National Project IV:
Sigrid Hutcheson and Anna Neumann in the first year, Jamie
Beth Catlin and Michael Mills in the second year, and Barbara
Carr and Terry Heitz Rogers throughout. While Catlin, Mills,
and Rogers have written particular chapters, their generosity
and intelligence inspire every part of this book.

Chilmark, Massachusetts   Zelda F. Gamson
January 1984

The Authors

Zelda F. Gamson is professor in the Center for the Study of Higher Education and the Residential College at the University of Michigan. She has long been a participant, observer, and student of the worlds of higher education. An undergraduate at three colleges (the University of Pennsylvania, Antioch College, and the University of Michigan) when it was not yet fashionable to try out different schools, she completed an undergraduate honors degree in 1958 at the University of Michigan in philosophy. A year later, she received an M.A. degree in sociology at the University of Michigan. Her Ph.D. degree in social relations from Harvard University in 1965 combined work in sociology with studies in social psychology and anthropology. Her dissertation on Monteith College at Wayne State University, a harbinger of contemporary efforts to bring an education of excellence to average students, led to a book coauthored with David Riesman and Joseph Gusfield, *Academic Values and Mass Education* (1975).

For seven years at the height of the activism of the 1960s and early 1970s, Gamson held an appointment at the Survey

Research Center at the University of Michigan, where she did research on student organizations, activism, and development. A reflective essay, "Michigan Muddles Through," which places those years in the perspective of the political culture of Ann Arbor and the University of Michigan, appeared in a Carnegie Commission volume (Gamson, 1973).

In 1970, she began teaching a graduate course in the Center for the Study of Higher Education on theories of innovations applied to undergraduate life. Soon after, Gamson taught a course on research design and on student development during the college years; she continues to teach versions of those courses. The Residential College, part of the College of Literature, Science, and the Arts at the University of Michigan, gave Gamson the opportunity to teach undergraduates and participate in shaping an innovative small college. Since 1973, she has taught a freshman seminar, a field work course, and a course on democracy in the work place; coordinated an interdisciplinary team of faculty in a course on political economy; served as associate director for curriculum development; coordinated an interdisciplinary social science program; and raised funds for and taught in an unusual semester-long, intensive research community.

Her research throughout these years has concentrated on various aspects of innovation and higher education: the impact of black students on white colleges and universities (Peterson and others, 1979), competence-based education (Grant and others, 1979), and higher education in Israel. Most recently, she has become interested in collaborative work structures and in the relations between education and work, which have led her to study cooperative work settings and colleges and universities as places of work.

From 1979 to 1981, Gamson directed National Project IV, Examining the Varieties of Liberal Education. In her continuing travel through the worlds of higher education, she has held visiting positions at Hebrew University, Stanford University, and the College of Public and Community Service at the University of Massachusetts in Boston.

Nancy B. Black is associate professor of English, Brooklyn College.

Jamie Beth Catlin is manager, Foundation Relations, University
Development, University of Michigan, and formerly associate director of National Project IV and associate director, Office of Academic Counseling, College of Literature,
Science, and the Arts, University of Michigan.

Patrick J. Hill is vice-president and provost, Evergreen State College, and formerly chairman, Federated Learning Communities, and associate professor of philosophy, State
University of New York at Stony Brook.

Michael R. Mills is a graduate student in the Center for the
Study of Higher Education, University of Michigan, and
formerly staff associate of National Project IV.

John Nichols is core curriculum coordinator and professor of
philosophy, Saint Joseph's College.

Terry Heitz Rogers is a graduate student in the Center for the
Study of Higher Education, University of Michigan, and
formerly staff associate of National Project IV.

Liberating
Education

You don't need me to tell you what education is. Everybody really knows that education goes on all the time, all through our lives, and that it is the process of waking up to life. . . . It takes a heap of resolve to keep from going to sleep in the middle of the show. It's not that we want to sleep our life away. It's that it requires certain kinds of energy, certain capacities for taking the world into our consciousness, certain real powers of body and soul to be a match for reality.

—Richards, 1964, p. 16

CHAPTER ONE

What Should
Liberal Education Mean?

April 1983. I surveyed the walls of my study trying to decide whether my restlessness was due to spring fever or to the despair I had been feeling lately about the state of the world. 1984 was just around the corner. *1984*. Was it to be Orwell's nightmare or something else? In Orwell's world, the people were deliberately turned into sleepwalkers. Specialization became a way of separating individuals from a common culture, from one another. Could we be approaching such a situation? Would higher education have anything to say about it?

I chewed on the eraser of my well-worn marking pencil and stared at what I had been writing about what had happened to undergraduate education since World War II. Even before the war, specialization had bent the undergraduate curriculum out of shape, eroding it outside of department majors (Rudolph, 1977). In spite of protests from educators and public leaders (Harvard Committee, 1945; President's Commission on Higher Education for Democracy, in Hofstadter and Smith, 1961), the trend continued unchecked throughout the postwar period (Levine, 1978).

I decided to look into the matter further and was relieved to learn that most colleges and universities had never let specialization take over the undergraduate curriculum completely. Students were still asked to have a general education in addition to

1

a specialized one. But when I looked closely, I saw that the distribution systems that had grown up to enforce a general education had become quite meaningless in many schools, since almost any subject could meet the requirements.

There seemed to be some hope in core curricula. As most schools moved to the distribution system, some colleges required that their students take a small number of general education courses. But then I read that core curricula were likely to turn into distribution systems (Blackburn and others, 1976). By the early 1970s, in any case, they existed in only 10 percent of all American colleges and universities (Levine, 1978).

Students and their parents seemed to have kept their faith in a broad education even if faculty members had not. For a long time, the mark of an educated person was being "well-rounded." The notion of "breadth," of being acquainted with the great works of Western civilization, continued to command enormous respect in the college-going public, where it was accepted on faith that the great works meant something grand. By the late 1960s, however, even this rather simple-minded belief had been profoundly shaken. How had this happened in so short a time? I learned that the story is a complicated one.

Whatever Happened to Liberal Education?

The story seems to have begun with federal support for research. In 1950, government support for research was $177 million (1980 dollars); by 1980 it was over $3 billion. The federal government underwrote the development of graduate programs, laboratories, and research institutes, which produced a class of academics whose main work was doing research rather than teaching. This happened just about the time that the baby boom generation, the largest in the history of the nation, began to reach college age. Affluence and the importance of a college degree for a good job brought a larger proportion of high school graduates than ever before into colleges and universities (Collins, 1979). After the launching of Sputnik in 1957, higher education really took off. The number of graduate students, many of them supported by government grants and fellowships, increased dramatically. Brilliant and not-so-brilliant Ph.D.s became college professors.

The bargaining power of the faculty was heightened considerably during the late 1950s and early 1960s, when there were not enough college professors to staff the swelling ranks of colleges and universities. Combined with the easy availability of government and foundation grants, this led to greater faculty control in institutions and over the curriculum. Academic departments began to exert more influence over the curriculum than they ever had, especially in research universities and selective liberal arts colleges. Given a free hand to teach the subjects they wanted to teach in any way they wanted, Ph.D.s across the country brought what Christopher Jencks and David Riesman (1968) called "the academic revolution" to the hinterland.

The tough model of the university college—high standards, advanced scholarship, graduate school preoccupations—spread unevenly but took hold in many schools that had to fight hard to attract faculty in the early years of expansion. By the late 1960s, most faculty members, even in small colleges, had become specialists in a certain discipline like biology or sociology, with special knowledge about a field within that discipline—microbiology or stratification. Faculty members who never again did any scholarly work after their Ph.D. dissertations—and the majority of Ph.D.s did not—thought of themselves as biologists or sociologists, not educators. The occupation may have been college professor, but the preoccupation had become a specialized field. Identifying so much with a discipline weakened faculty members' loyalty to the schools that employed them and to their colleagues in other disciplines. If a job went sour, they could go somewhere else. The disciplines grew more arcane, and it became harder for faculty members in the same school to communicate with one another (Sloan, 1979; Smith, 1981; Boyer and Levine, 1981; Bowen, 1977). In the larger schools, few college professors participated in the community of scholars, a term that began to sound faintly antiquated (Birnbaum, 1973). Important discoveries were being

ity of life in their institutions. The Carnegie Foundation for the Advancement of Teaching (1977) declared general education a "disaster area," and finally the gaps between the faculty and the students, even in the elite schools of the nation, could no longer be ignored. Few members of the faculty knew how to teach "skills"; many felt that was the job of education specialists and English teachers. Nor could "skills" be laid down as requirements, since many of the general education requirements in composition, mathematics, and foreign languages that had been common during the 1950s and most of the 1960s had been abandoned across the country (Blackburn and others, 1976). Even the most idealistic college teachers found themselves denigrating students. Faculty members in unselective schools drifted into a resigned acceptance of low student performance, sugar-coated assignments, and mutual boredom. Without much conviction or vision, more colleges and universities across the country introduced "developmental" or "remedial" courses (Levine, 1978). These were typically separate operations, financed with federal or state funds, in student services offices or in entirely new units that were organizationally distant from the liberal arts departments.

Then, as the economy began its downward turn and as the job market for liberal arts graduates began to shrink, the era of "defensive credentialism" (get a college degree just to hold on to what you have) and "vocationalism" (only study things that will help you get a job) set in. As a college education took on the meaning of yet another public good, students became consumers. And a decreasing number, even in the best schools, were interested in buying a liberal education. The word was out in the middle classes that higher education was no longer a growth stock, and students who ten years earlier would have gone on to graduate school shifted to law or medical school. Mediocre students were not interested in the traditional liberal arts subjects either, since they knew that they would have to find a place for themselves in more applied fields like engineering and business. And the students who had little choice scrambled for what was left—vocations and semiprofessions like human services, communications, and computer science. Unselective

schools were hit hardest by these sudden shifts in student pref-
erences, and many rushed headlong into concocting vocational
programs in all sorts of fields for which the job market looked
promising—computers, social work, nursing, and medical technology. Even traditional liberal arts colleges discovered that
they had become de facto vocational schools, as their students
shifted their allegiance from the liberal arts to business, engineering, law, and medicine (Geiger, 1980).

The accumulated effects of all the forces undermining liberal education might have ended it entirely at some schools. If
so, the faculty would pay a high price. Many disciplines in arts
and sciences, especially the humanities, found that they could
no longer attract the students they wanted, let alone those they
did not want. How could they bring the students back, after
such a long period of neglect? It was clear that a concerted response was necessary, but it was difficult to mobilize the faculty to the task, especially in schools most attached to specialization. The faculty as a corporate body had become so fractured
that it could not present a coherent conception of education to
students divided by race, class, gender, and age differences.

Renewal or Despair?

I asked myself whether the current situation held some
hope for a renewal of liberal education, for a new vision? Or
was it too late? Of what use was a liberal education in a fast-
moving technological society? What could it say in the age of
robotics and laser-beam battle stations? I knew that some academics had already given up, as commentators and journalists
talked about higher education as a dying industry. Some (Bird,
1975; Freeman, 1976) questioned the point of college at all,
arguing that a college education does not add much to people's
lives. If anything good happens to students in college, they
maintained, it is because they come from well-educated families or because they already have the qualities that colleges take
credit for (Astin, 1968; Chickering, 1971).

Reports by the Carnegie Council on Policy Studies in
Higher Education (1980, 1981), as well as works by respected

social scientists, have refuted some of these claims. Nevertheless, academics were deeply stung by the criticisms. Some have begun to write about higher education from many perspectives, ranging from restorationist to reformist stands. While their views of pedagogy and politics are clearly at odds, the restorationists and reformers agree on at least one thing: The postwar expansion of higher education was a disaster for undergraduate education. Restorationists want to shore up standards, get rid of remedial students, return to the classics, and turn back government interference (Epstein, 1977; Bennett, 1983). Drawing on earlier academic critics (Barzun, 1959; Nisbet, 1971; Hutchins, 1967), they argue that the undergraduate curriculum needs coherence and discipline. Reformers have their own solutions, which are based on their desire to preserve the populist gains of the past fifteen years. They agree with the restorationists that the question of the quality of education is critical, but their conception of quality is very different. Drawing on the findings of researchers like Astin (1968) and Chickering (1971), they assert that the new students benefit from higher education as much, if not more, than students from privileged backgrounds and should have the opportunity to get the best kind of education. Reformers see them as just as worthy and educable as the traditional students (Shor, 1980; Shaughnessy, 1977; Meisler, forthcoming).

Meanwhile, in the trenches, ordinary faculty members are still struggling with the situation. Early in the 1970s, grade inflation was a popular topic, and the first impulse was to go back to basics. The 1970s saw a resurgence of English composition and mathematics requirements after their abandonment in many schools in the late 1960s and early 1970s (Blackburn and others, 1976). Books on writing, workshops for instructors, and projects on basic skills appear regularly (Shaughnessy, 1977; Richardson, Martens, and Fisk, 1981; Tobias, 1978), and faculty members are slowly beginning to accept some responsibility for teaching basic skills—not only in open-door colleges but in selective ones as well.

A shift in thinking about undergraduate education began sometime in the 1970s. A national survey of faculties in the middle 1970s showed that half of them favored some sort of core curriculum (Levine, 1978). At faculty meetings in hundreds of colleges and universities across the country, an old question is being asked again: "What should every educated person know?" (Gaff, 1983). Specialists in different disciplines have begun talking with one another, often for the first time, about their fields and why they care about them. Many college and university faculties do not seem to get much beyond this point, but some have begun to formulate a conception of liberal education for themselves. This is a painful process, as faculty members who themselves may not have had a liberal education discover that not only their students but they themselves are also ignorant.

New programs and courses are being invented all over the place. Pacific Lutheran University has designed a core program consisting of eight courses and one seminar, "The Dynamics of Change." Carnegie-Mellon University has adopted a new core curriculum to give students experience with skills in several disciplines. Brooklyn College has decided to require that all students take a basic core of ten courses, in an updated version of a core curriculum it had abandoned in the previous decade. Harvard University, in a late but celebrated move, has introduced its own version of a core curriculum that resembles a distribution system (Keller, 1982; Shulman, 1979; Change Magazine Editors, 1979).

Suddenly, general and liberal education has become a popular topic. One cannot pick up a newspaper or magazine without encountering some discussion of the liberal arts. Foundations and federal agencies have sponsored a variety of projects (Hendrix and Stoel, 1982; Boyer and Levine, 1981; Commission on the Humanities, 1980); higher education associations, colleges, and universities have organized countless conferences on the undergraduate curriculum. Interest seems to be present in all sectors. Harvard, Stanford, and other major research universities have joined state colleges, small private liberal arts colleges, and community colleges in examining their undergraduate requirements (Gaff and others, 1980; Gaff, 1983). Traditionalists and innovators, humanists and scientists, and teachers and administrators are meeting together. Educators with an interest in adapting the innovations of the 1960s to the 1980s are joining with those who talk about computers and competences.

Motivations are diverse and often conflicting. Liberal arts faculty members, especially in the humanities and the social sciences, are looking for ways to lure students to their departments. Instructors who work with adults or poorly prepared students find themselves forced to think about what is fundamental in an undergraduate education. Those who work in interdisciplinary areas—women's studies, ethnic studies, American culture—and in vocationally oriented subjects—human services, labor studies, communications—raise questions about the elite bias in the liberal arts. Administrators who want to resist the pull of professional and vocational programs seek a good justification for maintaining support for liberal education. Politicians who have lost faith in the quality of higher education press for excellence. And spokespersons for the business world argue that a liberal education is more valuable for employees than a technical one (Beck, 1981).

I wondered whether all this energy implied that real change would take place, or whether it would dissipate as other educational campaigns have. Was liberal education to be a banner flown at academic processions while the forces described in *1984* marched on? What if we really tried to figure out what a liberal education meant in a way that was relevant to the conditions of life in the United States today? What if we tried to put it in terms that anyone could understand? Maybe that was worth a try.

But how to do it without boring myself and everyone else? An enormous amount had already been written about the subject, and more was coming out every day. Most of it was pretty airy stuff. I could not bring myself to write yet another high-flown discourse on liberal education. What, then, could I do? Suddenly, it came to me as I was listening to a tape of a discussion at one of the meetings of National Project IV. One of the things people in the project did best was discuss. So why not set up an imaginary commission? Call it the Commission of 1984. Select a small group of people from National Project IV to represent different sectors of higher education. With me as moderator, they could speak in their own words as much as possible (thanks to the transcripts of actual discussions), referring to the comments of others from the project who would not be on the commission. I would give them the opportunity to consult research and other literature and bring in some real students.

Reformulations: A Dialogue on Liberal Education in the 1980s

Cast of Characters

- *Roland Braithwaite:* professor of humanities, former dean of Talladega College.
- *Jamie Beth Catlin:* manager, foundation relations, Development Office, University of Michigan; former associate director of academic counseling, College of Literature, Science, and the Arts.
- *Laurent Daloz:* mentor, External Degree Program, Johnson State College, and educational researcher.
- *Raymond S. Franklin:* instructor in the Institute of Applied Social Science, District 65 of United Automobile Workers, and Hofstra University; professor of economics and sociology, Graduate School and Queens College of the City University of New York.
- *Zelda F. Gamson:* professor, Center for the Study of Higher Education and Residential College, University of Michigan.
- *Patrick J. Hill:* vice-president and provost of Evergreen State College; former chairman of Federated Learning Communities and associate professor of philosophy at the State University of New York at Stony Brook.
- *Bari Watkins:* dean of Rollins College; former director of the Program on Women, Northwestern University.

Gamson: I've asked you all here because there is a lot of interest in liberal education around the country right now, and that may give some momentum to a reformulation that might challenge the menace in *1984.*

Catlin: Before we get going, we are going to have to deal with the "religion" problem.

Gamson: What do you mean?

Catlin: Let me see if I can find what Caroline Bird says about it. (Pulls out a dog-eared copy of Bird's *The Case Against College* and reads from it) The liberal arts are "a religion in every sense of that term. When people talk about them, their language becomes elevated, metaphorical, extravagant, theoretical, and reverent" [Bird, 1975, p. 10] .

Franklin: In a way, believing in liberal education *is* like religion. It is what gives value to academic life. When we get together and talk about these things, we touch our moral commitments. We rub up against things that provoke some profound feelings. Past all the truisms, I know I feel a kind of joy when what I teach and study is connected to my moral beliefs. But it's a very private kind of thing.

Hill: That's the issue. People have experienced what they want to call "liberal education" but it has been a private experience.

Watkins: That's because liberal education in the past meant indoctrination into some timeless values thought to be shared by all educated people. Now, with the rejection of universal values by academics, "values" have become private matters.

Franklin: Right. Liberal education was born in an age that no longer exists. The world is different now and disappointments have accumulated about what it is supposed to be, until no one really believes in liberal education any more as a public responsibility. It has become obsolete.

Gamson: That's why we are called the Commission of 1984. We must see if we can retrieve or reformulate the meaning of liberal education for our times.

Hill: But our students are so different that it seems unlikely that we will ever be able to agree. In fact, liberal education may need to be different for different kinds of students. Younger students may need a different kind of education than older ones. The same goes for black and white students, men and women. Any statement that tries to cover all students in all schools will be so general that it will be meaningless.

Braithwaite: I agree that my students are different from yours, Pat, and I will grant that they need different things in their education. Therefore, our immediate educational aims will be different. For instance, you have to pay less attention to helping students with writing and math at Stony Brook than we do at Talladega. But I still believe that apart from those immediate concerns, there is a common purpose.

Hill: What is it?

Braithwaite: To improve people's lives.

Hill: So does bourbon.

Watkins: Come *on*, Pat. You know what he means.

Hill: I really don't, honestly. Improve people's lives in what ways?

Braithwaite: Make them think better, be more competent, more socially aware, more responsible. . . .

Catlin: (Loudly) Hold on! You're doing it. You're talking religion.

Gamson: Maybe he is and maybe he isn't. (Points to a pile of books and articles) I sent each of you a few of the most important works on the impact of college on students to read before this meeting. Suppose we start with Hyman, Wright, and Reed's (1975) *The Enduring Effects of Education* and Hyman and Wright's (1979) *Education's Lasting Influence on Values,* since they analyze the effects of education in the general population. Who looked at those two studies?

Braithwaite: I did, and the results are very impressive. They reanalyzed hundreds of surveys done over the years and found, first of all, that the more education people have, the more they know. That news may not be too earth shattering, but then when they looked at the effects of education on values, they discovered that college educated people, compared to people with less education, are most likely to support civil liberties, due process, and freedom from arbitrary laws; they want less protection from controversial ideas. They are also more in favor of equality and humanitarianism.

Hill: In other words, college educated people support democratic values.

Braithwaite: Yes, that's what their studies seem to show.

Franklin: Do they act on those values though? They *sound* very good, just the sort of thing that is taught in civics classes. But saying you support them is not the same as doing something about them.

Catlin: Howard Bowen's (1977) review of hundreds of studies demonstrates that college educated people participate more in community and cultural affairs. They vote more and have a highly developed moral sense. They also spend their money sensibly, do satisfying work, and raise their families well.

Gamson: But remember: The studies you quote cannot identify which aspects of college have which impacts. It could be the overall environment, or the opportunities that a college degree opens, or the contacts made in college, or. . . .

Watkins: (Interrupting eagerly) Yes, well, I found a really smashing study by Winter, McClelland, and Stewart (1981) that sorts all that out. They followed up graduates of an Ivy League college that sounds like Harvard or Yale and measured what they called "liberal arts competences"—things like analytic skill, independence, leadership, and emotional maturity. They related these competences to later life and found that they affected family life, careers, participation in organizations, personal feelings, and self-image. The effects were very positive, and they were more important than SAT scores and several other characteristics of students when they entered college.

Hill: I am skeptical about all this, but I must admit that Douglas Heath's (1968) study of Haverford graduates is pretty convincing. He found that their undergraduate experience had a continuing effect on their lives, much more than graduate or professional school. The effect was not just on their intellects but also on their characters and the way they lived.

Franklin: But what's so great about that? Obviously, people who have gone to Harvard or Yale become leaders and achievers. And it isn't a big surprise that a small Quaker school with Haverford's reputation would have effects on the character of its students. But that isn't where the vast majority of college students go. They are in community colleges, state colleges, and so on. They don't have the benefit of a fancy residential school.

Catlin: Bowen (1977) could not detect many differences in the way different schools affect their students. It seems that there is a bigger gap between those who go to college and those who don't than among graduates of different kinds of colleges.

Gamson: Still, it does make a difference which college we are talking about. Bari, didn't Winter, McClelland, and Stewart (1981) find that graduates of the Ivy League college come out with greater liberal arts competence than graduates of some of the other schools they studied?

Watkins: Yes, at the end, students in a state teacher's college and a community college didn't score as well on the liberal arts competences.

Franklin: I'd like to see students at those colleges do as well as Ivy League graduates.

Catlin: Do you think that extending liberal education to more people will make us a better society?

Franklin: No guarantee, but certainly it should help us resist the totalitarianism of *1984*. If liberal education means that more people will be critical, civic minded, and mature, then all power to it. We have extended access to higher education to more people but we have not spread the benefits equally. Community colleges should be giving their students a liberal education, including those in vocational tracks.

Hill: Are you talking about a real education or a phony one, as in many of our public schools in inner cities? I watched open admissions at the City University of New York [CUNY] and it was devastating. The faculty didn't know what to do with students who couldn't read and write. Instead of really giving them an education, professors handed them over to counselors and treated the curriculum as if it were a public utility.

Franklin: What's the matter with a public utility if it does its job well? We know that low-income students are much less likely to go to college. For all of its faults, CUNY did give a chance to thousands of people who are perfectly capable of doing college work. Many of them are probably more capable than students who go to expensive schools.

Gamson: Are you saying that all of the good things we have heard about liberal education should be available to the masses of people?

Franklin: Absolutely, and in the most serious and demanding way possible. We should see the presence of working-class people, minorities, women, and older students as an opportunity to test the belief—my belief—that a liberal education is for everyone. *And we ought to push them* as far as they will go!

Hill: We ought to let them push us just as far. They are as much a challenge to higher education as it is to them. Liberal education has been defined historically by middle-class, white, male realities. Now educators must change what they do to fit the realities of people who are very different.

Gamson: That's a good cue. I invited five students, one each from your programs at Hofstra, Northwestern, the State University of New York [SUNY] at Stony Brook, Johnson State, and Talladega to join our discussion. (The students enter.) Welcome to all of you. We have invited you to speak with the Commission of 1984 because we think you may be able to help us identify the meaning of a liberal education for our times. To prepare for this session, we reviewed some of the most important research in the past few years on the effects of a college education. Without going into too much detail, we saw that going to college and, possibly, having a liberal education seems to help people develop capacities that serve them well throughout their lives.

Northwestern student: I'm not sure that going to college has made that much of a difference for me. It's something my family always expected me to do. I went to a prep school in the East and college isn't that different. When I got to Evanston, I played mostly, joined a sorority, that sort of thing.

Gamson: I gather you took several courses in the Program on Women.

Northwestern student: (Looks over at Watkins, who shifts slightly in her chair) I took the introductory course because it fit into my schedule. I thought it would be a gut—you know, not too much work. Was I wrong! That course opened my eyes. I worked harder than I ever did in a course. The things I learned. . . .

Gamson: Like what?

Northwestern student: Like how aware it made me of women's lives. The course was important for the awareness and perception it started in me. We were concerned about *why* we saw what we did. It worked on my thinking. It didn't tell us just to regurgitate what we studied.

Catlin: Could you give an example of what you mean?

Northwestern student: Well, let's see. (Ponders for a moment) OK, we studied myths, Greek myths, and how men and women were portrayed in them. One of the topics was "Is woman to nature as man is to culture?" We studied women's functions through myths—how they are supposed to stay home and take care of the household and the children while the men go off to fight and have adventures.

Gamson: And how does that build your awareness and perceptions?

Northwestern student: By relating what we learn to what we do now. I test what I learn in class. With my boyfriend, for instance, I realized that the tone of voice I use with him is accommodating. . . . I am beginning to see that men interrupt conversations, that they control them with eye contact. I realize that the men I know take too much for granted, assuming that housekeeping is for women, for example.

Talladega student: You're talking about what you learn from women's studies, which is only one subject. I think a liberal education means being exposed to a lot of different ideas and knowledge. It means being a jack of all trades.

Northwestern student: But why? What difference does it make for you to learn a lot of different things?

Talladega student: I want to be able to explain things to other people and be understood. I want to be able to talk to anyone about anything.

Catlin: That sounds like what people used to say about a liberal education making you well rounded.

Talladega student: A little bit like that. . . .

Braithwaite: Let me explain something here. We have students at Talladega who haven't had the background of students in other schools (glances at the student from Northwestern). They haven't been to many places and they have had very few cultural advantages. So going to college opens up a whole new world for them. When Joe says he wants to speak to anyone about anything, he means that he will have a sense of himself as an educated person, as someone who lives in a wider world.

Talladega student: That's it. Talladega has changed my whole *life* because it has shown me that I can live in a more complicated world than the one I grew up in. My teachers are interested in what I think and they try to teach me how to tell others what I am thinking. I've also learned how to take an interest in new things and how to follow up on them.

SUNY-Stony Brook student: It's something like that for me too, even though I come from Long Island. We are Catholic and the family goes to church every week. My dad has spent his life in a large office downtown where he has worked his way up to being the head accountant. I never knew there were so many different kinds of people in the world, so many different ideas, so many different religions. I will *never* be able to think of myself and my family in the same way again.

Hofstra student: I am at least ten years older than the three of you and I grew up in the Bronx. I've been working as a shipping clerk sending things all over the world, but I didn't know what the world really is. What I've been studying in the Labor Institute has been an eye-opener for me, just to realize that there is a bigger world out there beyond basic survival.

Johnson State student: That's the point. Survival at that level is one thing, at another level it is something more. Look, I've been around. I grew up in a small town in Vermont, married at eighteen, had two kids, took a job in the paper mill, divorced, went on welfare. And let me tell you, education has been my *survival.*

Daloz: Yes, I have worked with Ella. . . .

Johnson State student: Let *me* explain. It's something like this: (She pauses, looks down to gather her thoughts) I thought, I actually *believed* that education was a one-time vaccination against incompetence and ignorance, that it was separate from everything else. Some sort of prize to be earned at the cost of hard work and scarce money. Well, liberal education has served me relatively well in the economic area and failed miserably in giving me protection from ignorance and incompetence. Instead of building up, it tore down the last vestiges of old beliefs and certainties. It didn't consolidate, it fragmented my entire life. . . .

Hofstra student: That's not what I meant.

Gamson: Let her finish.

Johnson State student: The point is, that fragmentation allowed me to start living—at age twenty-nine! Because I could see that learning will never stay put or be final. It will continue to complicate my existence and it will lead me down a lot of dead ends. It will rip away any uncertainties I insist on holding, it will forever show me how much further I have to go, but at least I know what learning is like now. (Quietly) It isn't hiding anymore. It's like setting an old friend free [Daloz, 1981, pp. 49-50].

A barrier seems to have given way, and everyone begins talking at the same time.

Gamson: OK, everyone! Let's go on. I think we are finally getting somewhere. You all seem to be saying that liberal education has had the effect of broadening your awareness of the world.

Johnson State student: And about yourself.

Gamson: Yes. Let's get back to that point in a minute. Let's just talk about this idea of broadening.

Catlin: Sounds to me like "join the army and see the world."

Daloz: It *is* kind of like a journey and a way of seeing the world, but without the army or a Eurail pass. But what, finally, is the difference between small-town Vermont and New York City? We're all on a journey through the wonders of the world, aren't we? We all struggle to make sense of things, yet see them afresh. And when we can help our students to do the same, what a wonderful thing to behold.

Catlin: Hmmn. Can anyone give some examples of when this seems to happen?

SUNY-Stony Brook student: I can tell you how it works for a lot of us in the Federated Learning Communities. We're just regular students who sign up for this program and wham! It starts.

Gamson: What starts?

SUNY-Stony Brook student: It's hard to describe exactly. A kind of mental volleyball. It is a different kind of learning than coming to school to obtain knowledge. You know, the teacher stands up there and lectures and that is what you take as knowledge and truth. In our program, the interplay between a student and a professor or students and other students is more like the development of *new* knowledge. It is not just learning academics. It is learning what is going on outside of academics, in your own life, current issues, in things that are going on in the world.

Catlin: That sounds great, but obtaining knowledge is what most people mean when they talk about a liberal education. You know, Plato and Aristotle, Shakespeare and Milton.

SUNY-Stony Brook student: Obtaining knowledge is part of it, but I wouldn't say that is the purpose of a liberal education.

Catlin: (Quickly) Oh, yes? What would you say the purpose is?

SUNY-Stony Brook student: I don't know, I haven't thought about it much. . . . I suppose it is to think better, to learn how to be critical, to be able to inquire into things, not take anything for granted . . . .

Gamson: That is very helpful. (Turning then to the other students) In fact, you have all been very thoughtful. The commission will certainly pay close attention to what you told us. Right now, though, we need a little more time to sort things out before we leave. Thanks for coming.

The students leave and the commissioners take a short break before reassembling.

Gamson: I think we got somewhere with the students. Let's see if we can use what we learned to help formulate what liberal education means in the 1980s. I'll call on each of you for a brief statement. (Looks around the room) Roland, how about it? What do you think are the most important purposes of a liberal education for our times?

Braithwaite: I am prepared to say that they have to do with what we teach—and that is a cultural heritage. At least one purpose of a liberal education is to transmit and preserve cultural heritage. The study of this heritage includes practice using all the tools needed to satisfy other goals of liberal education.

Franklin: But whose heritage? Surely, as someone from a black college you wouldn't say that the Western cultural heritage is the most significant one to transmit to your students?

Braithwaite: As a matter of fact, I would. Remember that the Afro-American heritage, as our students experience it, has to be understood as part of the Western cultural heritage. Our students have to live in two worlds. They are Afro-Americans conscious of a special background. At the same time, they have at least to learn to compete in a European system of standards, language, and customs. A liberal education has to help them deal with the Western world and improve their condition in the majority society.

Watkins: That may be so ideally, but it hasn't worked out in the real world, even in higher education where the perspectives of black people and women have been denied.

Braithwaite: We want our students to learn the ideas from the tradition and to carry them out at their best.

Daloz: Be that as it may, Roland, you and Bari aren't that far off in one respect. You both believe in what is taught. I want to say that a liberal education takes its justification not only from *what* is taught but from *the way* what is taught brings out a kind of awareness—not cultural heritage for its own sake but for starting a process of thinking and understanding. Weren't you all struck by how much the students talked about how they had come to a broader view about men and women, history, religion, ways to live? The purpose of a liberal education is to help learners reach an awareness that is increasingly inclusive, complex, and insightful, which ultimately results in the ability to experience the world more fully, in a more awakened way than before.

Catlin: You make it sound so *personal.*

Watkins: It is, Jamie. That's where real education starts, though that's not where it ends. In women's studies, for instance, my colleagues and I have noticed that there is a time when students start to recognize how they have accepted views of men and women that they come to see as wrong or unthinking. They ask themselves "How could I have accepted that?" That's when their liberal education really begins.

Gamson: Now that sounds like consciousness raising to me.

Braithwaite: Or indoctrination—the very opposite of what a liberal education should be.

Watkins: It's a pity it sounds that way—another example of how private our "values" have become. When we do not hold to any common values or culture, any talk about what we believe sounds like indoctrination.

Franklin: What we need to do is teach our students ways to think critically.

Catlin: Precisely. Most faculty would say that the purpose of a liberal education is the development of intellectual *discipline* and a capacity to think critically and clearly.

Braithwaite: What does that really mean? Some of our students are quite weak in the basic skills of reading and writing. Does that mean they cannot be liberally educated?

Catlin: Not until they master those basic skills. I don't think it's possible to think critically without being able to read and write competently.

Franklin: Even if they could do all those things superbly, it still wouldn't be enough. Some of our students in the Labor Institute at Hofstra have very poor academic backgrounds, but I wouldn't be satisfied if all we taught them are skills in reading or writing or in high-level thinking for that matter.

Gamson: What would you be satisfied with, Ray?

Franklin: I don't think critical thinking is just a matter of learning the skills of reading, or writing, or even of logic. It is the capacity to look at facts or materials and *evaluate* them. It's being able to move out of your involvement in a particular situation and gain a critical sense of why you are in it. It is developing some objectivity, some awareness about what you and others do—and why. Being in a situation but also being able to detach yourself to examine it. If that's "indoctrination," I don't know what people are talking about when they use the word. We aren't defining the situation *for* people or giving them ready-made answers. We are teaching them ways to define their own situation for *themselves.*

Daloz: Another way of putting it is to say that we want our students to form their own beliefs. These are not necessarily the ones they were raised in—or if they are, then they come to them through a process of thinking about them.

Franklin: We want to foster *critical* awareness, one that is critical not only of other people's ideas but of your own as well. Here is my short statement about the purpose of liberal education: It is to teach the skills and the commitment to think critically about all experience, including one's own. What we can give to students is the belief that they can *think* and the tools to do it well.

Braithwaite: Isn't this what used to be called "the examined life"?

Franklin: Partly, but it sounds so passive. When I said critical thinking involves more than good logic, I meant that it contains a commitment to do something.

Hill: I would say that is crucial. In essence, the purpose of a liberal education is to engender the habits and skills of critical thinking that enable students to apply what they know to the affairs of living.

Catlin: And that will improve the world?

Hill: It will be a start. If Americans are sometimes like sleep-walkers, it is partly because education has failed to help them use what they learn. People who are liberally educated should be able to apply what they learn to all areas of life. They should be intelligent and intentional about how they live—what kind of work they do and how they do it, whether or not their community should allow a nuclear power plant to be built, how their state should deal with economic crises, and so on.

Gamson: It is not easy to get academics to accept this view. Because it has been part of the elite tradition, those who speak for liberal education have taken pride in *not* being useful. It was the kind of education that was supposed to be free of the real world. Ivory towers and all that.

Braithwaite: Liberal education for minorities was always thought to be useful.

Hill: Right, and there are others who support this view as well. John Dewey fiercely attacked the split between theory and practice at all levels of education. Alfred North Whitehead talked about "inert ideas" as not only useless but even danger-ous: "If education is not useful, what is it? Is it a talent, to be hidden away in a napkin? Of course, education should be use-ful, whatever your aim in life. It was useful to Saint Augustine, and it was useful to Napoleon" [Whitehead, 1949, p. 14].

Franklin: In fact, he argued that the antithesis between tech-nical and liberal education is fallacious. Technical education helps people do things well, and liberal education helps them understand why.

Gamson: The trick is to learn how to move back and forth be-tween awareness and action.

Hill: For liberal education, though, the problem is how stu-dents learn to use ideas.

Catlin: There is a lot of interest right now in ways of teaching "generically"—teaching that helps students apply what they learn in a variety of circumstances, not only in college courses.

Watkins: If they really succeed, then I think we can say that a liberal education can be empowering. It helps students, especially those who have had little power over their lives, to understand what has shaped them. Through this understanding they see that their lives have been determined in certain ways. They stop blaming themselves and start acting for themselves.

Gamson: What's empowering about that? That's just telling them they are victims.

Watkins: You're right, but only at first. Some students go through that phase—you know, poor little me, society has done this terrible thing to me—but they usually don't stay there. They start developing a perspective on their lives from learning about other times and peoples and places. They see that they have some choices to make, the most important of which is to be aware of how they and history intersect.

Franklin: Just realizing that they can understand things they didn't understand before is empowering for people who have felt dumb or put down all their lives.

Watkins: Right. They start to own their own minds. As my student from Northwestern said, she just won't put up with things she took for granted in the past.

Franklin: The transformation in our students is sometimes astonishing. They begin to interpret their lives not simply in terms of personal attributes like good, bad, smart, dumb, but as part of their relationship to groups and classes on a national and world scene.

Watkins: The important thing is that they begin to see that what exists might be different—right, Ray?

Franklin: Yes, people and institutions made those things happen and they can try to change them.

Catlin: Is that what we said? That's pretty radical. Do you really think liberal education can change the world?

Franklin: Indirectly, perhaps. We should be very careful not

to overestimate the power of education. As an economist, I
know better.

Hill: Besides, the idea of liberal education in and for the
world is not all that radical. It goes back to the old Greek notion of liberal education as the way to prepare free men to participate rationally in public life or the Jeffersonian view that
enlightened citizens are essential if democracy is to work.

Braithwaite: This is hardly Athens in the fifth century B.C.
or even America in the eighteenth century. The slaves have been
freed. Maybe it is a measure of how bad things are that an old
tradition should sound so radical.

Daloz: Like the Bill of Rights.

Gamson: Whether it is radical or conservative—and it is probably both—we have staked out a territory. It is clear that we are
at an important moment. As we struggle to address the conditions in this country that seem to be pushing toward *1984,* we
must redefine the purposes of liberal education.

Watkins: Let's see if we can summarize. We started by saying
that a liberal education has to do with a certain kind of awareness, one that is broad and critical. We agreed that intellectual
skills and discipline are a very important part of this awareness,
especially as they lead to a critical examination of ideas, one's
own as well as others'.

Hill: Then we went on to say that it should have a strong contemporary, even practical, bent. It should give people a better
way of understanding their lives and the major forces shaping
the modern world. It also endows them with the intellectual
skills and the commitment to apply what they know to the
world—a responsibility for enlightened action. When that happens, people can become empowered.

Franklin: It is not just a sharpening-up exercise for the intellect, a collection of fashionable tidbits of knowledge. . . .

Watkins: Or an investment in a better job.

Braithwaite: It is moral at the core, *without* indoctrination.

Hill: The things *1984* was not.

Gamson: Goodness. There's more here than I thought. Maybe we should write a book about it.

Watkins: But just to be sure our ideas aren't confused with the usual ways of talking about liberal education, let's not call it that.

Gamson: What then?

Daloz: Liber*ating* education. Education for awareness.

Franklin: Critical awareness.

Hill: Use.

Watkins: Which can lead to empowerment.

Gamson: The opposite of *1984.*

CHAPTER TWO

Educating Students
for Critical Awareness

John Nichols: (director of Core, Saint Joseph's College) Do
you know the novel *Rabbit, Run* by John Updike?

Gamson: Don't you assign it in freshman Core?

Nichols: We do. The students' first reaction to Harry Ang-
strom is that he is a consummate ass. He deserted his family,
brought about the drowning of his daughter, was with a mistress
when his wife was giving birth. His life contradicts all the values
they stand for, all the good Catholic teachings.

Gamson: So, what do you do with the novel?

Nichols: We tell them that it is a religious novel, that for Updike, Rabbit is a kind of saint. Now, for our students, that is
shocking. There is no way they can see it as a legitimate interpretation of what this person did.

Gamson: What happens?

Nichols: The students argue with the teachers, the teachers argue among themselves.

Gamson: Why do you assign it?

Nichols: So that they will confront their ideas about religion
and faith. We want them to be more mindful about what they
believe.

29

It is difficult to understand a liberating education without seeing it in action—seeing students argue with their teachers
over interpretations of a novel, for example. This chapter and
the following two present accounts of a variety of approaches
to such an education. In this chapter, we look at two efforts to
bring students to greater critical awareness, the Core program at
Saint Joseph's College and the External Degree Program at
Johnson State College. Each goes about the matter differently.
For Saint Joseph's, awareness must come through the study of
certain subjects in particular ways at a small Catholic school
with a strong sense of tradition and community. For the External Degree Program, awareness is more individual and idiosyn-
cratic. Without a shared curriculum or even a shared collegiate
setting, students are expected to make sense of their lives on
their own, with the careful prodding of a mentor. In their very
different ways, however, both Core and the External Degree
Program have found ways to reach middle Americans.

Saint Joseph's College: What It Means to Be Human

> It is as though the liberally educated man
> had no incarnation. Somewhere along the line . . .
> the student should be able to experience what edu-
> cated men are supposed to handle. He must learn
> that, although his teachers are indeed specialists in
> one field, they are interested and competent in the
> major fields of human concern, that they are in
> fact embodiments of what the college wants and
> expects him to be [Nichols, 1980, pp. 7-8].

Saint Joseph's College is a small (1,000 students), private
residential college of Roman Catholic origins located in the
small town of Rensselaer, Indiana, 75 miles southeast of Chicago. For many years a men's college (it was when the statement just quoted was originally written), it became coeduca-
tional in 1968. In many ways, it is like many small, private,
unselective colleges in this country, colleges that are invisible to
most people (Astin and Lee, 1972). Quietly they go about their

business, recruiting students from shrinking pools, paying their faculty at the low end of the academic pay scale but asking them to do more than those at the high end. They will be particularly vulnerable in the coming Dark Ages of higher education, when enrollments of students eighteen to twenty-two years old will decline (Cheit, 1971, 1973; Carnegie Council on Policy Studies in Higher Education, 1980).

It is extraordinary that Saint Joseph's College should have come up with and taught since 1969 one of the most intellectually exciting general education curricula to be found anywhere in this country. Core, as the program is called, is an ordered series of ten courses totaling forty-five credits that are required of all students at the college. Unlike the common practice at other schools that put general education into the first two years, Core runs through the eight undergraduate semesters intertwined with the major. The courses in Core, which are built around themes, use materials and approaches from several disciplines. Core attempts to articulate the ten courses with one another and with a common rationale.

The central rationale for Core is its focus on the human condition, within a tradition of humanistic Christianity. It holds to the following six objectives:

1. To develop cognitive and communication *skills,*
2. To build a *community* of common seekers after truth,
3. To expand *awareness* of the many dimensions of reality,
4. To develop the *integrative* habit of mind,
5. To develop students' *values,*
6. To witness specific *Christian* values.

The order of courses is designed to make psychological as well as epistemological sense. The guiding metaphor for the curriculum is the funnel, with the narrow end at the beginning. "The Contemporary World" course, Core 1, asks students to place themselves in context by inquiring into what life must have been like in the early part of this century for their own grandparents at their age. Through literature, history, philosophy, theology, the natural sciences, and the social sciences,

Core 1 tries to come to terms with the major themes of the twentieth century. From there, Core 2, "The Roots of Western Civilization," Core 3, "The Christian Impact on the West," and Core 4, "The Modern World," investigate the historical roots of contemporary ideas and institutions. In the junior year, while students take the sequence of Cores 5 and 6 called "Man in the Universe," they are also asked to compare the "story of man as told by science" in Western culture with the alternative views of humans in other cultures presented in Cores 7 and 8, "Non-Western Studies," which are taken concurrently. Core 9 returns to the contemporary world in "Toward a Christian Humanism," which explores the nature of humans, religion, and Christian faith. Core 10, "Christianity and the Human Condition," is intended to help students make a "practical synthesis" through an intensive investigation of topics closely connected to their majors, such as respect for life, faith and reason, or the ethics of economic development. Each course in Core is divided equally into large lecture sessions and small discussion groups. Faculty members usually lecture in their fields of expertise, but they are often called on to discuss readings and topics outside of their fields in discussion classes, as in the presentation of John Updike's novels, in which literature instructors lecture and faculty members from other fields lead discussions.

Too often institutions seek an instant cure to educational malaise simply by revamping their curricula without preparing the faculty to teach differently. Had the Saint Joseph's faculty followed this path, they might never have revitalized the college. A crucial factor in their success was the establishment of an ongoing dialogue among instructors in the Core program about how to teach basic skills and integrate them into the content of required courses. The approach to skills at most institutions, as indeed it was at Saint Joseph's prior to the development of Core, is to leave skills to the skills specialists: the English instructors teach composition, grammar, and analysis; the speech specialists teach listening and speaking; the philosophers teach logic. Skills instruction is a one-shot affair, and students fail to relate what they have learned in freshman skills courses to later work in other disciplines.

The Saint Joseph's approach is integrative: It attempts to merge content and skills. All skills—writing, speaking, reading, thinking—are treated in relation to one another, and all ten Core courses develop skills in a sequential manner. By using theoretical works like Kinneavy's (1971) *A Theory of Discourse,* Moffett's (1968) *Teaching the Universe of Discourse, Student-Centered Language Arts and Reading Curriculum, K-13* by Moffett and Wagner (1976), Drake's (1976) *Teaching Critical Thinking,* and *An Introduction to Reasoning* by Toulmin, Rieke, and Janik (1979), the coordinator of Core provided Core faculty with a common vocabulary that cut across disciplines. Initial agreement upon a vocabulary enabled instructors next to identify course goals, describe connections from one course to the other, and devise assignments that would allow practice in skills.

To take one of the early examples of this approach, let us look at schemes the Saint Joseph's faculty invented to describe the goals of the writing program. They adopted three of Kinneavy's four "aims of discourse" as the goals of the four-year writing program: Expression, persuasion, and exposition are the three kinds of discourse presented over four years to students. The ultimate goal of the entire program is for students not only to practice each mode but also to be able to blend all three in a unified composition by their senior year.

Building such an approach to skills is, in effect, a faculty development project. Saint Joseph's faculty have worked for the past decade to develop a sense of responsibility among all Core faculty for teaching skills and for writing materials—study guides and suggested assignments—for one another and for students. The growing acceptance of this way of teaching skills can be charted in the attitudes of teachers at the college. In 1974, an English teacher said, approvingly, that his department "dealt with the diction problems of precision and appropriateness and taught units on how to use the dictionary, and we even did such 'Mickey Mouse' things as requiring everyone to bring his own dictionary to class for a dictionary check and tried to devise ways to ascertain that the book really belonged to the student carrying it around." Then, more critically, he outlined

Table 1. The Saint Joseph's College Core Writing Program

Core 1—Contemporary World	*Core 2*—Ancient World	*Core 3*—Middle Ages	*Core 4*—Modern World
(1) The aims of discourse 　(a) exposition: 　　scientific discourse 　　exploratory discourse 　　informational discourse 　(b) persuasion 　(c) expressive discourse (2) Organization (3) Techniques of development (4) Punctuation guide	(1) Persuasion (rhetoric) 　(a) organization 　(b) modes of appeal: 　　appeal to reason 　　appeal to emotion 　　appeal to strength of character 　(c) forms of persuasion: 　　deliberative 　　judicial 　　ceremonial	Research paper 　(a) primary sources 　(b) secondary sources 　(c) purpose and form of documentation 　(d) purpose and form of bibliography	(1) Expressive discourse 　(a) the personal essay 　(b) descriptive writing 　(c) creative writing: 　　satire 　　poetry 　　fiction
	optional: dialogues, myths, fables	optional: disputation, morality play	optional: manifesto, fantasy, social contract, criticism, pensée

Cores 5–6—Science	*Cores 7–8*—Non-Western	*Core 9*—Christian Humanism	*Core 10*—Seminar
(1) Observation (2) Exploratory writing 　(a) heuristic exercises 　(b) exploring models 　(c) analogy (3) Persuasive writing (science and public policy)	(1) Information discourse (2) Simulation and role playing	(1) Reflective writing (the autobiography) (2) Dialogue (At this level, students will be encouraged to make their writing a successful blend of exposition, expression, and persuasion.)	(1) The seminar paper (2) The policy-making paper
optional: science fiction, utopia/anti-utopia	optional: haiku, travelogue, 8-legged essay	optional: dialogue, prayers, liturgies, self-obituary creeds	

the problems of teaching basic skills: "Well, Core has replaced the composition course with all of those skills as it has replaced the introductory speech course with its compositional and elocutionary skills, the Western civilization history course with its research paper assignments, and the introductory logic course with its syllogistic logic. However, not only is the dictionary check gone, but so are all those skills" (Groppe, 1974, p. 1).

Despite such skepticism, this instructor joined his colleagues in 1976 in approving the requirement that writing be taught in all Core courses, according to the sequential approach sketched in Table 1. Three years later, the director of Core presented to the American Association of Higher Education a report that laid out the theoretical groundwork for an interdisciplinary and integrative approach to skills. His following comments capture the dramatic shift in thinking about teaching at Saint Joseph's as he describes how he, a philosopher, learned to teach *Rabbit, Run*.

> We would have two lectures on the novel by people from the English department, and then the rest of us would lead the discussions with groups of about eighteen freshmen—yes, musicians, philosophers, scientists, sociologists, communications people, and so on. It took me until last year to understand why the discussion leaders were appalled by the lecturers' talk of Harry Angstrom as a "deeply religious person" or even a "saint." The discussion leaders were judging Rabbit by their own value systems, whereas the lecturers were talking about him in terms of Updike's *text*.
>
> So I did some brief research into the section on "writing about literature" in Corbett's *The Little Rhetoric* . . . and into Panofsky's principles and methods of interpretation for iconography. . . . I devised a study guide for analyzing, interpreting, and evaluating *Rabbit, Run* for my students to use. At the end of our two weeks with the novel, all of

my students agreed with the lecturers' interpretation of Rabbit—and enjoyed very much being at odds with their peers on this!—but still very few of them liked the character much at all. I think their horizons were expanded by the experience of coping with the text on *its* own terms (it *is* a "religious" novel), and their evaluations of the book's issues were consequently much more informed and insightful. But to arrange for this to take place all throughout our Core curriculum, and for professors in any discipline to be able to make accurate and effective use of literature in their teaching, there is a set of skills that faculty have to acquire [Nichols, 1981a, p. 29].

The Core faculty is not a small, self-selected group: 60 percent of the Saint Joseph's faculty teach in Core as part of their regular work load. The college has had a hard time coming up with an appropriate way to describe the role of the faculty in Core discussion groups. "Colearner" is a common term, but people at the college, including students, do not like the familiarity and laxness it implies. Whatever term is used, it is clear that Core has had a deep impact on members of the faculty. They have been required to become learners outside of their own fields of expertise, which leads some of them to remember how it feels to be a student. Some have realized how limited their own education was. When Core began, few faculty members would have claimed that they were "embodiments" of the liberally educated person, as the writer of the statement opening this section suggests they should have been. This has been a humbling experience for some faculty members. As one of them put it, "Fifteen years ago I was king of the mountain. Now I have to listen to my colleagues." If the students are to become critically aware, it turns out, so must the faculty.

Everything at the college is turned to the end of creating a community of student and faculty learners in search of an understanding of what it means to be human. It is crucial that this search occurs within the themes and structures created in Core, which require great interdependence among students, among faculty members, and between students and the faculty. No longer can instructors and students go completely their own way as they often do at other schools.

Nichols (1981b) provides some basic facts about the students in 1980. Over 90 percent were white, 80 percent were Catholic, and 60 percent were male. The majority were first-generation college students. They were about ten to twenty points above the national average on the Scholastic Aptitude Test and between the 65th and 70th percentile in their high school classes. In their educational motivations, they were strongly vocational; half majored in a business-related field. Immediately after graduation, 70 percent took jobs.

As conventional thinking would have it, such students are unlikely to be drawn into investigations of the human condition. They are from middle America: fresh-faced, unquestioning, "good kids." Saint Joseph's students are not overwhelmingly interested in the higher professions or graduate school. They want to get their degrees, find a good job, and grow up.

These students are Saint Joseph's true mission. The instructors rarely complain about them or wish they had different ones, as faculty members at other colleges with similar students sometimes do. They are not out to uproot or humiliate them. Rather, they want their students to realize that there is something more spacious than what they have been taught to desire. As one faculty member put it: "I want them to be free of being tied to job, golf, TV, routines. I want them to learn how to live. Be free from the thought that there is nothing worthwhile in the past. Get out of this awful rut of life devoted to business, science, just a technical life. We give students a wide spectrum of problems, solutions, truths, mistakes. We want to force them out of their little prisons of a job and TV."

There is strong evidence that many students respond to Core in these terms (Nichols, 1981b). Several of my colleagues from the University of Michigan National Project IV staff talked at length to students at Saint Joseph's in arranged and

impromptu interviews. In a series of short vignettes in this and
following chapters, let us eavesdrop as students talk about what
education means to them.

The first two Saint Joseph's students are juniors: Dan
Kelley, an economics major, and Joe Fritz, a self-described hu-
manist majoring in mathematics and computing. (These names,
and those of other students mentioned here and in other chapters, are fictitious. Their characteristics and words, however, are
not.) Besides helping them to improve their writing and speaking skills—students almost have to talk in class since a good
grade depends on it—Joe said Core also had "deeper" effects.
Dan used the word "deeper" several times as well. When questioned about what he meant, Dan said that Core had led him to
look more deeply into himself and to think more clearly. Both
Joe and Dan said that Core had forced them to think about
things they wouldn't have thought about under ordinary circumstances—"and not to jump to conclusions." They felt that
Core had helped them deal with life better and that it had built
a better sense of community at the college by "opening" students, who could then understand one another better.

Another session involved students active in extracurricu-
lar life: Denise Calman, a senior majoring in history; Joyce Abbott, another senior in environmental geology; and John
O'Brien, a junior geobiology major. All three said that Core had
helped them with writing and speaking and that it had "broad-
ened" them and helped them to grow personally. It led them to
examine their own values by forcing them to look at "alternatives" and by increasing their compassion for others. The humanistic aspect of Core was especially important for John. He
drew an analogy between his academic experiences at Saint
Joseph's and an ellipse. His education had two focal points,
Core and his major. He thought the curriculum at other schools
was shaped more like a circle, with the major in the center and
general education at the circumference. At Saint Joseph's, studies in general education and the major reinforced each other.

Students in the student center and the laundromat were
informally interviewed. The first, a junior majoring in business,

said Core had made him more "well rounded." Like the others, he felt it had improved his writing and speaking ability and taught him how to examine his opinions as a result of learning about "alternatives." A shy person when he first entered college, he had become more comfortable with people because of Core discussion classes. The second student, a first-year business major, had only taken one Core course so far, but she liked the opportunity to meet and discuss ideas with other students. Two sophomores repeated the themes from other conversations. They said they had learned how to write and speak more effectively, had learned to think and define problems better, found it easier to open up to other people, and had become more inquisitive. One of them commented, "I'm not sure how everything fits together and where it is all leading." The other responded that he was not "too worried. Core has taught me that there are no easy solutions to most problems."

These interviews confirm the overwhelmingly positive results of the internal evaluation conducted for National Project IV (Nichols, 1981b). There is no question that Core helps improve reading, writing, speaking, listening, managing information, and thinking: Students in a broad survey were practically unanimous in saying that Core had improved these skills. It had also given them a greater appreciation for other points of view and of themselves as thinking people. Here are some of their comments: "Before I couldn't stand to read books and now I enjoy them," "Core has made me think and not merely accept what I hear or read; it has taught me how to think for myself and give my point of view," and "Core has made me less judgmental and more willing to listen."

Students also appreciated the interdisciplinary work and the idea of integrating what they learn. They talked about subjects being "tied together," of the intellectual terrain in which they are studying as "interconnected," of the world as consisting of "interactions." One sophomore compared this sense of coherence with the fragmentation of education at other colleges: "General education elsewhere is patchwork. At Saint Joe's Core is like a highway or mainstream. There is continuity

of thought even though you don't know where you're going. All
the teachers give their own perspectives and complement each
other. . . . I have friends who go to other institutions which
don't have a unified general education program. They have to
get off and on the curriculum—something people don't have to
do at Saint Joe's."

Certain courses, like those on non-Western cultures and
science, help students see connections among the various elements of the curriculum more than other courses. Some teachers are better integrators than others. But by the senior year—
called the "great awakening" at Saint Joseph's—students begin
to bring things together. Before then, they have to take it on
faith that they are heading in the right direction.

Along with a recognition of intellectual integration, perhaps even preceding it, is a sense of personal integration: of
being able to decide for yourself, of confronting received values.
What educators call the "confrontation with diversity" has powerful effects on students' values and growth. The diversity of
the disciplines combined with constant efforts to integrate
them, the contrasts among various cultures, the different ways
of thinking in the majors and Core, the alternative world views
represented in religious and scientific thought, and the variety
of beliefs and backgrounds among students and faculty confronted daily in discussion groups and readings are all harnessed
and put to use by the Core curriculum. For the first time in
their lives, students at Saint Joseph's participate in an intellectual community.

Saint Joseph's holds hope for higher education in the
1980s by demonstrating that it is possible to have an integrative
and thematic curriculum that does not surrender quality or
depth. It teaches us that the effort can be liberating not only
for students but also for faculty members. Finally, Saint Joseph's
tells us that a middling student body of no particular luster can
reflect on the most significant questions facing human beings.
"If you take Core seriously," as one senior put it, "you'll have
to sit down, sooner or later, and ask yourself 'What is the world
up to? What am I doing in it? What things do I value?' "

External Degree Program at Johnson State College:
Making Sense of the World

Who are we? We're quite ordinary. Our lives are full of sick kids, cold beer, death, close friends, dirty dishes, pride of accomplishment, love of children, hard physical work, clear north winds, bitter disappointments, and the smell of wood smoke. Some of us have lost our farms and we're seeking new directions. Others are secretaries on the way up, dissatisfied with the path that's been carved for us. Others simply see ourselves as somebody's wife or somebody's mother and we're beginning to discover that that's not enough.

Vermont is still like nineteenth-century America in many ways. People there have learned to make do with fewer material comforts. But they are in the twentieth century when they talk, as the comments just quoted reveal, finding new paths and meaning in their lives. Vermont is known in some educational circles for its innovative approach to the education of rural adults through the Community College of Vermont, which operates learning centers throughout the state, and through the External Degree Program (EDP) located at Johnson State College, one of the five state colleges.

EDP has adapted itself to the primarily rural population of Vermont. It serves close to 200 students who live all over the state in areas that are not within easy commuting distance of any of the campuses in the state system. An upper-division program, it accepts only students who have completed sixty credits of college work, either through courses or through the assessment of prior learning. Students in EDP complete the 122 credits required for the bachelor's degree by taking extension courses, weekend courses offered by Johnson State College, or courses on campuses near their homes. They may also do independent studies and internships. Each student builds a personal, hand-tailored program, which is spelled out in a learning contract each term and in an overall degree plan. These plans must include forty upper-level credits, thirty in one concentration. Sixty credits must be in liberal studies.

All students are assigned to a cluster of other students from their region who meet on weekends three or four times during the term. Each cluster is assigned a mentor who lives in the region. The mentor is quite unlike an academic adviser in a typical campus program. Because the students in EDP have little contact with Johnson State College—or any college, for that matter—the mentors must represent the college to them. For their students scattered around the countryside, the mentors must serve as the registrar's office, the campus hang-out, the faculty offices, the curriculum committee, the evaluation office, and the counseling center. The work is hard and, of course, underpaid.

EDP has a difficult time balancing its emphasis on flexibility with its equally strong belief in liberal learning. Like Empire State College, and the Goddard Adult Degree Program on which it was modeled, the individualized contract and the relationship between mentor and student encourages responsiveness to students' needs. But students do not always know what they need; even if they do, what they say they need may not be what the institution is willing or able to give. Requirements are a way to regulate the potential anarchy in such a system, but they are effective only if those who represent the institution—in EDP's case, the mentors—interpret them similarly. Like faculties in traditional institutions, the mentors are given latitude in how they carry out their work; differences, therefore, are inevitable.

Yet the mentors do manage to reach rough agreement on what constitutes a good education in EDP. How? It is clearly not because of the requirements they work with, since they interpret them quite differently. Rather, agreement comes from a belief in the potential of liberal education to help its students lead more enlightened lives and "engage productively with a changing environment" (Daloz, 1981, p. 10). EDP students come to their studies with a history. They are not empty vessels to be filled. Many are ready to examine their lives and their environments, sometimes at high personal risk. EDP places the readiness of older students for self-examination at the very center of its curriculum. As one mentor put it, liberal education in EDP is "the process of making new sense of the world —a process of transformation" (1981, p. 58).

How does this happen? All aspects of the program—the courses, the clusters, the mentors—are judged for their potential to stimulate students' development. In this, the mentors play a crucial role because students see them regularly. The mentors ask students to justify their academic choices and to articulate what they have learned in the program, necessary steps in the kind of development EDP represents. The mentors advise from six to twenty-five students, visiting them periodically to check on their progress and help them plan their programs. What might become merely paper pushing on a large university campus becomes teaching in EDP: "One mentor described his job as 'part accountant, part lawyer, and part philosopher-king.' As accountant, we help students slog through the slurry of paperwork; as lawyer, we help them design appropriate and defensible study plans and learning contracts; as philosopher-king, we work to help students examine their assumptions, question their values, and construct new, more comprehensive ways of thinking" (Daloz, 1981, pp. 58-59). It is, of course, the philosopher-king role that fascinates. Just how is this role conceived and how can it be applied to other teaching situations?

For a philosophy from which they could understand and test student growth, the mentors turned to William Perry's (1970) *Forms of Intellectual and Ethical Development in the College Years* and Jane Loevinger's (1976) *Ego Development;* both present stage theories of development. The mentor's role is to encourage movement from one stage to the next according to the Perry and Loevinger schemes through an effective mix of support and challenge. For example, a student in Perry's dualistic stage may honor authority and tend to view the world in absolutes of "right/wrong," "good/bad," and "us/them." The mentor must allow students at this stage first to talk about their current beliefs and then to "press the limits of truth" and "suggest alternative truths." Daloz (n.d.) suggests that students at

this stage may benefit from group discussions with other learners who are at the next higher stage. A group exercise could be
devoted to helping students examine several different perspectives.

The multiplistic learner, on the other hand, has "cast out
authority" and sees all truth as relative. At this stage, the learner may enter a "slough of despair," unable to make any sense of
the world. Here the mentor helps the student make connections. Once again he or she begins by having the student express
the multiplistic dilemma, as in the following example from an
exchange between a student and a mentor (Daloz, 1981, p. 41):

Student: It was possibly the knowledge that there were two
strongly conflicting points of view among the people who
would hear it and be reacting to it, and my feeling in being able
to identify the view of each side. But you can't take a position
if you feel both sides strongly because again you're caught between the two sides. And I suppose that's been the story of my
life these last couple of months. Being caught between the pro
and the con of the subject matter of a paper or between duties
at home and family relationships versus responsibilities at
school and life.

Mentor: It it worth getting educated?

Student: Well, I don't know whether I'd call it getting educated or not, but certainly I've taken in a tremendous amount
of new material.

Mentor: What's it done to your head?

Student: Sometimes it just rattles around in there and bangs
against everything else.

Several months later the student admits to the need for
new "connections" (Daloz, 1981, p. 41):

Student: I think there may be such a thing as being too detached.

Mentor: Oh?

Student: Yeah, I think detachment is a fine thing, but you
get tired of it after a while.

Mentor: You're feeling a need to reconnect again?

Student: Yes. I don't feel as though I've committed myself to anything.

The mentor can aid a student in the transition from multiplicity to commitment, Perry's final stage, by pressing for "a value hierarchy," having students "develop several different arguments," or suggesting "a comparative study or critical analysis."

The perceptions of student growth as outlined by Perry and Loevinger go far beyond the job of a mentor in an external degree program. Every teacher is to some extent a mentor, and the stage theories provide a framework for understanding students' needs. They offer a means to turn what might be casual conversations between student and teacher into learning sessions. Furthermore, the stage theories suggest that some assignments and teaching methods are more appropriate for certain students than for others (Weathersby, 1981). In EDP, the stage theories provide a conceptual basis for an in-house handbook, "Notes Toward a Simple-Minded Mentor's Guide" (Daloz, n.d.), used in the training of new mentors; they also provide a means of measuring student growth over an extended period of time.

> The scene is a graduation party. Karen has just received her degree in English literature after years of alternating work, study, and welfare. Her father raises his glass with a battered farmer's hand. "Well, now you got your diploma, what're you gonna be?"
>
> "Why, Dad, just the same as I've always been."
>
> "Well, you goddamn fool!" [Daloz, 1981, p. 54].

According to Daloz (1981) nearly all EDP students in 1980 were over twenty-five; the mean age was thirty-eight. More than 50 percent had full-time jobs, primarily in education (18 percent), business or clerical work (15 percent), and human services (11 percent). Almost 75 percent were women, the majority of whom had dependent children. Over 80 percent of EDP participants were part-time students.

Most students in EDP are ordinary rural Vermonters who decide that they "want that piece of paper," mostly to improve their work situation or earn more money. Take Betty Brown, one of the students in EDP interviewed for National Project IV. A business major, she has worked off and on over the years while raising twins. The rural community in which she lives is only a few miles from the town in which she grew up. Everyone in town knows her and her family and, while she sometimes dislikes their meddling, she also loves the closeness of small-town life.

In classic Vermont style, Betty would catch herself when she said anything too extreme. In an interview, she said first that the program was "expanding my curiosity. I've been short on basic liberal education. Philosophy courses have opened up a whole new world to me." Then more cautiously she added, "Of course, it doesn't change life completely. I can't see myself as having changed that much. I know husbands who were paranoid at first, mine included. Everyone's husband was a little concerned that it would make us more 'liberal' but everything is fine now." Then back to the excited tone: "I think more, I see a broader range of possibilities for action. I'm less judgmental. I haven't changed with regard to family and friends. I use my leisure time now to learn something rather than parking myself in front of the TV. If I wonder why about something I find out. I enjoy that. I'm more curious about government, politics, and my kids psychologically." And, finally, she attempted to connect what she is learning to her life in Vermont: "The program is giving me self-confidence to understand how little I do know. The limitations needn't affect my needs about thinking and reading. The notion that thinking makes something be—that's fantastic. The kind of person I may be up here in the woods makes it important that I take liberal studies to know what's going on."

The program's emphasis on development and the mentor and the individualized contract force students to pay attention to what happens to them in the process of their education. In the words of one mentor, it is education to help students "practice watching their own growth" (Daloz, n.d.). Some EDP students are highly articulate about the process of education itself, as well as its effects on them. This does not mean that they achieve the highest levels of intellectual and emotional maturity. The study done for National Project IV tried to determine systematically whether students' thinking becomes progressively differentiated and integrated, according to Perry's (1970) and Loevinger's (1976) schemes of intellectual development. Given that these students typically study part time, have other obligations besides studying, and lack the consistency of a regular campus, it would not be a surprise to find that change is limited. Yet evidence from the research indicates that students move in the desired direction. For example, while many students enter the program primarily for vocational reasons, they learn to view education in much more complex ways than as a means to a better job or higher pay. Their thinking becomes less dualistic, less simple. By graduation, the typical student in the study had moved from dualism through a more tolerant multiplicity to the edge of recognizing that knowledge is relative to context—Perry's (1970) highest stage of intellectual functioning. They view themselves as responsible agents in the world, become more skeptical about authority, and are more willing to make their own judgments (Daloz, 1981).

Waking Up to Life:
"The Notion That Thinking Makes Something Be"

For many of the students we encountered, not just those at Saint Joseph's or EDP, awareness took on an almost physical quality. Students came to see themselves as knowers, as people who control their own minds. They experienced the power of thought, as Betty Brown put it, "the notion that thinking makes something be." This notion consists of much more than bits and pieces of knowledge or mastery of academic skills. It is, in Mezirow's (1978) phrase, a kind of "perspective transformation" in which new learning is not just added on to old learning but, instead, transforms learning.

Students reached for a variety of metaphors to capture the feeling of transformation they were undergoing. Some spoke about life "before" and "after": Before, life was a prison; now, it is full of possibilities. One student in EDP contrasted her old life when her brain was "atrophying" as she "sat around making chocolate chip cookies." But now "life can only get wider." A young woman in the developmental writing program at Northern Virginia Community College contrasted the "prison of high school" with her writing classes, which encouraged her to think freely. Other students spoke of their growing awareness in quasi-religious terms. They felt "revived" and began "really seeing." As an older student from the University of Oklahoma's College of Liberal Studies said, liberal education "opens up the windows of your mind."

The students felt strongly about these matters. They talked in ways that combined thinking and feeling. Indeed, they took their education very personally. How does this happen? Somehow, in ways that we will examine in detail in later chapters, certain programs are able to establish linkage—connections between legitimate academic work and students' past or present lives (Cowan, Saufley, and Blake, 1980). For many students, higher education is an assault on self-respect, one of the many "hidden injuries" that Americans carry around with them (Sennett and Cobb, 1973; McDermott, 1969; Riesman, Gusfield, and Gamson, 1975). When linkage is established, however, students can become critical thinkers without being forced to take on an ill-fitting "academic" identity. The confrontation with diversity that is so necessary for intellectual and ethical development—called the "presentation of alternatives" at St. Joseph's and "developmental challenges" at EDP—forces students to examine their own beliefs without giving up who they are. Students become, in Richards's (1964) terms, more awake to the world.

We encountered many examples of this awakening in action. At Brooklyn College's New School of Liberal Arts, a two-year general education core curriculum was based on the simultaneous study of the literature, arts, sciences, and social institutions of one historical period; students met for four hours once a week. (The program was disbanded in 1980.) In this intense setting, students were almost wrenched into thinking. The following example, which shows the eruption of critical awareness for a student in a class on modernization, is described by the economic historian teaching it:

> In discussing the concept of modernization I questioned how Marx would interpret a set of events, then asked what Ricardo might say, or Keynes. My goals: to enhance recognition of various arguments, and the ability to manipulate them, leading someday to the problem of choice among them and the value implications of our choices. I am, as I have been all term, as careful as possible to keep my ideological preferences to myself, so the students don't choose Marxism or Keynesian economics or whatever just to please me. After an hour of playing what I call the law-school game (make them defend every possible side of the argument in a complex case), Donna—a very bright, articulate, but quiet student—erupts. "Don't *you* [me!] have *any* values? You're *always* just presenting the various cases, identifying who's who, pushing us to be able to analyze from five different directions. What about what you believe?"
>
> The class get dead quiet—are they interested, scared at a direct and relatively emotional challenge to me, both? (The unstated rules by which the class has been moving along have obviously been broken.) I try to smile or whatever, let the silence sit there, and look around. Florence, who has hardly said a word all term, starts tentatively, then gets more aggressive in the quiet way some of the students from the islands have when they finally decide to open up: "I know what you mean, but don't you realize that these are the

values in his teaching . . ." and off we go (or they
go—I can finally watch and direct traffic) [Margon,
1979].

When linkage is established and diversity introduced, students come to see that they can make what they learn their own. They become, in a word, committed to learning and its uses.

CHAPTER THREE

Preparing Students
to Use What They Learn

Hampshire student: The lab situation is great. It teaches you independence, allows you to be creative and follow your own interests.

Braithwaite: Could you give me an example of following your own interests?

Student: Yes. I wanted to study whales, and I decided to go to Washington to get information from a team of scientists at the Smithsonian. They kept giving me a runaround, slamming doors in my face. I finally got to work with them, though. They even invited me to join the team that rushes to reported whale beachings.

Braithwaite: You sound like a graduate student.

Student: In a way, that's true. It is good to feel trusted and responsible. When people work in the lab they seem to be enjoying themselves. A friend of mine wasn't planning to go to graduate school for a while, but he did go to visit the lab of a man at Berkeley whose work he had come across in his senior project. This professor was so impressed that he offered my friend a fellowship to Berkeley because of his understanding of how to carry out research.

Educating for critical awareness increases students' commitment to learning. Educating for use gives them the capacity to apply what they learn. As the Hampshire student just quoted suggests, a combination of these two modes of education can be liberating. But a useful education is typically thought to be training in practical skills like repairing an automobile or running a computer. The situations in which knowledge and skills are to be used are also thought to be quite narrow—generally, similar to the situation in which they were learned. Knowing how to repair an Oldsmobile may help in repairing a Volkswagen but probably not a television. Skilled teachers, however, are always looking for ways to teach the skills that will help students transfer what they learn to a number of different school subjects and "real life" situations (Bruner, 1960).

This chapter shows that education for use need not be limited to narrow skills. Hampshire College and the Radcliffe Seminars, both for superbly prepared students, offer opportunities to apply learning. They do so very differently. Hampshire is a young, innovative college with students between eighteen and twenty-two. In an intense residential setting, students are required to shape their studies in terms of their own interests. In order to survive, Hampshire students must develop general arts of inquiry and use them in a variety of academic and non-academic settings. At Radcliffe, the older women who take a course or two in the nondegree Radcliffe Seminars learn a different lesson about the uses of education. In the environment of a venerable women's college, they receive practice in making choices.

Hampshire College: How to Ask Questions

We start with the student's own concerns, whether they be scientific, quasi-political, or very personal. We are able to design courses and support individual and group examinations that catch students where they are: They may ask a political or ethical question and before they know it, they are doing work in physics, biochemistry, chemistry, or computer science [Lowry, 1981, p. 33].

Hampshire College is a small (1,200 students), private liberal arts college located in the rolling countryside outside the college town of Amherst, Massachusetts. The setting is idyllic, the students among the finest in the country. Founded in 1970, Hampshire opened after many years of planning with a structure that challenged many accepted practices in U.S. higher education (Patterson and Longsworth, 1966). Instead of standing independently, like most liberal arts colleges of its size and resources, it shares courses and other activities with Amherst, Mt. Holyoke, Smith, and the University of Massachusetts. Instead of traditional disciplinary departments, Hampshire brings together several disciplines within four schools according to their characteristic mode of inquiry: humanities and arts, natural sciences, social sciences, and language and communication. Instead of requiring students to take particular courses, they are told instead to complete projects and papers on topics of their choice. And instead of letter grades, students receive detailed evaluations of their performance.

Students at Hampshire proceed through three academic divisions that serve as graduation requirements. Division I is a breadth requirement in which students must ask a significant question and answer it by means of different frameworks and methods in the four schools. In order to pass Division I, students must complete projects and papers in each school. Division II, the equivalent of a major, requires that students build depth in one area through whatever means are appropriate: courses, field work, papers, and independent studies. To pass Division II, students take a comprehensive examination, usually oral, based on course evaluations, papers, projects, and a proposal for work in the next division. In Division III, students complete creative or advanced work in their Division II area. In the first two divisions, students design an individual program and examination with a faculty committee; the Division III paper or project also requires that a written contract be worked out with a faculty committee. The Hampshire program runs the danger of encouraging premature specialization and self-centered individualism, so Division III also requires that students take an integrative seminar with advanced students from other areas and engage in a community service project.

The Hampshire curriculum places a strong emphasis on paying attention to the learning process itself. Students are pushed to develop the general art of inquiry in all areas of their lives. They are encouraged to "learn how to learn" and to watch how they are doing it (Bateson, 1974). As students put it in interviews: "If there's any topic I'm interested in, I can track it down" and "I'm aware that the world has more to teach."

Such comments from older, more mature students would be striking but perhaps not surprising; they are extraordinary coming from students age eighteen to twenty-two. How does the college produce such results? The first answer lies in the weight Hampshire places on framing good questions. Students are encouraged to do what professionals do: ask questions, comb the literature, try different solutions. Students quickly learn that nothing will be given to them without strenuous effort. One student contrasted other schools, where students "get paint and a canvas with forms of the picture already arranged so all you have to do is dab on the paint as you are told," with Hampshire where "you choose the colors; you decide what you want to paint and how you are going to go about doing it."

In separating evaluation from performance in courses, Hampshire frees its faculty to join students in wrestling with a problem without worrying about playing favorites or biasing grades. Hampshire students talk about "working with" rather than "taking a course with" faculty members. They spend a lot of time with the faculty identifying problems, clarifying questions, experimenting with solutions, designing ways to test answers, reviewing findings, and critiquing papers. There are differences between individual faculty members and among Hampshire's four schools, but the faculty at Hampshire must, at minimum, treat students as intelligent and responsible people capable of doing serious intellectual work.

In the School of Natural Sciences, for which we have detailed information from National Project IV, three goals stand out as different from science teaching at other colleges: interdisciplinary instruction, concern for educating women, and a strong emphasis on hiring effective classroom teachers. Interviews with science teachers at Hampshire, like those with teachers in Core at Saint Joseph's, revealed a group of faculty engaged in analyzing how and why they teach. They spoke of a Hampshire style of teaching: a strong commitment to uncompetitive, collaborative modes of teaching rooted in the need to combat scientific illiteracy and sexist education. Faculty attitudes at Hampshire are "tinged with a missionary zeal": "We adhere closely to Hampshire's early dream of interdisciplinary and open-ended teaching of science. Part of this attitude is based on the fact that Hampshire opened during a time of great student unrest. Students were hostile to science and a faculty member cited Vietnam and pollution as two reasons for the hostility. Natural science took this attitude very seriously. We have had to 'try harder' from year one and the result has been that we have recruited a faculty who are enthusiastic about Hampshire's blueprint for education and receive a lot of pleasure from teaching in Hampshire's style" (Lowry, 1981, p. 31).

In recent years, a small group of science faculty have met weekly and questioned whether some modes of teaching are more conducive to nurturing women scientists than others (Lowry, 1981). They have been able to define two common modes of teaching often used in discussion classes—the "quiz kid" model and the "gladiatorial spectacle" model. Both seem antithetical to Hampshire's goals. The first is an example of the worst kind of recitation. "It is characterized by the teacher giving out a question that requires a single 'right' answer, then giving the class two thirds of the answer." The second type occurs in team teaching when two teachers have "a go at each other from different sides of a question." Both methods tend to make students feel "dumb"—passive observers of a performance put on by their teachers.

The alternatives, as the Hampshire science faculty sees it, are more collaborative and less dependent on the charisma of the teacher: students working in pairs or small groups, tutorials, or small class discussions that attempt to involve all students—regardless of quickness or native talent—in a common quest. Since the characteristic mode of inquiry in the natural sciences involves using the laboratory, students have chances to work with one another. The laboratory itself, a large space with moveable desks used jointly for experiments in biology, biochemistry, geology, chemistry, physiology, and environmental science, is set up to encourage interdisciplinary work. A large percentage of women on the faculty are in the natural sciences, the result of a concerted effort to attract women scientists. The women faculty members have strong bonds among themselves, and they tend to encourage mutual support and cooperation among their students. The science faculty is willing to start with students' concerns about the social and ethical aspects of science, which lead them to study ecology, sexuality, alternative energy sources, nuclear energy, and biochemistry. Students who are not concentrating in science are thus more likely to become actively engaged in doing some work in science. This interest, plus the large number of women faculty members, may account for the extraordinary representation of women among Hampshire's science concentrators: More than half of Hampshire's science graduates are women (Lowry, 1981).

Obviously, a system like Hampshire's depends on self-motivated students. On the whole, Hampshire attracts such students—certainly, these are the ones who usually succeed. More than one quarter of the students in each entering class are transfers, people who often feel that they were inhibited from following their own intellectual interests in other colleges. There are as well a cluster of first-year students with powerful urges to define their own pursuits. From superior high schools and educated families, Hampshire students exhibit a kind of intellectual courage that is unusual among young people of their backgrounds.

We got a sense of this in our interviews with several of them in 1980:

> Michael Marcus, freshman: During the year after high school, I was doing music on my own. I like to work independently. I liked the opportunity to explore what suited my fancy. With the five-college participation, it was the best of both worlds.

Chris Anderson, history concentrator: I wanted to go to Stanford. Hampshire was the only other place I considered. I was attracted by the independence. I came here and am doing all the things I wanted to do and didn't have a chance to do elsewhere.

Jeannie Lukens, natural sciences concentrator: I wasn't smart enough to get into Amherst. But they party all the time! They aren't curious about learning anything. They study only what the faculty tells them to.

Attraction to independence is rarely the same thing as being independent, and even Hampshire students have a hard time adjusting to freedom. The Hampshire program combines clearly defined ends with apparently undefined means for reaching these ends—the opposite of most colleges and universities, which tell their students what they must do but not why. Students at Hampshire seem to accept the ends but struggle constantly with the ambiguity and unrelenting freedom of means. Many succumb to a disease of the will known as "Hampshire drift." One freshman we interviewed, Eric Freedman, had chosen Hampshire because he had gone to an alternative high school and wanted the same kind of education in college. He was taking four courses but still felt unsure about what he was doing. He was concerned that he hadn't settled yet on any grand scheme for his inquiries. Eric was being inducted into the Hampshire way, one that allows for a good bit of questioning about the world—which often translates into questioning oneself. One faculty member described this as the Hampshire obsession. Students spend a lot of time at various points in their college years worrying about whether they are getting the right kind of education. They have what one of the students called "pangs of questioning." What am I doing here? Why am I doing this? If they alight on some answers, students are then likely to complain about feeling harried, about never knowing when they are going to finish. They become, in a word, academics.

Individual research is isolating, and there is not much of a student life at Hampshire to relieve the pressure. The school is too new to have an independent student culture and students share few common academic experiences. There is no question, however, that the emphasis at Hampshire on figuring things out for yourself is highly motivating. Students may have to take their equivalent of sabbaticals to clear their minds by dropping out for a while, but those who finally complete the Hampshire requirements do stunning work.

As several interviewers from the National Project IV staff learned when they spent as much time answering questions as asking them, Hampshire students quickly learn to add "inquiry" to their lexicons. What does this really mean? For some, it is the best way to get to the bottom of a subject; one student said that he felt he knew how to understand anything if he carefully inquired into it. Jeannie Lukens pointed out how the science faculty at Hampshire operated compared to faculty on other campuses. At Hampshire, "Faculty took the time to answer 'dumb' questions like 'How many molecules are in this room?', while off-campus professors sometimes say 'I don't know,' but it is probably not that they don't know but that they don't want to answer. They have a certain amount of material to get through in the class and they can't get behind schedule. Hampshire has taught me to take the time to look beyond simply studying a text. I have become more self-critical since being here. I have learned to enjoy the actual process of learning and not to concentrate solely on the outcome, like a good grade or a future graduate school."

For other students, "inquiry" means not taking things at face value, not trusting experts too much. Chris Anderson said he no longer saw knowledge "as a textbook." Continuing, he described how he was "writing a paper and reviewing it. I keep changing it. It's not the way I want it to be, but it has to be done. The standards here are very high; they are set by the students. That's the challenge—to accept some level of your own achievement and then move on. An 'A' is easy. I always feel sneaky when I come away with an 'A' from another campus."

Education, as Hampshire students see it, is an unending road whose contours are set in cooperation with their teachers. But it is up to the students to find their own path, follow it to the end, and decide when they have gone far enough. Occasionally the path will lead to a dead end, more often to a detour, and frequently through a maze. In the process, the students learn to articulate where they have been and how they have gotten there.

Radcliffe College:
Finding "the Self That Does Not Yet Exist"

A teacher of literature said the Seminars are much the same as other undergraduate programs—to teach skills such as reading, writing, communicating, and thinking in a way that makes them transferable to other courses and life. But she then took a step beyond this by referring to "the other self that does not yet exist" and her efforts to push students to this other self.

Everyone recognizes Radcliffe College, but only the cognoscenti may know that Radcliffe is organized differently from other colleges. Radcliffe was established in 1879 to offer women an education that was equal to what their brothers received at Harvard College. From the beginning, all instruction at Radcliffe has been provided by members of the Harvard faculty—initially by a small group, then later by the entire faculty of arts and sciences. At first, Radcliffe students were instructed separately from men. Men and women students began to sit in the same classes during World War II.

The current agreement between Harvard and Radcliffe, signed in 1977, retains Radcliffe's status as a separate institution with its own endowment, but it turns over all tuition monies to Harvard. Students apply to both Harvard and Radcliffe through a joint admissions office, and the diploma they receive upon graduation bears the seals of both institutions. Since 1975 there have been no restrictions on the number of women who may be admitted; the admissions process is now "gender-blind." Radcliffe participates in general policy decisions about undergraduate instruction and administrative appointments in the faculty of arts and sciences.

The relationship between Radcliffe and Harvard has become more equal over the years, but there is no doubt that Radcliffe still lives in Harvard's shadow. Having achieved its initial goal of equality between female and male undergraduates, Radcliffe turned to another item on its agenda—one that clearly distinguishes it from Harvard: "As it enters its second century, Radcliffe is focusing renewed energy upon its second and larger purpose—the promotion of higher education for all women. Thus at the time that it provides a number of educational opportunities and services for women undergraduates, the college has also initiated a variety of innovative programs designed to promote and enhance the education of women more generally" (Downey and Ware, 1981, p. 4).

Three clusters of programs serve this purpose. The research cluster includes the Henry A. Murray Research Center, a repository for longitudinal social science data on the changing experiences of American women; the Arthur and Elizabeth Schlesinger Library on the History of Women in America, a world-renowned collection of a wide range of materials documenting the contributions of women to American society; and the Office of Institutional Policy Research on Women's Education at Harvard and Radcliffe, which identifies significant issues affecting the education of women at Harvard and Radcliffe.

The second cluster of programs—public lectures and discussions—includes the Charlotte Perkins Gilman series, which sponsors presentations on topics and issues of special interest to women, and the Bunting Institute Colloquium series, which offers presentations of research in progress by institute members.

The third cluster includes programs for the personal and professional development of women. The Radcliffe Career Services helps women of all ages to define the meaning of work and success in their lives through individual counseling and workshops, and the Mary I. Bunting Institute, a postdoctoral fellowship program, supports women scholars and artists in residence for a year at Radcliffe to pursue independent study, research, writing, and other creative work.

The final program in this cluster is the Radcliffe Seminars, the unit that concerns us here. The Seminars were established in 1950 to give educated women in the Boston area an opportunity for "full use of the liberally trained mind" (Borden, 1950). Seven courses were offered that first year to seventy students. Over thirty years later, the program has an enrollment of over 1,100 students in seventy courses. The Seminars allow students to study a wide variety of subjects at the intellectual level of a senior honors seminar or a graduate course. Each year different courses are introduced. The new courses, often designed in response to student requests and changing interests of the faculty, are reviewed by committees of the Radcliffe Seminars Program and the Radcliffe College board of trustees.

The program operates on an open admissions basis. There are no formal entrance requirements, and the course fees range from $260 to $300. Scholarship assistance is available. Seventy-six percent of the students have a bachelor's degree; of these, 39 percent have a master's degree and some students hold the Ph.D. degree. Many participants are Radcliffe alumnae and the percentage of graduates of the Seven Sisters colleges enrolled in the Seminars is high. The Seminars provide the opportunity for some students to prepare for advanced degrees and to explore professional interests as well as to pursue subjects out of pure curiosity. Certificate programs are offered in management and landscape design. For each Seminar satisfactorily completed, Radcliffe awards four units of academic credit. The Seminars do not, however, grant degrees. Evaluation of course work is done either by a letter grade or on a pass/fail basis. Students overwhelmingly choose to enroll for a letter grade.

The subjects offered in any one year range across the variety of academic disciplines. In the two certificate programs, changing electives complement required courses. Within the three subject areas in the Seminars program—liberal arts, management, and landscape design—some of the course offerings are "Art, History, and Meaning: The Baroque Age," "Topics in the Psychology of Women," "Calculus II," "Organizational Behavior," and "Introduction to Plant Communities in New England."

Although many courses are not directly focused on women, they are more likely to include a feminist perspective than similar courses offered in traditional departments. Classes are small, and they encourage freewheeling discussion. Instructors, some of whom are former Bunting Institute fellows, come from the faculties of colleges and universities around Boston. Most are women selected for their commitment to teaching as well as for their scholarship. The Seminars are often as much an opportunity for the teachers to explore as for the students. One faculty member, a teacher of English at a state college nearby, said: "The Seminars offer me a unique opportunity and challenge as a teacher. The student body is superb. But more important for me, and for my personal and intellectual growth as a teacher, is the chance to develop and offer new courses—to try my hand at topics and subjects that the more traditional college curriculum committee might take years to approve. My Radcliffe course is always a course for me as well as for my students" (Parry, 1981, p. 8).

Carole Steiner and Lisa Keveles, both in their late twenties, had taken different turns in their lives. Carole, who had a B.A. degree and an M.A. degree in education, had worked in a program for children with learning disabilities. Married to a successful psychiatrist in the Boston area, she had given up her job to care full time for her two-year-old and saw her life as in an intermediate stage—devoted to motherhood but looking to the future. The Seminars gave Carole a taste of the future. A chooser of the path of least resistance when she was in college, she was convinced for the first time, as a result of her work in a Seminars course, that she could trust her own ideas. The expectations of the Seminars instructors were critical in helping her feel she could do intellectual work of quality. A "good girl," Carole usually did what her family expected of her—and that was not much when it came to a career and success. As one of the staff members from National Project IV described her after an interview: "She has envied her husband's involvement in his work and has wanted to experience that more herself. But it wasn't until the Seminars that she began to become clearer about what *she* wanted. A special tone is set in the classes by an emphasis on the job of learning, that it is *fun* to have a mind of your own. At the same time, there is a strong emphasis on women in transition and the women's movement. Courses directly express the belief that women need training or retraining. Careers and career change are presented as definite options."

A career change is precisely what Lisa Keveles had in mind when she enrolled in a Radcliffe writing course. An enormously self-confident woman who would not entertain the slightest skepticism about her talents, Lisa had given up a responsible job at a television station to devote herself completely to freelance writing. At the small women's college she had attended as an undergraduate teachers had discouraged her, but she persisted in her ambition to become a professional playwright and novelist. Unmarried, she was different from many of the other students in the Radcliffe Seminars, who enrolled because of changes in their family situations. Lisa hoped that being in Radcliffe's environment would open doors to the writing world. The writing course had already encouraged Lisa about her skill as a writer and helped her hone that skill even more. She liked the small classes that allowed contact with the instructors and encouraged comradeship among the students, who supported and criticized each other's work. She felt this experience had made her a better writer. She described the support as "endless, not only from the class but from the Seminars staff as a whole."

Both Carole and Lisa illustrate the different ways students experience Radcliffe's concern to help women "become who they can be" by seeing more options in their lives and acting on them. The very act of enrolling in a course is itself an indication of some change, as Carole and Lisa's stories make plain. Women enroll for different reasons: interest in a particular topic, instructor, or skill; interest in general, intellectual, and personal enrichment; and interest in help at a time when they are thinking about, or have already begun, making important changes in their family or work lives.

Whatever their original reasons for attending Radcliffe Seminars, the evaluation for National Project IV shows that the Seminars have effects beyond the initial decision to enroll

(Downey and Ware, 1981). A large proportion of the students said that the Seminars had bolstered their self-confidence, given them a greater sense of their own competence, provided an opportunity to reevaluate their own values, and introduced them to new perspectives on themselves and other women. The sheer job of learning, reinforced by exacting but sympathetic teachers, stimulating fellow students, and the supportive and confident ambience of Radcliffe, releases hidden talents and energies. As they master complex subjects, students feel more competent in other areas as well. They begin to make changes in their lives —taking the plunge into graduate school, renegotiating childcare arrangements with their husbands, taking on a new job. Quite a few capitalize on their course work to make career changes. Paula Blanchard, a writer who completed a biography of Margaret Fuller as a result of a Seminar, brings these elements together in an account of her own experience. "I had reached a point in my vocational life when I needed to take a big risk, and I didn't have the courage to do it on my own. The seminar was Jane Cohen's course on biography and the big risk was writing a book. . . . The course was demanding, but I think we all felt an unusual sense of community and trust after the second or third meeting. We were all women, mostly over thirty, and there was a sense of shared vulnerability and shared purpose. Possibility became contagious" (Parry, 1981, p. 9).

Making Education Usable:
"Knowledge Is No Longer a Textbook"

It is obvious that students at Hampshire and Radcliffe learn more than the particular subjects they study. In defining their own interests, students at Hampshire acquire a variety of intellectual and personal skills: how to ask a fruitful question and marshal information, how to handle ambiguity and suspend judgment, how to persevere. At Radcliffe, students learn how to assess themselves, receive support and criticism, set priorities, and test options. They come to be less afraid of risks and more able to capitalize on what they already have.

Linkage, as we saw in the preceding chapter, encourages

the development of critical awareness when it is coupled with exposure to diversity. It is also the first step in learning how to make knowledge usable, for it shows students that they can connect what they learn to their own lives. But to do so with control and competence, students need something more. They need skills that can be exercised in a variety of circumstances—what the recent literature calls "generic" skills.

As Whimbey and Whimbey (1975) put it, "intelligence can be taught." At schools like Radcliffe and Hampshire, where students arrive with well-developed capacities, generic learning can take place indirectly, although even with such students, too much should not be assumed about their emotional maturity or willpower. At less selective schools, generic skills must be taught more intentionally (Sadler and Whimbey, 1980). According to Woditsch (1977), these generic skills have five components, many of which are implicit in what Hampshire and Radcliffe students learn: (1) *selective attention*—controlling the stimuli on which the person focuses, (2) *sustained analysis*—breaking a complex problem into its component parts, (3) *drawing analogies*—testing what is known for its similarity to a new situation, (4) *suspending closure*—setting priorities or synthesizing factors before reaching a conclusion, and (5) *avoiding presumptions*—testing solutions before adopting them. When students bring these capacities to critical awareness, they are ready to make education their own. They are ready to engage in enlightened action.

CHAPTER FOUR

Helping Students
Make Choices
in Their Lives

Catlin: What do you want to happen to your students?

George Jefferson: (Instructor in the Institute of Study for Older Adults, New York City Technical College) I want them to see that they do not have to act out society's expectations of old people.

Catlin: How can you do that in just one course?

Jefferson: You can't, really. But you can start the process. My current students are mostly transplanted rural blacks from the South. They have had everything programmed for them in their lives. They do not question authority and they are ill equipped to deal with the different values of a contemporary, urban, Northern, white world. They do not take advantage of what is there for them, and they will not push to get what they want or should have.

Catlin: But how can a course on the politics of the Middle East teach them these things?

Jefferson: By drawing lessons that show them that other people have gone after what they want, and they can do it, too.

What George Jefferson is describing is termed *empowerment*—having the resources, skills, and personal qualities necessary to control one's own fate and to make a difference in the world (Cowan, Saufley, and Blake, 1980). It has a strong element of self-esteem, the belief that one can trust oneself to handle whatever comes along. It also carries a sense of options, a recognition that there are choices (Freire, 1970; Meisler, forthcoming). Educational institutions are probably less important in developing empowerment than other institutions like the family, work places, and communities. Yet in so many words, students in Chapters Two and Three told us that they felt empowered. Saint Joseph's students described new confidence in themselves as thinking people, EDP students a sense of personal and intellectual growth. Hampshire students learned that persistent and systematic inquiry could make a difference, Radcliffe students that they had more options in their lives.

Perhaps these students would have come to these realizations anyway; the backgrounds and academic preparation of Hampshire and Radcliffe students certainly helped. But what of the students without such advantages? It is especially difficult to imagine that formal education can change the passivity and helplessness of people who have been systematically blocked from power. This final chapter on the three aspects of liberating education presents two vignettes, both about programs for groups of people who have been among the least powerful in the United States: blacks and the elderly poor. Talladega College, a small school in rural Alabama, offers a traditional liberal arts curriculum to young students drawn primarily from Southern black families. The Institute of Study for Older Adults at the New York City Technical College teaches courses in a variety of subjects to elderly people in centers scattered around New York City. Working against considerable odds, Talladega and the Institute of Study for Older Adults offer examples of the empowering effects of a liberating education.

Talladega College: What It Means to Take Responsibility

There is a town called Sunflower, Alabama (population: 500). And there is a student from Sunflower who is unaware that she won't be able

to do anything she'll want to in this world. There is
something about this school that never tells her she
can't.

Dean Roland Braithwaite's depiction of Talladega College
in 1980 builds on a long history. Founded over 100 years ago,
Talladega was the first college in the state of Alabama open to
freed slaves. With funding from the American Missionary Association, a predominantly Congregationalist group, the college
came more and more to stress the liberal arts. This was not a
casual commitment. It stood definitively on one side of the controversy between those who advocated training in the practical
trades—the position taken by Booker T. Washington and best
represented by Tuskegee College and Hampton Institute—and
those like W.E.B. DuBois who spoke for a more general, humanistic education for blacks (Bowles and DeCosta, 1971). Talladega's models were the best liberal arts colleges in the country.
Inspired by the general education curriculum at the University
of Chicago during President Robert Hutchins's tenure there,
Dean James T. Cater, whose ideas exerted a strong influence on
Talladega years after his retirement, suggested a scheme of
courses in general education in the 1930s. In many ways, Talladega has been more faithful to the original ideals of liberal
education than the school on which it patterned itself. The curriculum remains relatively unchanged since the days of Dean
Cater. Since the 1950s the college has offered only the bachelor
of arts degree. Freshman survey courses in the humanities, natural sciences, and social sciences, in addition to mathematics,
English, and language courses, are still required.

Although it took over a white man's curriculum—and a
most elite one at that—Talladega brought a black perspective to
the liberal arts. It has always recognized the necessity to prepare
its students for careers, but it has aimed high—toward the professions rather than the vocations. Its students have succeeded
magnificently over the years. During the 1960s, for example,
Talladega ranked eighteenth among the top 100 colleges and
universities of the nation in the percentage of its graduates who
were awarded the M.D. degree (Manuel and Altendorfer, 1961;

Tucker, 1978). Talladega ranked first, among black colleges with twenty-five or more male graduates receiving the M.D. degree, in the percentage of M.D.s and science doctorates among its alumni. A follow-up of Talladega graduates between 1960 and 1978 showed that 80 percent attended professional and graduate schools at a time when the national average was considerably lower (Tucker, 1978).

The college takes great pride in these statistics as an expression of its commitment to individual achievement and social responsibility (Gurin and Epps, 1975). Talladega tells its students that they can do anything; they can shape their lives and learn in college what they need in order to do it. They can become leaders. But not just for themselves. They have a responsibility to become professionals who serve other black people.

Talladega College was a center of the civil rights movement in the 1960s, and for good reason. The college constantly reminds its students that they stand in a long line of black people who have had to overcome overwhelming obstacles. Since its founding, the entire ethos of the school has been dominated by the memory of the *Amistad* incident that led to the growth of the American Missionary Association, which eventually proved to be the main financial support for the fledgling institution. The *Amistad* was a slave ship on which a band of slaves mutinied off the coast of Cuba, took over the ship, and attempted to sail it back to Africa. The ship entered U.S. waters and was taken in custody by the Coast Guard. The American Missionary Association was the main support of the slaves in the resulting hearings, which ended with the freeing of the blacks (Braithwaite, 1981). A seal on the floor of the lobby of the college library commemorates the *Amistad* incident. Out of respect, no one walks on it.

Such a symbol carries more information than words. Faculty members and administrators tell the students "legendary stories of determination" that invoke the "names of the founding freedmen." These are things that do not have to be explained to students after a while; they are part of a "Talladega understanding" (Braithwaite, 1981). The Talladega understanding carries heavy freight, for it tells students that at once they can do good for their people while doing well for themselves.

Changes in the student body, as well as in the institution, may complicate these old heroic truths. Long-time faculty members feel that students today are different from their predecessors, less socially conscious, more concerned about vocational success, less prepared academically but also less willing to put in the effort to overcome serious academic deficiencies. Such things have been said about college students in other colleges and universities, but for Talladega they are a threat to everything it holds important.

In their struggle to come to terms with a new president and young faculty members fresh from specialized graduate programs, few of whom share their feelings about the heritage of Talladega, older faculty members fear that the college may be slipping away from them. While they may have to adapt to new times and new students, the college still holds to its own vision with considerable tenacity. The chapel story, as told by Roland Braithwaite, is emblematic:

> For years we had a chapel service on Sunday morning that was exactly like what you'd find at the Harvard chapel. I'd play Bach and everything would go along in a very orderly manner. But then came large numbers of students from fundamentalist families. We had to bring in some of the elements they are used to, like gospel music, things I was never forced to deal with. I talked to the choir director and other people on campus and I said, "Look, we're not going to have two competing ideals here at this small school. If the choir is going to sing Bach, the same kids who sing Bach will sing gospel. The kids who want to sing gospel will sing Bach. Everybody is going to do everything. We're just going to roll and take in the whole situation, the urban North and the rural South. We all have to learn from each other. It is important not to separate these things. It just kills your purpose.

Small (about 750 students), rural, and upright, Talladega offers its students a family feeling. Freshmen have big "brothers" and "sisters" assigned to them when they arrive. They visit members of the faculty in their homes, but call them by their last names. The religious influence remains strong, even though Talladega is officially an independent college. Although chapel is no longer required, many students go anyway, dressed up in their Sunday best.

The majority of Talladega students come from rural backgrounds and the immediate geographical area. They are, for the most part, first generation college students from families with modest incomes and relatively low socioeconomic status. The majority of incoming students have high school grade point averages of B or better, but two thirds of them arrive with deficiencies in basic academic skills (Braithwaite, 1981).

John Cook's grammar was atrocious. He had had trouble expressing himself when he first came to Talladega, but after a speech course and a lot of encouragement from his teachers, he came out of his shell. Although he was still less articulate than the other students with whom we spoke, he seemed more thoughtful.

His family was poor, but two of his sisters had graduated from Talladega. There were 100 students in the graduating class of his small-town Southern high school; of the twelve black graduates, two went on to college. When he first came to Talladega, John was not serious about studying, but slowly he began to work harder. And he had to work hard because things did not come easily to him. In economics, his major, he had to get special help from his instructors and fellow students.

For John, as for many students, a liberal education at Talladega meant getting an overview of a lot of things that "gets you to think about different subjects." He connected this with one of his most meaningful experiences in college, reading the *Wall Street Journal* (a requirement for economics majors). He learned about many things he had not ever thought about before, about business and industry and foreign policy. He talked about getting a new understanding of the world around him, especially of the relationship between current events and life back home.

These realizations led him to see that education could change people's lives, and he tried to convince high school friends back home to go to college. But this was almost impossible. "All they worry about is getting a crummy job to buy a car or get married. They are often unemployed. Some are in the army. They think college is a waste of time. But I keep telling them, do you want to do what you're doing now for the rest of your life?"

John thought things were going to get worse in the country, especially for blacks. Even though he had to make himself do it, he went home regularly and tried to convince his friends to go to college. He knew he did not have much of an effect on them, but he felt more optimistic about the kids in his neighborhood. There were several he kept after, telling them that they should work hard in school and better their lives.

Lucille Deems came to Talladega from a public high school in Brooklyn, New York. Several other colleges tried to recruit her in her senior year of high school, but she decided to go to Talladega because a godbrother who had gone there told her she would get a lot of personal attention. Lucille was not disappointed. A sophomore when we spoke with her, she talked about the concern and helpfulness of the faculty as she pursued her degree in psychology and planned her future in rehabilitation work. Like John Cook, Lucille appreciated being exposed to a variety of subjects. The most important things she had learned were to depend on herself and to take her work seriously.

Martha Jackson, the youngest child in a college-educated family from Birmingham, Alabama, was majoring in early childhood education. Like Lucille, she chose Talladega for its personal touch. Education at Talladega meant a little bit of everything, but most of all it taught her to depend on herself. The faculty, students, and staff pushed this lesson: "I learn a little from everybody about values, knowledge, and critical thinking. My ideas have changed a lot. I've learned that the world is a very competitive place. I didn't know that before. No one spoon feeds you here. Instructors talk about this all the time. They keep telling you to make the most of your four years, to assess your values, to keep the lines of communication to others open."

Taylor Brown was a couple of years older than most seniors at Talladega. From Charleston, South Carolina, he had worked as a brickmason and a hospital orderly for two years to save enough money to pay for college. An uncle who was a high school teacher told him about Talladega, and Taylor applied there because, as he put it, he did not feel ready for a white school. After finishing his B.A. degree in biology, Taylor wanted to go to medical school. He talked about how much more confident he felt about himself not only academically but also in personal relationships: "I am more confident about my knowledge. My performance on tests has taught me that I am better academically than I thought. I've learned to deal with people better. I have better relationships with the opposite sex. I think about what kind of relationship I want: Do I want to be a gigolo or have a serious relationship?"

In spite of the faculty's worries, Talladega continues to foster confidence and a sense of responsibility in its students, whose ambitions are high for a group with such shaky academic skills. The performance of Talladega graduates continues to be impressive: Almost half of the class of 1980 went on immediately to graduate and professional school. In a survey conducted for National Project IV, over 70 percent of the students said that Talladega had strongly influenced the ways they thought about school, friendship, work, the wider world, and themselves.

What is it about Talladega that has these effects? There is apparently nothing special about the curriculum or even about the teaching at Talladega. Rather, the answer seems to lie in the quality of daily life at the school, which is suffused with the example of the black struggle, its dignity, and its capacity to "go beyond." Whether contemporary students accept the responsibility to carry on this example—John Cook certainly has —is an open question at the moment. Whatever the outcome, it is clear that Talladega teaches its students a sense of personal responsibility. In commenting on the experience of being black in this country, Herman Blake, the black founding provost of Oakes College at the University of California at Santa Cruz, said that blacks must constantly face an environment that humiliates them. At Talladega, the environment is a loving teacher.

Institute of Study for Older Adults:
How to Stop Being a Victim

Goldie made me feel like Gulliver among the Lilliputians. At least seventy-five, she did not reach five feet. She proceeded to tell me the story of her husband. He had an illness as a young child which affected the normal growth of his legs. So he stands four feet six inches. She said he has had a chip on his shoulder all his life as a result of his size and all the teasing he has had to endure. He takes it out on Goldie by putting her down all the time. One of the problems with her taking a class is that it has made this tendency of his worse. Goldie is using the class to help understand her husband and how she can cope with his belittling her. But she is having a hard time. She is glad that he is still working at the age of eighty because having him around the apartment all day would be too much.

After telling me all this, she leaned toward me and with her Brooklyn Jewish accent said "So . . . what should I do? Leave him?"

The Institute of Study for Older Adults (ISOA) is a program for poor elderly people that brings liberal arts courses to nursing homes, centers, and hospitals throughout the New York City area. Most educational programs for the elderly, including those offered by four-year colleges and universities, tend to be recreational or practical. The few that teach liberal arts subjects, such as Elderhostel, attract middle-class, educated people. By most measures it would seem that a liberating education would be impossible at ISOA. Its students inhabit a world of physical limitation, poverty, and isolation. They are unprepared academically and too poor to pay for their courses. Many cannot travel beyond their residences, and they take their courses in ISOA under circumstances that are far from ideal.

The program itself lives on "soft" money (insecure grants) from the New York City Department for the Aging and grants from foundations and private corporations. In order to ensure the continuation of funding from these sources, the staff of ISOA spends an enormous amount of time in meetings and writing reports and proposals. Located within the Division of Continuing Education at the New York City Technical College (formerly New York City Community College, the oldest and largest in the city), one of the campuses of the City University of New York, ISOA has informal ties with staff members in the agencies that are part of the "aging network" in New York City —agencies that provide nutrition, social service, health care, and referral services to the elderly. These agencies are constantly vulnerable to cutbacks; ISOA is doubly so since education for the elderly is seen as a frill compared to basic survival services like providing food and shelter. Yet with little money, a fragile institutional perch, and a shifting "campus," ISOA has been able to serve between 4,000 and 5,000 people a year in 150 courses at 75 centers around the city.

ISOA students take classes in philosophy, anthropology, psychology, literature, comparative religion, and world affairs. They listen to lectures and have impassioned discussions. Although many of the old people cannot read long assignments and write term papers, they confront serious intellectual content by the sole test that matters for people in ISOA: its enhancement of life. ISOA operates on the assumption that stimulating old people intellectually will free them from the limitations of their lives by helping them to understand their condition. The only way this can possibly happen is if the students see a connection through the subjects taught and the teachers selected. The classes are free and do not carry credit or grades. Courses are taught in nursing homes, hospitals, and senior centers. Students participate in selecting the subjects to be taught. In some centers, the old people lobby for different courses, and it is not uncommon for more to turn out to vote on what is to be taught than actually take the course. Once the subject is selected, a qualified instructor is lined up from among moonlighting faculty members from other New York schools, freelance professionals, or retired professors. The courses meet for nine weeks at the sites; each session lasts ninety minutes. At the end of the course, students receive a certificate if they attend seven out of nine sessions.

The atmosphere in the classes is highly charged, as students engage in intense discussion with each other and their instructors. For them, what they learn in class *is* life. Two examples are cited here, the first from a course on the Middle East taught at a nursing home and hospital for the aged and the second from a psychology course in a high-rise apartment development.

In the course on the Middle East, the instructor, a fifty-year-old black man, spoke loudly and with feeling, moving briskly around the room waving his hands. He told a story about the rattlesnake who bit the housewife who took it in from the cold. He used this story to illustrate the U.S. government's offer of asylum for the Shah of Iran.

About forty students were in the room; three were in wheelchairs. They all closely watched the instructor, nodding as they listened. At one point he asked a question and got three responses at once. When the instructor said that the United States should never have allowed the Shah to come here, two students made sudden and highly emotional outbursts. One old man started fidgeting. His hands clasped and unclasped on the handles of the walker in front of him. His mouth trembled as he opened and closed it. His legs shook. He suddenly rose and leaned on his walker with one hand and used the other to point to the instructor. His voice shook as he said two incoherent words of disagreement. As the two words came out, the instructor said, "Thank you, sir. Thank you, sir."

The teacher of the psychology course, a retired New York University professor—small, frail, himself a senior citizen —stood at the front of the room. There were about fifty people in chairs scattered around in no apparent order, but mostly facing the teacher. The topic of the class was anger and under-standing it. The discussion was very lively, for brief periods un-controlled. Most of the students had something to say. Some expressed their views so that the whole class could hear, while others conducted private conversations. The room was buzzing. A lot of advice was being given. One woman was in favor of ex-pressing anger right then and there, but a man said that didn't get anyone anywhere. The instructor said, "For every truth there is an opposite. The important thing is to know thyself."

Taken as a group, the ISOA students range from fifty-seven to ninety-two; the average age is over seventy. Many have physical handicaps, and all are low income. Fifty-five percent are widowed, and 75 percent are female. About one third are black or Hispanic; most have strong ethnic identifications. The average number of years of schooling is 10.4 (Burgio, 1981).

For the old people in ISOA, the end of life meant strip-ping down to essentials. Of all the students we met around the country, they were the most eager to tell us what they had learned. And among the ISOA students, blind Dora Marmel-stein was the most eager. She did not talk about her blindness because she was more preoccupied with problems with her son. Recently divorced, this son had become "totally different," lashing out at her and blaming her for his problems. Dora's blood pressure had begun to climb. How did a class in psychol-ogy help her? Dora found a way of using it directly. She said that the class had helped her realize that "I am a person and don't have to bear the burden of my son's problems." She was not blaming herself any longer and was standing firm with her son, insisting that he seek psychological help and stop picking on her. As a result, her blood pressure was down and she was feeling much better physically.

Evelyn Golden was born deaf, and recently she began going blind. Her previous schooling had been limited, hardly more than eight years. In the psychology course, she had learned to her astonishment that even though she lacked two senses, she had three more. She never knew that she had five senses. She never knew that she had an unconscious and that dreams might mean something. The class had opened up a new world for her. In spite of her physical disabilities, she said that the class helped her realize that her problems were minor compared to others. She reads lips and speaks fairly clearly. "The biggest happening," she said, "as a deaf person, is to 'hear' others. It helps my mind work better."

Finally, Sally Bernstein, one of the oldest and best educated students in ISOA, talked about how she had been ready to give up on life when her husband died, until she became active in the center where the ISOA courses were being taught. She was especially proud of having organized a cooking class for men. What had she learned from the ISOA classes? The most important discovery was that there was a lot she did not know. Her main point, whether it was talking about her involvement in the center, or men learning how to cook, or the class, was that "elderly people should not give up on themselves. They need to have something to continue working for."

We were struck by the unusual openness of ISOA students, an indication of the lack of intellectual stimulation in their lives and of their freedom to take risks. As an administrator at the college put it, elderly people may be the last constituency for a genuine liberal education. Whether or not this is true, they certainly provide the purest example of the empowering effects of an examined life. For many of them, *college* was a term of awe and wonder; only in old age did they have the opportunity to fulfill a long-held wish to go to one.

The National Project IV study of ISOA focused on the effects of the program on the students' quality of life (Burgio, 1981). It asked whether they became more competent socially, more satisfied with life, and more active in their neighborhoods. These are major impacts to expect from such a limited educational program, yet the results suggest that ISOA courses have helped many students overcome loneliness and isolation. Few of the students in the survey were more satisfied with their lives—if anything, ISOA students were likely to be less satisfied than those who were not enrolled in the program—but they were virtually unanimous in saying that life was more interesting and more worthwhile as a result of their participation in the program. Their friendships and social lives had been enhanced, and they were more active in their relationships with others. The students had already told us how they applied what they learned to relationships with family members; behind these social effects lay intellectual ones. The psychology course, for example, gave Dora, Evelyn, and Sally a structured opportunity to see their lives in a larger framework. Out of this larger understanding, they could turn back to their particular situations and act in different ways. Even when they could not do much because of handicaps and illness, the students could at least use their minds to transcend their pain. As a nursing home resident put it: "I almost forgot I was in a wheelchair. The wheelchair wasn't important, our minds were. In class you don't feel like you're on exhibition, or that no one has any use for you. . . . The teacher made us use our minds, made us think. Not much else around here does that. Thinking is very important, otherwise you become a vegetable—something less than human" (Dabney and Chaiken, n.d., p. 6).

Becoming Empowered: A Feeling That You Can Do Something and Do It Well

Whether they are young or old, male or female, bright or dull, black or white, in a selective school or an unselective one, many students say that the kind of education they have experienced bolsters their self-confidence. What do students mean by this? They mean that they have come to believe in themselves, to trust themselves to handle more than they have in the past. They feel competent and able. These feelings are rooted in a general sense of mastery, which seems to derive from successfully engaging in difficult academic tasks. Which academic tasks are mastered and what is considered difficult varies according to the different programs and students' academic preparation. What counts for well-prepared students is mastering patterns of inquiry and critical thinking, while less well-prepared students are more often concerned with mastering basic skills.

By mastering academic challenges, students find that they can master other things as well. Frequently in interviews students described how much more confident they felt about being able to mobilize themselves for whatever comes along. While well-prepared, well-supported students spoke about internal struggles to become autonomous, less-privileged students described their struggles to resist succumbing to the academic, social, and financial difficulties that plagued them. The fact that they were enrolled at all was a triumph for many, and they had to marshal extraordinary energy and self-discipline to remain in college. They talked about learning how to set their own goals and follow through on them, to take responsibility for themselves.

Not only did the students come to think of themselves as competent people who could handle themselves but some also began to behave differently. In classes, students who had been silent and fearful got up their nerve and spoke, even when they were not entirely sure that what they were saying was right. They came to understand that there would be no reprisals if they made mistakes; some even saw that making mistakes might be a way to learn.

They began to stand up for themselves outside of class as well. Women, in particular, spoke of becoming more assertive. The elderly women in ISOA, for example, described how they began talking back to domineering husbands and sons. Women at Radcliffe learned how to take more risks in their families and careers. Through the resources of the mind and the will, they see that they might be able to exercise greater control over their fate. However, whether they can do so depends on more than mind and will. ISOA students may learn to stand up to members of their families, but they cannot very well control the economic and social forces that dominate their lives. Radcliffe Seminars students may see a world of career possibilities opening before them, but larger forces have as much to do with their future as boldness or even the backing of Radcliffe College.

CHAPTER FIVE

Creating a Lively
Academic Community

We never educate directly, but indirectly by means of the environment. Whether we permit chance environments to do the work, or whether we design environments for the purpose makes a great difference.

—Dewey, 1916, p. 22

A strong academic community has a sense of its purposes. The environment Dewey referred to and what is taught, and how, echo that sense (Martin, 1982). In their different ways, the programs described in this book express a sense of purpose —even a vision—of what a real education means. Like many academics, the educators in these programs do not find it easy to articulate their visions. Yet when they succeed in doing so, they connect what they do to a vision of liberation for their students. So, for example, Saint Joseph's College believes that Core should embody a vision of Christian humanism. Radcliffe College holds up an ideal of autonomy and informed choice. Talladega College tells its students that they have a responsibility to the black community. The Institute of Study for Older Adults (ISOA) believes that its elderly students have the capacity and the right to greater power over their lives.

These ideals are not simple responses to students' desires. Rather, they are expressions of what people in the programs think a liberating education ought to be. Core at Saint Joseph's does not unquestioningly accept the limited aspirations of its students; it pushes them to aspire to more enlightened lives than they have experienced. Hampshire College teaches its women students that they can become creative and accomplished scientists, despite their own doubts that they can. Talladega constantly warns its students to resist the temptation to make it on their own.

Obviously, these visions must be appropriate to the students being taught. That the elderly population from which ISOA draws has few educational, social, and economic resources means that the program cannot expect the kind of academic performance that schools like Hampshire or Saint Joseph's can from their students. Furthermore, ideals that are expressed in similar terms may, in practice, mean different things. Empowerment at ISOA means enabling students to gain control over the basic necessities of life; at Radcliffe it means choosing from a wide array of options. Even the justifications for studying certain subjects—mathematics, for example—differs. At Talladega, studying mathematics is likely to be seen as important for an educated citizenry. At Radcliffe, it is important as a way for women to enter technical fields.

Ideals must fit institutional environments. For programs in research universities like the Federated Learning Communities at the State University of New York at Stony Brook, the worth of the disciplines must be incorporated into its educational ideals. For programs like ISOA and the External Degree Program (EDP) at Johnson State College, an appeal to educate students of all ages will be more acceptable since their institutions see themselves as serving the general population.

But creating the conditions for a liberating education is as much a sociological question as a philosophical one. If colleges and universities are to be environments in which such an education takes place, they must design *structures* that overcome the isolation of faculty from one another and from their students. They must build *communities* that encourage faculty members to relate to one another not only as specialists but also as educators. And they must provide continuity and *integration* in the curriculum.

In their own ways, the programs we have examined have created academic communities for students as well as for faculty members. The term "academic community" has often been equated with "community of scholars," thus restricting it to the faculty and, occasionally, to graduate students. But an academic community can also involve undergraduates. Such a community thrives on students and faculty members getting together and talking. Even individualized programs like those at Hampshire and EDP reach for ways of getting students and the faculty together. They then become environments in which the faculty and students discover how exciting it is to discuss questions that matter. For many commentators on higher education, this is the beginning and the end of a true education (Schwab, 1978; Brann, 1979; Wegener, 1978).

The best example of this principle in action is the Federated Learning Communities (FLC) at the State University of New York at Stony Brook, a program that has intentionally cultivated academic community. FLC groups existing courses at Stony Brook around a broad theme, such as world hunger, social and ethical issues in the life sciences, human nature, and technology, values, and society. The federated courses, ranging from three to fifteen over one to three semesters, enroll students who travel as a subgroup through the courses, which also include students not enrolled in the full FLC program. The faculty members who teach the federated courses meet weekly over two years to exchange points of view and plan joint efforts. A seminar that helps students integrate materials from each course in the federation is taught by an additional faculty member called a "master learner" along with a graduate student, both of whom take the federated courses with the undergraduates. In addition, all the instructors who teach the federated courses team teach a core course for all FLC participants once a month to integrate and apply the content of their courses. Over time, the responsibility for directing the core course shifts from the faculty to the students. In the semester following the completion of the federated courses, students may pursue an interdisciplinary project under the direction of two FLC faculty members. Student projects have included papers on nuclear energy, the effects of photography on society, and the impact of computers on higher education.

In a major research university where faculty members are typically more preoccupied with their research and graduate students, FLC transforms the nature of the undergraduate experience of academic and social fragmentation to one in which the meaning of academic community is felt vividly. In several studies of the program, students consistently refer to a sense of community as one of its most important characteristics. They become comfortable in talking with the faculty and learn to give and receive assistance from other students. As one student put it, "I have come to appreciate the importance of academic discussion with my fellow students. I spend much more time discussing what I learn in school with my friends. FLC has opened doors to getting to know fellow students in an intimate academic community where we could help each other and lean on each other. . . . Learning slowly became . . . fun" (Landa, 1981, p. 1).

The faculty in FLC has also learned the value of academic community. One observer of the program reported that a master learner "stressed the warmth of personal interaction with students in the program and the strengthening effect it had on him. He meant much more than conviviality or creature comfort but seemed to reflect a feeling that intellect flourishes when there is stimulus and motivation derived from the zest and cooperativeness of a group of fellow inquirers."

The College of Liberal Studies at the University of Oklahoma offers an example of an academic community for adult students who spend most of their time working alone. After completing assignments, readings, and an individualized learning contract in humanities, natural science, and social sciences at home in consultation with a faculty adviser from the university, students attend a three-week, team-taught seminar in each of the three disciplines on the Norman, Oklahoma, campus. In their final year, students return to campus for a four-week integrative seminar taught jointly by three faculty members from three different fields. Such a seminar in energy taught by an historian, an engineer, and a geographer in 1980 brought twenty students together around a large table. Ranging in age from the middle twenties to the late fifties, the students included a small-town banker, a farmer, a rock singer, and several housewives.

At this session, the historian was talking about the nineteenth-century utilitarians. The students did not hesitate to interrupt him with questions and comments. There was a lot of joking—at one point, the instructor launched into the song "Eating People Is Wrong" by Flanders and Swann. The discussion turned to the welfare system in the United States. One student complained about welfare chiselers. The instructor said that in other parts of the country that are not booming like Oklahoma, people have no choice but to go on welfare. The geographer pointed out that welfare goes not only to the poor and the unemployed but also to farmers and big businesses. This comment evoked an impassioned discussion about the definition of welfare, the consequences of different forms of welfare, and what was morally right. This went on for a while until the historian brought the discussion back to John Stuart Mill.

Students realize how special their programs are. Saint Joseph's students, especially those who had applied to other schools or had siblings studying elsewhere, contrasted the challenge they encountered in Core with what they saw as inferior curricula at other schools. Students at Hampshire have a contrast ready at hand in the local consortium of five colleges. They spoke of how the bright students in some of the four other institutions in the consortium worked for grades and did only what their teachers told them, while Hampshire demanded that they make their education their own. Students at Stony Brook were articulate in describing the differences between FLC and standard education: "It is a different kind of learning experience than coming to school to obtain knowledge, where the teacher stands up there and lectures and says this is what you take as knowledge, this is truth. In this program the interplay between a student and a professor or other students leads sometimes to the development of new knowledge. Because you feel confident here to put forth an idea that people somewhere else would think was a little flaky. You may be talking to a professor and he says, 'Hey, you know, I never thought about it that way before.' "

Winter, McClelland, and Stewart (1981) found that a sense of specialness increases the development of liberal arts competences, especially leadership. This sense does not seem to result from any single aspect of the college experience. Instead, it seems part of a "hidden curriculum" that provides opportunities for direct participation in an active, intellectually alive community. The programs, therefore, are more likely to become "our world" for students than are typical departments and programs. They are places in which students come to feel that their membership is assumed, that it "goes without saying" (Perry, 1970). This is not only the first experience of academic community for them but also is often their first experience of any kind of community.

Students who feel insecure about their abilities or frightened by the academic world find protection in their programs. In interviews, they described the faculty as "caring," "trusting," and "available." They referred to their programs as "homes" and "families." A student in the New School of Liberal Arts said, "across the street" (as she referred to the rest of Brooklyn College) was a "different world" from "our own nest." A student in Hofstra's Labor Institute of Applied Social Science, a black woman with a full-time job and three children, started out at a community college. In contrast to the impersonality of the community college, the labor studies program "is like family. I feel disappointed when someone drops out. We're working people together. We're treated like adults." Another student said that compared to the four-year campus she had first attended, the Hofstra program made her feel as if she were "on the ground. It's given my life 'a life.' " At the developmental writing and mathematics program at Northern Virginia Community College, Project Intertwine, a student talked about how much students came to trust one another. They "learned about life from the experiences of others. There was one woman who talked about how she was beaten by her father and we all accepted that."

Secure and sophisticated students are more likely to say how their programs affect them intellectually, but like other students, they also feel nurtured as people worthy of learning. A woman in her fifties who had worked her way up from a secretarial to an administrative position in an aerospace company described the College of Liberal Studies at the University of Oklahoma as a place where there "is kindness. I have never seen a put-down. There is constant encouragement, never diluted with 'Yes, but . . . .' The whole setup says to the students that they are being taken seriously as thinking people."

It is difficult to separate the social from the intellectual aspects of these little worlds, since they are such total environments for their students. Although fun, encouragement, and a sense of being special are the source of their success, these are means rather than ends. We are speaking, after all, of communities in which hard intellectual work is the main focus. As a faculty member in the New School of Liberal Arts at Brooklyn College often said to his freshmen, "I want you to feel comfortable—so I can then push you damned hard." The students in the programs are not typically "isolates who have now been blessed with a few intimates. They are people who have suddenly discovered that intimacy has a function in learning; that discussion in a trusting atmosphere is crucial to intellectual discovery and moral honesty; that recognition that professors have opinions and ideals leads to examining one's own view points" (Landa, 1981, pp. 3-4).

Such worlds may seem too cloistered, too protective for the good of their students. For some students, this may be true. But for most, the closeness and intensity of these worlds seem to enable students to move out into the wider world, much like students in the schools examined by Winter, McClelland, and Stewart (1981). The key here is the extent to which students have the opportunity to use what they learn in other courses and settings. The faculty members we encountered outside the programs who have taught students from them sounded much like faculty describing students in experimental programs: The students talk more, ask more questions, are unwilling to take too much for granted (Gaff and Associates, 1970; Riesman, Gusfield, and Gamson, 1971, Meiklejohn, 1981). As one faculty member who teaches both in the College of Liberal Studies and a department at the University of Oklahoma put it: "My students in the regular college like to be *told*. Students here like to *ask*." A faculty member at Saint Joseph's College observed: "After they go through Core, they're never the same again. They just question a lot more." A graduate of the Stony Brook program said that in other courses, "if I don't understand a particular concept or I don't agree, I will question it until I *do* get the understanding. I use the tools I have learned in FLC in the other courses that I am taking. I don't take things at face value. I go and I question. I have found that while it takes a lot of time and effort, if you go to professors and you bug them enough, they'll answer your questions."

The Power of Context

One of the lessons to be learned from several of these programs is that it does not take a lot of money or a residential institution to build such communities. Rather, attention to how the curriculum is structured to affect social relationships is critical. Radcliffe, Hampshire, Talladega, and Saint Joseph's can rely on the natural conditions that are conducive to the formation of academic communities—a clearly defined area called a campus, a history, and a sense of tradition—but EDP, ISOA, the Oklahoma program, and several others cannot. They must, therefore, be more self-conscious about how they function as educational environments.

One important component of community is the provision of facilities for students and faculty members to get together outside of class, preferably near classrooms. This is more important for commuter institutions than for residential ones, where opportunities for informal interaction are built into the physical layout and rhythm of daily life. In the New School of Liberal Arts at Brooklyn College, four-hour classes required breaks. During the breaks, students and faculty members could get together in the modest coffee lounge located near classrooms and faculty offices. The Radcliffe Seminars are taught in comfortable rooms in the gracious building that also houses a fine din-

ing room on the Radcliffe campus. In the College of Liberal
Studies at the University of Oklahoma, students live in dormi-
tories for the three or four weeks that they are on the Norman
campus to attend their seminars, eating together and with the
faculty in the common dining room and going to classes in the
adjoining building in the continuing education section of the
campus. The Federated Learning Communities' lounge and
mailboxes for the students and the faculty are near the administrative offices in the science building. The lounge is used almost constantly for informal get-togethers and meetings, although the program had to fight to get the space and scrounge
for furniture in faculty members' attics and basements.

Many of the programs have carved out niches for themselves within their institutions. These niches are organizational
as well as physical. They use everything within their control—
physical facilities, faculty roles, teaching styles, the curriculum
—to express their visions of education. EDP, ISOA, and the College of Liberal Studies bring education to their students and
operate with unusual time schedules—short intensive seminars,
clusters, and weekend courses. The New School of Liberal Arts'
four-hour classes, EDP's clusters, and Oklahoma's campus seminars all represent efforts to intensify the educational experience, particularly for commuting and geographically dispersed
student bodies. The seminars at Stony Brook, the Division III
seminars at Hampshire, and the interlocked Core curriculum at
Saint Joseph's are different ways to structure integration among
elements of the curriculum.

One striking feature of some of the programs is the way
in which members of the faculty coordinate with one another in
their teaching and students participate in shaping the curriculum. In ISOA, potential students in the centers for the elderly
vote on the courses they want to be taught. At Saint Joseph's
College, student representatives are required to be members of
the Core planning committee. At FLC, students increasingly
take responsibility for running an integrative seminar.

Faculty work together in a variety of ways: planning curricula, coordinating their courses with one another, team teaching, and jointly reviewing students' work. For example, faculty

in the New School of Liberal Arts who taught in the ancient world curriculum for poorly prepared students met for a week before classes to work out course objectives and integrate the syllabi. The group included a reading specialist, a writing teacher, a counselor, and instructors in the courses (social institutions, literature, and art) that were to be part of the ancient world curriculum. The following is an account of the group's work:

> Fighting a natural tendency to create reading lists on the first day . . . or to define their own disciplinary "turfs," this group of faculty focused instead on the needs of the students. What would these students need to learn within a year if they were to perform college work successfully? . . . By the end of the week, the faculty had broken down . . . complex goals into smaller, testable objectives, . . . assigned responsibility for presenting and testing them, and then reintegrated them back into a traditional college curriculum based on readings in the Old Testament, *The Epic of Gilgamesh,* Sophocles, Plato, and Homer [Black, Hey, and Margon, 1981, p. 28].

Throughout the year, the group planned occasional joint class sessions, organized field trips, visited each other's classes, and went over students' work together.

In Core at Saint Joseph's, faculty meet to plan readings and assignments. Faculty members teaching in the Federated Learning Communities attend a seminar before and during their association with the program; in the seminar they relate what they do in their individual courses to the theme of the federation. At Hampshire, the divisional system brings faculty together on committees to decide whether a student is ready to move on to the next division. In EDP, mentors struggle together over whether students meet the program's requirements. In the University of Nebraska's individualized university studies program, faculty "fellows" meet together to review students' study plans. In the College of Liberal Studies at the University of Oklahoma, members of the faculty from different disciplines teach seminars jointly. Having to work with people from other disciplines can be enormously frustrating. In the blunt words of a faculty member from Saint Joseph's: "I don't plan a Core course all alone; I have to do it in anguished and exasperated dialogue with a whole set of other prima donnas who are just as pin-headed as I am in virtue of *their* training, except that they have *other* specialties."

Gradually, the instructors become used to explaining what they do to other "prima donnas." It helps if they are placed in situations that redefine how they teach. Several of the programs have, indeed, created new faculty roles—the mentor, the counselor, the adviser—or new ways that faculty members play traditional roles—the colearner, the master learner. These changes in faculty roles often have the effect of minimizing the faculty's psychological distance from students. The clearest example is at Hampshire, where the faculty cannot rely on a grading system to control students. "Inquiry" at Hampshire is another way of saying that the faculty and students are on the same side with respect to a problem or body of material (Elbow, 1979). In EDP, mentors are not responsible for covering a body of knowledge; they are stimulators of a process in which students come to decide what to study, why, and how. At Saint Joseph's, the very notion of "colearner," however uncomfortable it may sometimes be for students and faculty members, is an attempt to recognize that they share a common quest for understanding and mastery. The same is true for the master learner at Stony Brook.

This balancing act is a tricky business, because the faculty does know more than students. Even if they are not experts in the particular subject they are called on to teach, as at Saint Joseph's or in team-teaching setups, the instructors do know more than most students about how to go about learning something new. In the Federated Learning Community's term, they are "master learners." It is difficult to make faculty accessible and human and at the same time maintain their authority (Gamson, 1967). Yet students in the programs do not appear to reject the authority of their teachers, as students often do when traditional controls are removed. Why? Because their relationships with faculty members are embedded in curricular structures and communal forms that legitimize both the accessibility and the authority of the teachers. They come to know their teachers in more authentic and less stilted circumstances than the typical undergraduate does and, therefore, are likely to see the faculty in more realistic ways. More important perhaps is the fact that the programs are built on discourse and critical thinking, which means that students can express disagreement with the faculty legitimately in the daily life of their programs.

The key to a liberating education does not lie simply in faculty members' good will or rest on convincing them to adopt this or that teaching technique. Rather, it grows from structures that build in opportunities for dialogue and active student involvement, which then change the way faculty members behave as teachers and students behave as learners. Like collaborative research teams, teaching groups in secondary schools, and integrative mechanisms in industry, such structures are the basis for organizational and individual vitality (Little, 1982; Kanter, 1983).

CHAPTER SIX

Inspiring Teachers
to Revitalize Teaching

Knowledge should be a refreshing and vitalizing force. It becomes so only through stimulating intercourse with congenial friends with whom one holds discussion and practices application of the truths of life.

—The I Ching, 1976, p. 224

An almost inevitable cultural gap makes it difficult for instructors in most colleges and universities to deal with differences between themselves and their students. They tend to concentrate, therefore, on the students who most resemble them or who are easiest to influence. When they cannot find such students in satisfying numbers, faculty members are likely to withdraw from teaching. Their zest dries up and they find themselves caring less about their students. Thus begins a vicious circle in which they and their students merely go through the motions of learning and teaching (Hill, 1974).

In numerous colleges and universities, this situation is essentially the end of the story. But in many of the programs we have examined and in other schools as well, teaching remains a vital activity (Gamson, 1982). At some schools, one reason is that the single course carries less weight than it does in most undergraduate curricula; individual courses have been dethroned in favor of an encompassing curriculum and educational vision.

This has several effects. First, what happens in the classroom is more visible to other faculty members and students. Second, responsibility for what students are to learn is shared among colleagues—conscientious teachers are released from an "Atlas complex" that holds them responsible for everything their students learn (Finkel and Monk, 1983). Third, students and teachers come to see connections among the courses in the curriculum and are more likely to have a common understanding of why certain subjects are important.

These arrangements release hidden reservoirs of energy. At the New School of Liberal Arts at Brooklyn College (NSLA), the style of teaching came closest to what most people mean when they speak of "class discussion." Classwork was usually based on the study of a single text selected as a key work in the historical period in which students were taking a cluster of related courses. Here is an account written by an observer of a class conducted by a literature professor we will call Brown:

> As I walked into Brown's class, I was immediately adopted as a class member. I introduced myself and took a seat next to a tall and quiet young man—Chicano or Puerto Rican—who showed me the page and line that the class was studying. The room held about twenty students comfortably; they sat at tables arranged in a square horseshoe design; there was no teacher's desk. The teacher wandered back and forth at the front of the room. His shirt sleeves were unbuttoned and fluttered as he walked. His tie was loose and his watch was buckled onto his belt. He talked almost constantly, quickly, and with much emotion. He joked with the students and carried on a conversation with them about Milton's *Paradise Lost*—a dialogue, not a lecture or even a discussion.
>
> They were talking about "the inferiority of women" as reflected in *Paradise Lost* when I came in. Three young men at the end of one table were laughing and making comments slightly off the

topic. Brown responded quickly to them, returning a joke for a joke—not abusively, but very directly. These young men later became very involved in the conversation. Two young black women also participated very regularly, their comments almost totally related to the women's viewpoint that was left out of *Paradise Lost*. Brown talked about the lack of self-confidence of women, about loneliness, about self-love, about motivations for love, about self-esteem—all in the context of Milton—and the students responded with interpretations of the literature based on their own experiences. It was obvious that they came to understand Adam and Eve as Milton portrayed them.

All of this was happening very quickly and Brown was being loud and pushy with his students —but never abusive. He yelled at them to "shut up"; he screamed a verb correction at a young woman who missed the verb "flew." He talked constantly, but he accepted interruptions and he always listened carefully. He responded to all comments students made, and the conversation was, indeed, directed by them. Brown redirected it only by questioning what students said. (In fact, he verbally responded to students' grimaces as often as to their words.) It was obvious that the students were immersed in Milton. They scanned the text easily for proofs of their assertions. They were intently trying to understand Adam, Eve, and Milton on the basis of their own experience.

This class has several noteworthy features. First, there is the way the observer was immediately included in the group. The student who invited her to share his text was undoubtedly following an example the teacher had set early in the semester: All students should participate in the study of the assigned text. The arrangement of the tables removed the teacher from the center focus and enabled students to speak face to face, thus reinforcing the message that all should participate. Second, the instructor's open and brash style provided an interesting combination of informality and high expectation. Neither a bland facilitator nor a distant expert, Brown started with the students' own experiences of love or loneliness and moved from their personal responses, through consideration of the text and development of counterarguments, to a more critical, detached stance. Students were learning to examine their own experiences, to think critically—by providing evidence, formulating questions, avoiding logical fallacies, and presenting counterarguments—and to think abstractly about philosophical issues.

Brown's style ("loud," "pushy") is his own, but the discussion approach he used was typical of classes in the New School of Liberal Arts. There are several reasons for this: The program was directed primarily to freshmen and sophomores, graduates of New York City public and parochial schools, who were quite passive about learning. The instructors felt a particular urgency to have students speaking in classes, since they could not lecture their way through four-hour classes all term. They were, therefore, forced to pay attention to pacing and to devise classroom activities that would make difficult texts come alive. The interdisciplinary nature of the program and the absence of traditional departmental structures encouraged teachers to seek connections among disciplines and between what they taught and what mattered to their students. When they succeeded, the classes changed. Students contributed more, and they became engaged with their teachers and with one another. These relationships affected encounters outside of class as well. For example, the writing teacher in the one-year preparatory program on the ancient world was meeting with students we will call Claudia and Marguerite about their outlines for a paper comparing Telemachus in *The Odyssey* with Theseus in *The King Must Die*. The students had reached the point in the term when they were expected to write papers with clearly expressed thesis statements. After reviewing Claudia's outline and suggesting that she use only one of several good ideas to organize her paper, the instructor turned to Marguerite:

Marguerite showed me two versions of her outline; she was still having trouble formulating her ideas. Her confusion led to a freewheeling discussion among the three of us that lasted about an hour and a half. I used my old tutoring technique of writing down Marguerite's more interesting statements, so she would then have something on paper to work with. For much of the conversation Claudia assumed the role of questioner and again demonstrated her keen intelligence. One of her questions was especially provocative: "What was Theseus's goal? Compare that to Telemachus's goal. How do their goals affect what happens in the two works?" At the end of the discussion Marguerite still did not have a final outline, but she had done some real thinking about the assignment [Mlynarcyzk, 1979].

Such encounters emerged spontaneously out of the program's structure. No coherent philosophy, no specific social goals, no set of liberal arts objectives were defined at the start of NSLA. Only later, after several years of practice, did the faculty members realize that they had come to a similar version of teaching. They came to see that discussion was a crucial part of what and how they taught. But what exactly was discussion, they asked? Was it a pedagogical technique only or was it also a subject that could be taught? Certainly, it was clear that discussion was a way to "get students over the belief that they have nothing to learn from one another . . . that teachers know everything." Several instructors worried that discussion could become an unfocused bull session and insisted that it be keyed closely to the texts. Others felt comfortable with more open-ended approaches. They used the *New York Times,* films, or weekly quizzes to generate questions that opened a debate that was meaningful to the students. One faculty member videotaped student performances of a Shaw play, "partly to get the students involved in the play but also . . . to get them to see themselves as others see them. In all cases, the faculty seemed to be interested in getting the student to 'own' what he or she was doing in college, whether through questioning and discussion, performance, focus on life histories, or whatever" (Black, Hey, and Margon, 1981, pp. 15-16).

Liberating Teaching: Active, Articulated, Demanding

The NSLA instructors looked around and saw that their program was far different from the usual approach to undergraduate education. Yet it seemed to work for themselves and their students. This led them to call into question some traditional notions of the academic enterprise, especially the view of the teacher as dispenser of knowledge and the student as passive consumer. They came to speak of teaching and learning as an active process, one in which students and faculty jointly participate. In this, they were neither unique nor advanced. Paolo Freire (1973) criticized the "banking" conception of education (in which students are receptacles into which bits of knowledge are "deposited"). On the basis of observations of college classes between 1969 and 1971, Kenneth Eble bemoaned the state of college teaching and concluded, critically, that "the professor giving out, the students taking in, is the central way college teaching takes place" (Eble, 1978, p. 8). In *Teaching as a Subversive Activity*, Neil Postman and Charles Weingartner (1969) urged that asking questions be at the center of teaching, and they pointed out that this mode of teaching is at least as old as Socrates—and just as dangerous now as it was then. Throughout the 1960s, Carl Rogers encouraged teachers to take a learner-centered approach to teaching. In *Freedom to Learn*, Rogers (1969) documented some early attempts made by elementary school, college, and graduate school teachers to become "facilitators." Freire (1973) and Shor (1980) urged teachers to become "problem posers" working to break students' dependency and passivity.

Much work has been done by cognitive psychologists on learning as an active process (McKeachie, 1980; Weathersby, 1980). More than twenty years ago, Jerome Bruner (1960) wrote of the importance of helping students connect what they learn in classes to other situations based on the active mastery of general principles. From an entirely different perspective, writing teachers like Kenneth Bruffee (1980), Peter Elbow (1973), and Mina Shaughnessey (1977) have developed classroom techniques that support what is currently called a "learner-centered philosophy" that "starts with the student" (Hendrix and Stoel, 1982).

The NSLA curriculum based on historical periods hardly started with the student, and yet the faculty was able to establish linkages with the students' lives in the process of teaching (Cowan, Saufley, and Blake, 1980). By pressing his students to answer questions that mattered to them, Brown, for example, helped them see *Paradise Lost* as still living and open to debate and controversy. In contrast, classical texts and knowledge in general tend to be purveyed to undergraduates predigested, as if they were not as problematic as they really are (Kuhn, 1962; Bell, 1968). The disciplines are volatile at frontiers, where physicists, for example, debate about the nature of the universe (Lin, 1981) and psychologists and literary critics blur their genres (Geertz, 1980). Instead, students need to grapple with the process that animates the search for understanding, not in their "finely honed disciplinary form; rather more in the form they first came knocking on the human mind—opaque, recalcitrant, misleading, and unyielding" (Woditsch, 1977, p. 26).

In classrooms, a question—"How many molecules are in this room?" "What was Milton's attitude toward women?" "Should anger be expressed?"—guides discussion. These questions lack simple answers, and the teacher's role is to lead students through a variety of techniques and activities toward progressively more accurate and more complex responses to such questions. Each individual's experience or perception—the teacher's as well as the student's—adds to the total understanding of the question at hand. When students begin to realize that the search for understanding is embedded in their own experience, they can see that their "conceptual abilities are omnipotent" (Woditsch, 1977, p. 26). They are then ready to be active learners who can question and challenge, inquire and research, discover and invent. Thus *Rabbit, Run,* as it is taught at Saint Joseph's College, challenges students' comfortable assumptions about morality, Hampshire stresses learning how to ask a good question, the seminars at the Federated Learning Communities confront students with the differences among the disciplines and somehow reconcile them, and the External Degree Program requires students to work out their own learning plans.

Liberal education is sometimes defined as an initiation into "the conversation of mankind" and, indeed, teachers and students use "talk" to describe what goes on in their classes. But what exactly is meant by "talk"—or, for that matter, by "dialogue," "discourse," or "discussion"? These words are used frequently in descriptions of teaching in the various programs we have been examining. How, as skeptics like some of the instructors in NSLA asked, is discussion different from a "rap session" or just "shooting the bull"? The answer is that discussion is different when it is treated as something to be learned in its own right. Discussion, as the NSLA faculty realized, is not only a means but an end, "not merely a device, one of several possible means by which a mind may be brought to understanding of a worthy object. It is also the *experience* of moving toward and possessing understanding" (Schwab, 1978, p. 106). It is, indeed, one of the several ways that students learn the generic arts of expression.

While discussion is closely connected to helping students become active learners, it is also important as one way they learn to articulate. In many of the programs, students not only need to learn something in an active way, they must also try to express what they are learning, sometimes even while it is going on. This emphasis on articulation means that thought must be communicated—it must be made public. In the process of communication, thought itself becomes clarified.

Classroom discussion is only one arena in which skills of articulation can be learned. Classes that are too large for discussion can be divided into smaller study groups (Bouton and Garth, 1983). In the Federated Learning Communities, while the faculty members who teach the federated courses often lecture, the program seminars outside the regular classes give students the opportunity to ask questions and construct their own understandings. Students also learn to articulate when they work together on course materials or projects.

At Hampshire, the natural sciences laboratory courses work in this cooperative way. At the University of Michigan's Residential College, groups of students work with faculty members on a collaborative research project. At Brooklyn College and Beaver College, peer groups critique each other's writing (Bruffee, 1983). At the University of California at Berkeley, underprepared minority students in introductory mathematics courses work through problems together (Bouton and Garth, 1982). In several universities in Great Britain, student "syndicates" work out assignments in a variety of subjects (Collier, 1983).

The African-American Music Program at the State University of New York at Old Westbury offers an intriguing example of articulation in music. The program is organized around instrumental music taught at beginning, intermediate, and advanced levels. Even at the beginning levels, students with no musical background are expected to improvise. For the first element of improvisation, evolution, they are required to sing a melodic idea suggested by the minor ninth chord. After they complete a number of exercises on evolution, they move to revolution, repeating the same process using a dominant thirteenth chord. Then they move on to resolution, this time using the major seventh chord. Eventually, students learn to take the three parts through the keys at various tempi. All of this happens in front of the class, and students learn to listen closely to their peers, provide helpful criticism, and take responsibility (Lawrence, 1981).

Even programs that do not offer courses can push for high levels of articulation. We have seen how the College of Liberal Studies at the University of Oklahoma brings students to campus for short, intense seminars. In programs that assess the prior learning of adults, articulation of what has been learned from experience is as important, perhaps more important, than the experiences themselves. Certainly, the relationship between mentor and student in external degree programs like that at Johnson State represents superior articulation. When programs work well, they uphold an ideal that an adviser in any college or university might try to attain. Meta-thinking, an important component of articulation, is closely connected to learning those

generic skills that make knowledge transferable and useable.
Several of the programs ask students to assess their progress
regularly. Others, like Saint Joseph's College and Hampshire
College, require a project in the senior year that integrates and
applies what students have learned. Frequent program evaluation, when it is authentic and asks students to reflect on their
experiences, is not generally thought of as part of the educational process. Yet as we will see in Chapter Nine on evaluation,
a number of the programs assess themselves regularly and use
students as respondents and even as researchers.

Teaching, as we have been describing it, is neither easy
nor laissez faire. "Learner-centered" but not "learner-directed,"
instructors must plan exercises and assignments and carefully
direct what goes on in their classes. Like the effective teachers
studied by Schneider, Klemp, and Kastendiek (1983), they
make heavy demands. They make these demands because they
believe that their students are capable of accomplishing more
than is normally expected of them. The result is that many students do. Thus, poorly educated, disabled old people talk of the
unconscious and U.S. policy in the Middle East at the Institute
of Study for Older Adults. Saint Joseph's freshmen learn sophisticated literary analysis. Talladega students read the *Wall Street
Journal*. Stony Brook students in the Federated Learning Communities debate the great issues at the frontiers of the disciplines. Hampshire students do research at the graduate school
level. And students in NSLA's preparatory year program who
began barely able to put together a sentence compare Theseus
with Telemachus in formal essays.

Liberating the Faculty

In the old days, I was virtually not answer-
able to anyone *but* my students either for what I
taught or for *how* I taught *my* classes. I tended to
be the big answer man for them—sole arbiter of
truth in content and justice in grading. We just
didn't talk all that much with one another, and I
surely didn't listen all that much to them. Core

really tends to *explode* all that. . . . In discussion groups, I *have* to listen to my students, and they to one another as well as to me, as we wrestle with the content. And not infrequently, one or the other of them knows a *lot* more about the topic under discussion than I do. Yet I have to evaluate his performance and give him a grade. It becomes a topsy-turvy world; one feels inept and threatened, humiliated and frustrated. If one does not despair and surrender, it all becomes very salutary after a time. I find that I tend to respect and trust, have faith in and hope for, and downright love students far more than I used to. And I even believe that these feelings are mutual [Brinley, 1974, pp. 4-5].

This teacher from Saint Joseph's College has been forced to question his old ways and to understand anew why he teaches. He described his old ways in tones of authority: "my students," "sole arbiter of truth and justice," "big answer man." The qualities to which he turns in describing his new views on teaching are gentler, more receptive: "listen," "respect," "faith," "trust," "love." One way to describe the changes this man has undergone is to say that he has been liberated himself. He found himself in a situation—the Core program—that forced him to confront his way of teaching and to look for a new approach. This led to a struggle about his sense of himself as a teacher and, eventually, to a new conception. Although they are about the same age as faculty members on the average in U.S. colleges and universities (Fulton and Trow, 1975; Bayer, 1973), come from typical graduate schools in a range of disciplines, and have decent publication records, teachers at Saint Joseph's and some other programs in National Project IV have gone through similar transformations.

In graduate school, students are expected to learn the traditions, knowledge, and methods of a discipline but are left to pick up the craft of teaching by osmosis—if at all. Given their rather typical profile, therefore, it is not surprising that teachers in the programs usually plunged into their first teaching jobs without thinking much about how to conduct a class. With their own experiences as students and perhaps a few graduate teaching assistantships from which to draw, they typically began by imitating their own teachers. A veteran teacher who has been at Hampshire College since its opening observed: "For many of the young faculty originally hired, Hampshire was their first or second teaching job. They tended simply to reinvent their old classes, to seek refuge in the teaching models with which they were familiar."

Thus, the principal concern of teachers when they started teaching was to present their discipline coherently at a level suitable for their students. What is the matter with this? Most teachers would be happy with it. Looking back, however, these teachers feel something was missing. A science teacher, describing her early approach to teaching, implies that good teaching is something more than what she thought then: "I was concerned about being a good teacher in the sense that I knew the material. I mean, most science teachers really think of presenting the material, but they don't necessarily think of how they are doing it." A teacher from Stony Brook's Federated Learning Communities called his early style of teaching "the inspired presentation of material"—a form of "intellectually responsible showing-off, teaching as if to say 'Look at me! Aren't I smart?' " When done well, this is an exhilarating experience, and it is little wonder that new teachers try to do it if they can.

However, not all teachers can pull off the "inspired presentation of material" approach. Even among the teachers in the programs discussed here, those who succeeded now look back and see an undercurrent of discontent that they did not perceive at the time they began teaching. Sometimes it was reflected in an inability or unwillingness to lecture, other times in a queasy feeling that what they were teaching made little sense to students. They recalled teaching when they first began with words like "insecurity," "doubt," "anxiety," even "guilt." For many, these feelings were more than a beginner's nervousness. The Hampshire College science teacher just quoted remembered that she began to "sense that my concern about knowing the material was not the way to teach." Another talked about searching for a "natural" way of teaching and groped for examples of what she meant: the one-room schoolhouse, or perhaps the "open" classroom, or people learning on their own when they really want to find out something.

The discontent among the teachers came from several sources and was expressed in different ways, but it seems to point to a common desire to "make connections" not normally made in college settings. Making connections among the disciplines was one. They began to search for a broader view of the world that might help their students fill out their understanding and integrate the various courses they were taking. While they still identified with their disciplines, these teachers felt that staying within the confines of their fields prevented them from asking certain questions. They began to look for approaches that would broaden their own research and improve their ability to communicate with colleagues from other disciplines. Part of the desire for more connections among the disciplines stemmed from a yearning for more intellectual community than they found in their institutions, where teaching was typically a solitary and lonely occupation.

Teachers also found the connections with their students missing. A teacher in the Stony Brook program wrote about "feeling that my experiences as a teacher had never been quite what I wanted them to be, but I was at a loss when it came to understanding why. It seemed to me that those moments when I had come closest to absolute confidence and command in front of the class were haunted by a kind of loneliness, even when my audience was with me all the way" (Bordo, 1979, p. 1). She had a mental image of how a class should operate—as "a kind of communal conversation"—but it was "something that I felt helpless to make happen." Other teachers were disturbed by the obvious fact that only a small percentage of their students got actively involved in thinking, let alone feeling joy in learning. One faculty member talked about a kind of "academic strip mining," as he saw his colleagues put all their efforts into the best students and essentially throw the rest away. Like the effective teachers studied by Schneider, Klemp, and Kastendiek (1983), these teachers were unwilling to write off a broad spectrum of students because they were average or unprepared for college. Indeed, some seemed to prefer working with students who were not "stars," who learned slowly, who had lost their way in the educational system. These students presented a challenge to them, and they learned from trying to reach them. A teacher in Brooklyn College's New School of Liberal Arts who had attended a Quaker high school, Vassar College, and Columbia University described her first encounter with poorly prepared students at Queens College:

> I was stunned by their writing. This demanded, immediately, enormous changes, and I began to become critical of my teaching. I was confronted with students who couldn't write, really couldn't write. I had to think about the whole process of learning and writing. Then, just pragmatically by talking to colleagues dealing with the same problem and keeping up with what people were beginning to publish about how to teach writing, I found ways of doing it. At that point, I began to be fascinated with the process of teaching writing.

A science teacher at Hampshire College who had attended Smith College, Harvard University, and the Massachusetts Institute of Technology talked about how she learned to deal with students, especially women, who thought they were "dumb" about science:

> The rightness of answers inhibits the freeflowing and critical inquiry that education should promote. I try to find another way to ask questions so that they open up the possibility of discussion and trial and error without making students feel that they're venturing forth into an area with a right answer. . . . My awareness of the need to do that came from my experiences with my children when they were little. They would bring home drawings from school and they were very proud of

them. If I said, "That's a nice house" and it wasn't a house, the kids felt bad. And if I said "What is it?" the kids felt bad because they felt they hadn't drawn it right. So you learn to say "Tell me about it," something that is much more provocative and gets them to put in the meaning that they have for the picture. I think that kind of approach works on the college level, especially with students who have some fear of the subject or some sense that they are dumb. The word "dumb" came up in many of our student interviews. It casts a certain amount of judgment on the kind of teaching style where the goal *is* to make the student feel dumb.

Thus, the teachers seem to have been heading for a vision of the educational enterprise that is broader than the conventional one. Even when they began their academic careers, they seemed to sense that education could mean more for their students and for themselves. Although they held attitudes that supported interdisciplinary study and the inclusion of students who have often been neglected in higher education, they did not start out to be educational innovators. When they joined their programs, they did not do so in order to improve their teaching styles or to engage in a grand experiment. In fact, some happened to be in their programs through what can only be called fortuitous circumstances, as in the case of several women who took jobs in their institutions because their husbands' work brought them to the area. Other teachers were often participants for reasons unrelated to the goals of the programs in which they taught. Several of the faculty members in the Federated Learning Communities who may have joined the program out of boredom started questioning old assumptions about the limited capabilities of Stony Brook undergraduates. Some questioned their earlier teaching practices, experimenting with new ones and testing emerging ideas in their classes. The effects were often slow and incremental.

One teacher talked of feeling her way along, as she learned from chance "encounters and insights here and there." She described the loneliness she felt as she weaned herself from old ways of operating in the classroom. Faculty members at Saint Joseph's spoke with much feeling about their fear of stepping beyond the boundaries of their disciplines to teach Core discussion sections on materials from other disciplines. Many of the teachers in the programs stood alone. They were looking beyond ways of teaching that they already knew to methods that were untried in their own experience and rare in the world of college teaching. As they experimented with different subjects and techniques, they had to put themselves in front of their students. This self-exposure was unsettling. More than status as an expert is called into question when teachers stray beyond their disciplines. Observers of the various clusters at Stony Brook have witnessed the full extent of the teachers' struggles in the program over the years. Katz (n.d., p. 5) wrote of the "profound questioning of one's skills of enabling students to learn, not to speak of the even profounder challenge to one's personality." Taylor (n.d., p. 2) noted that teachers joining the program invite "shattering uncertainties" and "anxieties of a kind that most have not faced since graduate school." In many of these programs, the faculty is forced to recognize what it is like to be a student, especially one who does not take easily to the world of ideas.

Mina Shaughnessy (1977) observed that the greatest barrier to good teaching is teachers' ignorance of their students. As they sought new grounding for their teaching, faculty members in several of the programs began by observing their students more carefully in classes, through systematic data collection, and in discussions with their colleagues. In the setting of Hofstra University's labor studies program, for instance, teachers came to see that they needed to help their students overcome fatalism. They described their students as people "who have no faith in their own capacity to control, determine or plan their own destiny. For some 'making it' seemed to be luck—'hitting a number.' . . . For our learners it seemed essential to develop both self-esteem and respect for their working class culture and heritage" (Silverman, Franklin, and Kessler-Harris, 1981, p.4).

As they search for new ways to reach their students,

some of the teachers in the programs have become quite sophisticated about educational theories and their application to teaching. Indeed, their teaching practices apply many of the principles found in the most advanced thinking about cognitive and life cycle development. Like others around the country, some instructors have begun to read Piaget (Piaget and Inhelder, 1969) and Perry (1970, 1981). They have also been willing to cross departmental boundaries, as they turn to psychology, sociology, and education for ideas that will help them construct a coherent pedagogy. This is a significant change in college teaching, for faculty members have long scorned the study of pedagogy.

The result is that teachers in many of the programs feel excited about teaching. They display little of the condescension to students, dyspeptic talk about poor preparation, and despair about the capacity of the classroom to affect students' lives that characterize faculty writing about students (Gamson, 1982). If they do not run away from the pain involved in changing, faculty members become acutely self-reflective. They begin to analyze the values, assumptions, and habits that color their teaching. They talk about how participation in their programs has allowed them to express commitments they had kept locked away from their institutional lives, such as working for racial, sexual, and economic equality; contributing to the improvement of life in their communities; and participating in the arts. By teaching in new ways, they have come to see themselves differently as professionals. Although some of their colleagues will not go near their programs for fear of draining time away from research or other pursuits, the closer a few of them venture, the more enthusiastic they seem to become.

At Stony Brook, a hard-nosed and skeptical faculty group has ended up convinced of FLC's value. A professor in the English department said that she had been hesitant about joining the FLC because she feared it would devalue the disciplines, like several of the experimental programs she had observed in the 1960s. This fear turned out to be unfounded. A sociologist described being dragged "kicking and screaming" into the program—and then discovering how much fun it was to argue and gossip with colleagues from different fields. A philosopher spoke of the effects of his colleagues on his teaching: "I was astonished about how much I did not know about my own teaching. The weekly reports on my class, the master learner, the opportunity to observe others in the classroom, and the constant discussion of teaching techniques have all profoundly altered my attitude about teaching. I was infinitely more relaxed in my classes in the spring term and (I think) a better teacher. I have every expectation that this new attitude will stay with me for a while" (Taylor, n.d., p. 7). From such contacts with colleagues in other disciplines and the attention paid to pedagogical issues, faculty members in the programs come to see their participation as generating valuable working relationships and sometimes lasting friendships. In the University of Nebraska's University Studies Program, faculty fellows from different departments have worked together to such an extent that they finish each other's sentences. Like some of the teachers in the other programs, they have learned that they can enjoy talking with people from other disciplines and let their teaching be evaluated without feeling spied upon or judged by inappropriate criteria.

In their own ways, faculty members become aware that "the medium is the message"—that teachers educate as much by *how* as by *what* they teach. This principle has a symbolic level: Teaching style becomes a metaphor of an attitude toward human relationships. What finally distinguishes the teachers in these programs from individuals in other colleges and universities who are searching for better ways to teach is that they work in the context of a program that structures their relationships. Like the students, they take sustenance from their programs. They feel pleasure in their relationships with students and take pride in their accomplishments. As one teacher put it, "The best summary statement of my motivation is what happens to the students." The programs make it possible for faculties to find out that their students know more than they do about some subjects. Thus begins the mutual entanglement of students and teachers: The faculty is open to its students and works from their abilities, thus enhancing the students' ability to contribute and, in turn, making teachers both more open and more demanding.

CHAPTER SEVEN

Modifying Course Content to Encourage Critical Awareness

Knowledge does not keep any better than fish. You may be dealing with knowledge of the old species, with some old truth; but somehow or other it must come to the students, as it were, just drawn out of the sea.

—Whitehead, 1949, p. 102

When faculty members talk about what should be included in the undergraduate curriculum, they quickly get caught up in a discussion of "what every educated person should know." Asking this question implies that certain subjects must be included regardless of who the students are, what kinds of faculty are available, and what the history of the institution has been. Such an essentialist view of content is misleading, since the undergraduate curriculum has been profoundly influenced by external forces: (1) changes in economic and cultural conditions, (2) the composition of the college-going population, (3) the rapid increase in the growth of knowledge, and (4) the device of awarding credentials to succeeding waves of professionals (Rudolph, 1977). These forces have come to particular schools in different ways, with the result that there has not been a common undergraduate curriculum for a long time (Blackburn, 1981; Burke, 1982).

Furthermore, essentialism flies in the face of the obvious difficulties colleges and universities have in reaching agreement on the undergraduate curriculum outside of the disciplinary major. As long as the faculty holds to an essentialist ideal of the One True Content, philosophical differences and competition among teachers will degenerate into arguments about whether philosophy is more important than history or literature more important than mathematics. Territorial disputes lead almost inexorably to a distribution system—which begs the question about what is important to teach by letting the students decide. Instead, colleges and universities must accept the fact that the content of the curriculum must be pluralistic—that is, it must supply different plans for students to follow.

Such a notion holds terror for many faculty members. Someone almost immediately asks, "Does this mean that anything goes? If so, you don't really care about *content*. All you care about is *process*." We have encountered comments like these in faculty discussions of the curriculum across the country. They imply that essentialism equals seriousness about content and pluralism equals frivolousness. But if we are to make any progress on the matter, we must recognize that it is possible to be serious about content and hold a pluralist view of what is to be taught, just as it is possible to hold to an essentialist view and not be serious about content. Indeed, content may matter more in a pluralistic curriculum because pluralism is likely to force an examination of the potential of different contents to educate students in certain ways.

Once and for all, let us dispense with the notion that there is one content that all students in this country ought to study. Let us say finally, even regretfully, that not all may need to read Shakespeare or Plato. For a liberating education, a faculty must select subjects that will help students achieve a broad critical awareness with the commitment and skills to apply that awareness. Within this broad conception, many different subjects and texts can be taught—including Shakespeare and Plato. In some schools, for example, the study of women is seen as a legitimate part of a liberating education because it extends the understanding of the human condition by bringing attention to people whose experience has been inaccessible, even to themselves (Minnich, 1981; Martin, 1982; Watkins, 1981). Black studies and studies of other groups that have been denigrated or ignored in the standard curriculum (workers, for example) offer some schools the opportunity to stretch their students' awareness in other ways (Radzialowski, 1981; Stack and Hutton, 1980). Non-Western cultures, international studies, environmental studies, humanities, and technology have all been suggested as suitable content at one school or another.

Choosing appropriate content is a complex matter for a teacher or an institution interested in a liberating education, for attention must be paid not only to the intrinsic characteristics of texts and assignments but also to their potential for stimulating the changes in students they believe should occur. This presumes that enough is known about students to make such a judgment. Yet most faculty are unaccustomed to deliberately selecting what they teach on the basis of an assessment of who their students are, however much they would like to stimulate changes in them. The first step, then, in designing a curriculum for a liberating education is to assess students' prior experiences, skills, commitments, and needs. This assessment need not be a costly or even elaborate affair. As we will see in Chapter Nine on evaluation, an attitude of continuous examination of students' needs and reactions is most important.

At the same time, as we saw in Chapter Six, liberating education, properly done, depends on faculty members who believe in what they are doing. Just as the faculty underestimates how important it is for students to care about what they study, so administrators and reformers underestimate how important it is for faculty members to respect what they teach (Gamson, 1979). Curricular rationales, as well as the choice of texts and assignments, are relative to the contexts in which they are taught—institutional constraints, educational ideals, student characteristics, and faculty capacities and interests. In illustration, we take a subject considered to be a necessary component of college work—writing—taught in two very different institutions: Project Intertwine at Northern Virginia Community College at Manassas and the Preparatory Year Program of the New School of Liberal Arts at Brooklyn College.

Writing as Development: Project Intertwine

Northern Virginia Community College (NVCC) draws many people into its developmental courses who do not know how to think abstractly: "They are often reality bound and find it difficult to build concepts involving any experience which they have not had" (Grizzard, 1981, p. 3). These people often are afraid of school and at times think of themselves as stupid. This is especially true for writing, an activity they avoid if they can and suffer through if they cannot. It is, therefore, a challenge for teachers to combat students' low opinions of their minds and their undeveloped capacity for thought, while also teaching them to write decently.

Such students are typically tested at the beginning of the term and placed in special writing classes to prepare them for the regular introductory writing course. English 001, verbal studies laboratory, a writing course that is preparatory to admission and carries no credits toward degree requirements, works with such a group of students. The course has a deceptively simply objective: to prepare students to take freshman writing courses at Manassas, which means being able to write an essay of several paragraphs at a "C" or better level. This general objective is broken down into seven parts: (1) stick to a single, limited topic, (2) write a variety of kinds of sentences, (3) follow a recognizable pattern of organization, (4) write a topic sentence with clear, logical examples used for support, (5) write a thesis statement, (6) support the thesis statement with well-developed paragraphs, and (7) avoid major grammatical and spelling errors.

This list, a familiar one for writing teachers, was determined from a survey of introductory writing teachers at NVCC. How Intertwine goes about teaching students to do these things —and what else they learn in the process—is grounded in the situation of NVCC and the philosophy of Intertwine. NVCC's approach to teaching developmental English is based, first and last, on the belief that the most important barrier to learning among its students is their lack of confidence in themselves as people who can use their minds. The job of the course, then, is to teach them not only the rudiments of conceptual thought and the basic skills of writing but also an attitude of intellectual openness and practice in using thought in daily life.

The course, first offered in 1977, is rather like a laboratory in human development; hence, the considered choice of the term *developmental* English rather than *remedial* English. One of the English instructors contrasts developmental and remedial approaches:

> In remedial writing the teacher is . . . a doctor who prescribes specific doses of writing and rewriting, lecture, and individualized instruction to remedy some sort of illness. . . . We call our course "developmental writing." The classroom is less like a hospital than like an arena for social interaction. Every attempt is made to encourage total development of the student by working with and rewarding what is already present. "Total" means a spectrum of things: remediation, coping with school, examining attitudes toward the teacher and the self, enhancing self-concept. . . . It means approaching the teaching of writing humanistically, examining and building on what is there rather than identifying and installing what is missing [Bizzaro, 1981, pp. 7-8].

The course draws heavily on discourse theory, which suggests teaching techniques based on how people naturally learn to write. The text by Schor and Fishman (1979) used in the course argues that the first problem in writing is to find something to write about. Students are given writing assignments based on a series of class exercises meant to generate interesting material. Later, students learn sentence structure by working on material based on structural linguistics.

The exercises, the heart of the course, serve several functions in addition to providing essay topics. They help to turn the class into a group, force students to confront questions of value and choice, and encourage them to set goals. A counselor who works with developmental students leads the group exercises with the instructor, writes along with the students, and participates in class discussions. Working closely with colleagues, the counselor and the instructor have tried different exercises, discarding some and adding others. The exercises described here have proven the most durable.

The first exercise is intended to convince students to accept the importance of using standard English. They are asked to imagine that they are writing teachers who must come up with a way to handle the following situation:

> The meanest looking man you have ever seen has just decided to enter your classroom on the first day of class. You watch him duck beneath the door, step inside your classroom, and fill the front row. You ask him to write something for you and you discover he doesn't write edited American English. He does not punctuate, write sentences, or write paragraphs.
>
> He approaches you later in the cafeteria to ask how you liked his essay. You think only about the three pencils he squashed while he wrote. What would you say to him? [Bizzaro, 1981, p. 14].

The next exercises (adapted from some NASA training materials) are designed to teach students how to limit a topic, stick to it, use detail, and write a thesis statement. Students are first asked to imagine that they have been traveling on a space ship to the moon that has been forced to land 200 miles from the rendezvous point. Their job is to rank fifteen objects—matches, water, first-aid kit, map, and so on—from the ship in terms of their contribution to reaching the rendezvous. Students do this individually and then they meet with other students in a small group to reach a consensus about the ordering of the fifteen objects. The counselor follows with a discussion of the dynamics of the group as it worked on the problem: "How did you decide on the order?" "Who was the leader of the group?" "Was anyone able to sell the group on the entirety of his original rank order?" In the days following, students write about topics related to the exercise.

Another exercise also asks students to make decisions in a situation of constraint, but this time the constraint is severe and the information general. Students are asked to imagine that in the aftermath of a meltdown at a nuclear plant, twenty people varying in age, gender, race, and social background are crammed into an underground shelter of a department store. There will be just enough food, water, and air for nine people to survive the months before the fallout clears. The students must, first individually and then as part of a group, decide which nine should survive. Again, a discussion follows the exercise, one that is usually heated, and then the students write several papers on the values that emerged in the exercise, the strengths that would qualify them as survivors in a similar exercise, a justification for the retention of one of the twenty characters, and finally a justification for their own retention.

The lifeline exercise is introduced later in the term. Students are told to sketch a lifeline indicating important events in their lives. Then they are asked to draw a line showing how they see themselves in the future. Students write narrative essays, with time set aside for groups to proofread and make suggestions for improving sentence structure.

These exercises force students to use their minds in an active way. The space ship exercise teaches them to work as rationally as possible on a problem with others. The nuclear disaster exercise helps them recognize that making choices involves assessing different values and shows them how to go about identifying and articulating those values. The lifeline exercise leads them to analyze their lives and to see that they can make some choices about how to lead them.

Throughout, there is a constant effort to establish linkage with students' experiences. In NVCC's terms, students "whose family structure has not included higher education" need "certain bridges of understanding" (Grizzard, 1981, p. 55). One of these bridges is to teach basic skills in a way that is at once respectful and demanding.

Writing and the Classics:
The Preparatory Year Program

The faculty at the New School of Liberal Arts (NSLA) was as vehement in rejecting remedial education as the faculty at NVCC was, but from an entirely different standpoint. Open admissions at the City University of New York brought its share of students to Brooklyn College who had serious writing problems. But faculty members did not accept open admissions as part of their mission in the way that it is assumed in a community college like NVCC. Although they were willing to work with open admissions students, they were not comfortable with the language and tactics of remedial work (Black, Hey, and Margon, 1981). Instead, they insisted that, even though open admissions students lacked the requisite academic preparation to enter regular NSLA classes, they should study what other students studied, only more slowly. Then they were expected to be ready to enter the regular program.

The Preparatory Year Program, which started in 1974, consisted of regular NSLA semester-long courses stretched out over a year. In most years, students were offered a choice of two periods; "The Age of Revolutions" and "The Ancient World" were offered most consistently. For each cluster of courses within each period, faculty members and counselors worked together to integrate readings, assignments, and tests across the courses and to discuss student attitudes and progress. The content courses furnished the material for skills courses in reading and writing. Students read classic texts. In the ancient world period, for example, they read parts of the Old Testament, Plato, Sophocles, Homer, and *The Epic of Gilgamesh*.

A look at the ancient world Preparatory Year offered in 1979–80 indicates the scope and expectations of the NSLA program for inadequately prepared students. The social institutions and literature instructors who would be teaching all year met in the summer of 1979 with the reading specialist, the writing specialist, two counselors, and an art instructor. Instead of starting with the syllabus, they focused on what they thought the students would need to learn within a year if they were to be able to handle college work successfully. They came up with a staggering list: improvement of students' self-image, attitudes toward learning, oral communication, and study skills; development of spatial and temporal concepts; introduction to the vocabulary and techniques of the three academic disciplines covered in the courses; distinction between opinion and argument; familiarity with methods of argument and logical fallacies; precision in observation; and traditional competencies in vocabulary, comprehension, grammar, and mechanics. They broke these goals down into an even larger number of objectives and assigned them to particular people who would be responsible for testing them. Only then did they turn to the syllabus.

Like English 001 at NVCC, the writing workshop at NSLA made use of in-class writing that drew on students' experiences. But at NSLA, students' experiences were defined by what they were reading in their other courses. The first in-class writing assignment started with a discussion of the importance of individual and collective pasts in defining identity. The four-hour teaching blocks and the integrated one-year curriculum produced an intensity that is rare in the experience of the best-prepared students in higher education, let alone open admissions students. In the hands of skilled instructors, the ancient texts made fundamental human concerns come alive: "Should law ever be broken?" "How important is the family?"

Like the instructors in the writing course at NVCC, those at NSLA were concerned that students learn standard English. But they seemed to view their students as tougher—and maybe they were, since many came from the poor neighborhoods of New York City. The faculty did not hesitate to point out errors; at NVCC, such action would have been labeled an inappropriate dialect for the college setting. Consider the following example from a faculty discussion of nonstandard English:

[The instructors were beginning to] despair
of making headway with grammatical errors despite constant work with . . . the grammar text,
and frequent proofreading of exercises drawn from
student papers. Earlier . . . the Prep faculty had resisted the idea of correcting grammatical errors in
speech openly in class. . . . But now they suspect
that persistent grammatical errors in writing will
not be overcome until speech patterns are altered.
Furthermore, the time seems ripe. The students are
comfortable with one another. The reading teacher
has discussed—by chance—a recent *New York
Times* article on black English [in class]. The literature teacher agrees to present the idea to the class,
allow discussion of pro's and con's in group counseling, and then come back with their decision.
Agreement comes easily and correction begins immediately.

At the end of the next class, the literature
teacher notes four errors corrected in class: "he be
doing alright"; "mens" for "men"; "where he was
at"; and a double negative. Public corrections get to
be a game with some which spills outside the classroom. Passing through the hall one day, the literature teacher overhears a student calling to a group
of friends: "I be waiting for you." With split-sec-
ond timing, the teacher calls out: "I *will* be waiting
for you" [Black, Hey, and Margon, 1981, pp.
30-31].

The teachers treated their students seriously; at the same
time they recognized that they needed special attention. Skeptics have raised their eyebrows at the idea that students such as
those in open admissions programs could understand *The Odyssey, Oedipus Rex,* or Socrates' *Dialogues.* Yet properly prepared, they could not only read them but make them part of
themselves. For this to happen, however, teachers had to be
much more self-conscious about what went into reading and

understanding these works. Before reading *The Odyssey,* for example, students were introduced to Greek culture and given a preview of what they would be reading. Like the exercises at NVCC, discussions and assignments in the Preparatory Year required complex intellectual capacities. Students discussed poetic style and read the texts aloud. They were instructed in how to determine character, distinguish between physical and character traits, test their intuitive reactions against what they were reading, and bring in evidence to back up their positions.

Intertwine and the Preparatory Year Program were successful in their own terms: More than 60 percent of the students in Intertwine completed a regular English course at NVCC between 1977 and 1980, and close to 70 percent of the students in the Preparatory Year went on to the second year in the regular NSLA program. Yet, what was taught in the two programs was different. At NVCC there was less book learning and more in-class exercises, an approach that is appropriate to a community college but out of place in the academic culture of Brooklyn College. Indeed, one could not imagine two more different kinds of content for teaching writing. Within its limits as a single course, English 001 at NVCC went beyond a standard approach to writing by drawing on a variety of sources, including students' experiences in class and outside of class. It integrated what went on during the term by building writing assignments on the common experiences provided by the classroom exercises, in a sequential and increasingly complex manner.

NSLA taught skills on a similar pedagogic philosophy, but it had the advantage of enrolling students full time for a whole year. The broad scope of the year-long curriculum integrated writing with content courses and content courses with one another; later assignments built on earlier ones. It was probably successful, however, because it was able to connect the classic texts with students' own experiences, which, in turn, helped them understand what are difficult works even for well-prepared students. The students knew the significance of being given *The Odyssey* and *The Dialogues* to read, and they felt proud and accomplished to work through them. To comprehend these texts, they had to learn not only how to read the texts in their own right but also how to make them understandable in their own lives.

Despite these obvious differences, the two programs were similar in certain respects. Students learned much more than how to write; they developed a pragmatic attitude toward the use of standard English and toward its users, trust in the goodwill of teachers, a sense of group responsibility, and a strengthening of the will and of the sense of personal control. Some of these features were taught intentionally and some were present in the "hidden curriculum." In both programs, the instructors' faith that their students could handle the academic demands of the course infused everything they taught intentionally.

They were able to do this because they were demanding teachers who required that students be active and articulate. But what about the content that they taught? Did anything go? We think not. Although we have argued for a pluralistic view of the content of a liberating education, we think that certain common principles guided the selection of content at NVCC and NSLA.

Liberating Curricula:
Diverse, Integrative, Experiential, Critical

The idea of breadth is common to many discussions of liberal education. Indeed, breadth is the essential trait that sets off liberal education from specialized education (Hirst, 1974). Calls for experience in many disciplines (Halliburton, 1977), endorsements of a wide survey of cultures (Brubacher, 1977), and current concern for the cultivation of a global outlook (Bowen, 1977; Leestma, 1979; National Assembly on Foreign Language and International Studies, 1980) are common in writing on the undergraduate curriculum. Those who speak about liberal education from the perspective of the professions and vocations also assume comprehensiveness: Workers in business and government must be "generalists" who can coordinate data from many angles, solve many different kinds of problems, and deal with many different kinds of people (Beck, 1981). Human services

workers are expected to help their clients with a variety of social, personal, and economic problems and must, therefore, have
a broad education to be effective (Cohen, 1981).

Breadth refers to the sheer number of subjects encom-
passed in a curriculum; it says nothing explicit about how to go
about selecting certain subjects from the enormous number of
possibilities. Liberating education suggests a principle of selection: *diversity*. If education is to bring students to a broad
awareness of their lives from different perspectives, then they
must study a variety of subjects and points of view. Exactly
what subjects and which points of view depend on student
characteristics and the purposes of particular programs and institutions. For the Federated Learning Communities (FLC) at
Stony Brook, diversity comes from juxtaposing the approaches
of three or more disciplines to an overarching contemporary
problem. For Core at Saint Joseph's, diversity means exposure
to alternative world views and cultures. Even single courses like
English 001 can build in diversity by incorporating students'
diverse backgrounds in class assignments and discussions, by
drawing on work in several disciplines, and by varying assignments so that different capacities can be exercised. A course
that is not usually considered part of a liberal education can
also reach for diversity. In the African-American Music Program
at SUNY at Old Westbury, for example, majors must take a
year-long course in African-American music that draws on history, economics, and sociology to understand the development
of African music. For example, in studying music in the 1930s
in the United States, students learn about the effects of the Depression on the economics of the band. They trace the impact
of the Communist Party on racial integration and the subse-
quent careers of black musicians.

Diversity implies nothing about how subjects are organized in relation to one another. Hence, we introduce another
principle: *integration*. Subjects can be integrated with one another or they can be fragmented. One of the problems with current undergraduate curricula is the failure to pay adequate attention to the connections among the subjects taught (Conrad
and Wyer, 1980; The Carnegie Foundation for the Advance-

ment of Teaching, 1977). This is a serious failure; for a long time, the essence of a liberal education has been seen to be the development of an integrative habit of mind (Newman [1852], 1959). Arguments for integration continue today (Hazzard, 1979). Researchers are beginning to come up with evidence showing that curricula encouraging the integration of ideas and skills produce the greatest growth in their students' capacity to think critically, whereas distribution requirements without an integrative rationale do not have this effect (Winter, McClelland, and Stewart, 1981; Forrest, 1981). Writing across the curriculum, an approach to teaching writing within regular courses much like what NSLA did, is gaining favor across the country (Griffin, 1982). Calls for more integration are coming from traditionalists, who see the great books or core curricula as ways of overcoming the fragmentation and instrumentalism of the undergraduate curriculum (Brann, 1979; Boyer and Levine, 1981), and from reformers, who argue that student development, particularly of adult students, depends on more curricular coherence (Chickering, 1981).

Achieving integration demands a good bit more effort than diversity, which does not ask individual faculty members or departments to change their normal practices much. Integration pushes in the opposite direction. If the students should not be asked to integrate what the faculty cannot, ways must be devised to make the faculty do it that either bring the disciplines together in new ways, work around them, or eliminate them altogether. What devices are used in a particular school will depend on imagination, resources, and traditions.

Let us consider examples from some of the programs we have been examining. The most common device for integration is the special seminar that comes at the end of a sequence of study. The team-taught seminars at the University of Oklahoma's College of Liberal Studies for students who complete their requirements in social sciences, natural sciences, and humanities are one device. The senior seminars at Hampshire College on contemporary issues for students with different concentrations and the senior Core courses at Saint Joseph's, in which students address ethical and social issues from the perspective of their majors, are others. Less common are mechanisms that require faculty members to work together in planning a curriculum that has a common, integrative rationale, as in the New School of Liberal Arts at Brooklyn College, where teachers in a cluster of courses in the same historical period coordinated with one another. Other examples are the faculty seminars in the FLC at Stony Brook preceding the term they teach and the special integrative seminars while they teach and the student-faculty planning group for Core at Saint Joseph's. In individualized programs where a common curriculum or seminar does not bind courses together, advisers and mentors work with students to help them integrate the various subjects they are pursuing, as at Hampshire College and the External Degree Program.

Diversity and integration speak to the scope and the organization of a curriculum. We still do not have a basis for selecting *what* is taught. This question has exercised commentators on the curriculum for a long time. At one time, the basis for most curricula was religious. One studied what was deemed to be proper in the eyes of God. As knowledge and higher education became secular, the modern disciplines, especially the sciences, provided the basis for the curriculum in most colleges and universities (Rudolph, 1977). We argue, in contrast, that the basis for a liberating curriculum is experiential. A curriculum grounded on students' experiences establishes a linkage between what they already know and what they study. The opposite of experiential is academic—knowledge presented as if it had nothing to do with the world as students experience it. For the disciplines to avoid being merely academic, they must "reach down into their struggles with *life* and show students how that struggle can illuminate what they experienced themselves"; they must confront the student with "exemplars of those real problems that circumscribe the human condition and that are amenable to some resolution only through the exercise of conceptual thought and its tools" (Woditsch, 1977, p. 25).

The term *experiential* has been used in recent years in several different ways: as denoting what is learned from personal experience, especially in programs for adults; as specific classroom techniques, such as role playing and simulation games;

and as work outside of class, such as internships and original research. By experiential, we mean content that is based on experiences that students have already had or that induces certain direct experiences. Experiential must not be taken as focused primarily on the self. What is taught may start with students' experiences, but it quickly moves beyond that to what others have experienced in other times and places and to general frameworks of understanding. Put another way, life sets the agenda for the curriculum. This means that biology taught as a liberating subject might start with subjects that are familiar to students—sexuality or IQ, for example—and then show them how the principles of the field can illuminate such subjects (Carlson, 1981). Sociology taught as a liberating subject might start with students' experiences with authority at school or work and then turn to the writings of Max Weber to help them understand those experiences in a more fundamental way.

A curriculum that is experiential can include many different subjects. Some programs start with characteristics likely to make their students' experiences different from those of others, showing them why this might be so and how they compare to the experiences of other groups. The Program on Women at Northwestern University and the labor studies program at Hofstra University are examples of this approach. Other programs, in contrast, start with more universal experiences; the best example is Core at Saint Joseph's College. Others start with pressing issues like world hunger, as in the FLC at Stony Brook or, conversely, with ancient questions like justice, as in NSLA at Brooklyn College.

Whatever the particular subjects under study, a liberating curriculum must include content that helps students move back and forth between awareness and application, engagement and detachment. For this to happen, the curriculum must also be *critical*. Its opposite is a curriculum based on unexamined assumptions, whether they be held by authorities or ordinary citizens, conservatives or liberals. The primary task of a liberating curriculum is to help students reflect on their lives and society and to do so aggressively, testing and probing experience.

An important expression of a critical attitude in several

of the programs is the way they encourage students to analyze how different institutions—the family, schools, work organizations—have shaped their ideas and values. This critical attitude is most obvious in the Program on Women at Northwestern and the labor studies program at Hofstra, but it also animates the selection of course topics at the Institute of Study for Older Adults, the way the mentor in the External Degree Program and the faculty at Hampshire challenge students to articulate what they are learning, and the comparative devices built into the structure of Core at Saint Joseph's, the FLC, and NSLA. All are different approaches to getting students to think critically.

The selection of what is to be taught in most colleges and universities is usually not principled—that is, not based on some principles that give a philosophical and pedagogical justification for subject matter. We have said that a liberating curriculum is diverse, integrative, experiential, and critical. Whether or not they agree with these four principles, faculty members must be much more self-conscious about why they wish to teach certain subjects. They have a responsibility to press one another to say why they teach what they do. They will find, in the process, that their subjects take on new life.

CHAPTER EIGHT

Politics
of Creating Change

New settings arise from and exist within a context of existing settings over which [they have] little, and frequently no, control. The new setting is not only in danger from within but from without as well, and the interaction between these sources of danger sets limits. . . . To assume that a new setting will fulfill all of its purposes and will last forever is to assume a degree of control . . . that has no justification in experience or social theory.

—Sarason, 1972, p. 249

A curriculum is not only a set of subjects and courses; it is also an expression of an institution's political economy. A curriculum states what the institution considers important for students to study and, therefore, what value certain fields have. It channels students to some courses and departments and not to others, thus affecting enrollments, how faculty members spend their time, and ultimately the distribution of resources. When a curriculum also becomes a program with its own place, students, and faculty—in Sarason's word, a "setting"—it is subject to all the dangers from within and without in his warning.

Even in the best of circumstances, changing a curriculum in a typical college or university is not a casual matter. It depends on some consensus about the importance of the under-

131

graduate curriculum in the first place, and it requires that departments work together in unaccustomed ways. Deliberations about the curriculum flush out unexamined differences among the disciplines about the nature of knowledge and what constitutes good teaching, bring buried conflicts to the surface, and enforce competition. Most faculty members are not particularly unhappy with the curriculum, partly because they do not think in curricular terms outside of their disciplines. Even those who think there might be a better way of educating undergraduates are often reluctant to take the first steps toward change because of costs in time and potential estrangement from colleagues. Little wonder, then, that reforming the curriculum in colleges and universities has been likened to moving a graveyard: hard to do and who wants to anyway?

Given this state of affairs, it is extraordinary that the programs in National Project IV were created in the first place. Each program has a different genesis and history, and each has had to confront different institutional circumstances. Yet they offer some general lessons about creating and sustaining a liberating education. Let us look at some of them as they have survived one of the most difficult periods in higher education. We turn, first, to the institution that has sustained the most complete curriculum change, Saint Joseph's College.

Reviving the Core: Saint Joseph's College

Saint Joseph's reform of its curriculum drew on the solidarity of a small community. At a time when other schools around the country were throwing out even the weakest of general education requirements, Saint Joseph's College was working out demanding requirements. Whether or not they were in step with the rest of higher education at the time was irrelevant to the faculty and administrators at Saint Joseph's. The adoption of Core was an act of self-definition, conducted at first without large grants or national publicity.

Core is the core of Saint Joseph's College. It has raised fundamental questions not only about the nature of knowledge and of general education but has also required what one observer called "radical surgery" of the institution as a whole: how members of the faculty spend their time, how they teach, how they relate to one another and to students, how departments do their business. And they submitted themselves for the operation willingly, once they came to see that they needed it. How did this happen? Getting faculty members to agree to a set of ten courses—and only ten—that would constitute their college's statement about general education, with all students taking them in the same order, getting them to teach outside their departments and in collaboration with one another and even with students—this is equivalent to moving the heavens.

Yet this is what Saint Joseph's did, in a relatively short time, with a minimum of acrimony and an extraordinary degree of consensus. The story begins with a new president, who gave the first push in 1966. He and members of the faculty had been reading several important publications that seemed to have implications for the college: the Second Vatican Council document, "The Church in the Modern World" ("Pastoral Constitution. . .", 1966); the National Catholic Educational Association's (1966) report, "The Danforth Report and Catholic Higher Education"; and articles on curriculum in professional journals. The renewed vision of the church and of the community in the Second Vatican Council challenged the faculty profoundly. As John Nichols said: "The Catholic Church at the time of the Second Vatican Council redefined itself as a community rather than an institution. As an institution that was affiliated with the Catholic Church we asked, what does that mean for a college? What does an intellectual community mean? Community is not only a legitimate goal for higher education but a necessary goal. Liberal education must define the human in larger than male, white, middle-class, American, Midwestern terms."

The president and key faculty members were dedicated to renewing the college from within, and this meant that the whole institution would have to examine what it was doing and why. To start the process, the president established a series of "president's seminars" on general education in which everyone at the college had to take a public stand on the nature of general education. These discussions led to the formation of a select faculty committee to begin work on the curriculum. A Title III grant from the Department of Health, Education, and Welfare in 1967–1968 subsidized the work of this committee, which included teachers from all academic areas, not just those who taught courses in general education. From then on, things moved quickly. The committee stated two points on which there appeared to be strong faculty consensus: (1) a new general education program should be a common experience for students and as many of the faculty as possible and (2) it should be interdisciplinary and integrative. In 1969, the committee presented its design of Core to the faculty for its approval—which it gave by a three to one margin—and it was ready to be implemented on a semester-by-semester basis, a process that took four years.

It did not hurt the new program that the number of credits required in Core was actually a reduction from the previous number of distribution requirements and that members of the faculty received the highest form of encouragement by promotions and salary increases for participating in Core. But the most important incentive was psychological: Core brought a new vision and sense of purpose to a college that had been drifting.

Things have not been easy since then. Prospective students have undoubtedly been turned away from the college because of the rigid requirements of Core, and vocationally minded and insecure students must be persuaded regularly that Core is worth their time. There are pockets of skepticism on the faculty as well, in business and physical education particularly, which do not teach in Core. Even the more convinced teachers find the going rough. Some of the courses are widely recognized as less popular with students mainly because their instructors have had a hard time getting the hang of teaching interdisciplinary topics and leading discussion groups.

Saint Joseph's College and individual faculty members have gotten a good deal of attention for their efforts. Core has been written up in important publications on the curriculum (Levine, 1978; Boyer and Levine, 1981; Conrad, 1978; Gaff and others, 1980). It has participated in several large projects besides National Project IV. And it has received the validation of outside grants from the Lilly Endowment, the Department of

Health, Education, and Welfare, the National Science Foundation, and the National Endowment for the Humanities. This has brought even more internal commitment to the program, as Saint Joseph's faculty members attend conferences that put them in touch with educators across the country.

We turn now to a series of programs that do not represent as thorough a change for their institutions as Core did at Saint Joseph's. As one of several undergraduate programs in large institutions, they have not required that most of the faculty be involved with them. Nevertheless, the programs have had to find ways of achieving acceptance: by gaining a toehold at the periphery, fighting to get into the mainstream, burrowing in, and playing the system. The programs with the most difficult time have been those for adults, which for faculty members and administrators have proven the least understandable and the most difficult to incorporate into the mainstream.

Getting a Toehold: The External Degree Program

The External Degree Program (EDP) has had a rough time finding a secure institutional base since it was founded in 1977. Operating out of the Office of External Programs in the Vermont State College system, it could afford to live with the insecurity of working with five different institutions that "alternately ignored, smothered, and rejected" it (Daloz, 1981, p. 1) while it depended on a three-year start-up grant from the Fund for the Improvement of Postsecondary Education. Once the grant ended, it had to find a better arrangement or probably go under. Johnson State College, one of the collaborating institutions in the first three years, offered EDP a spartan but safe berth.

Why was Johnson State interested? Among the heads of the colleges with which EDP worked, only the president of Johnson State saw its potential as a source of new students, when enrollments were just beginning to be a problem in the Vermont state system. Johnson State had the reputation of being open to all kinds of students and, with EDP on board, it could point to the service it was performing for Vermonters. The connection with EDP also reinforced Johnson State's ties to the Community College of Vermont, the institution most closely connected to the founding of EDP, thus ensuring another ready source of students.

Some members of the faculty were less farsighted than the president, and they worried about salaries and competition for resources that were already meager and only likely to shrink. Yet they did not oppose the incorporation of EDP into their college, as the faculty at one of the other state colleges did. Slowly in EDP's first three years and at a quickening pace once it was part of the college, the Johnson State faculty came to know the program. A few teachers moonlighted as mentors. Several taught weekend courses. From its office in the administration building, where the president's office is also located, EDP has taken pains to work itself slowly into the rest of the institution from its rather shaky perch. A former teachers' college, Johnson State has struggled for academic respectability. Early in EDP's incorporation, the college curriculum committee approved a plan to appoint a faculty advisory board to set program policy. Representatives from the college were also put on the regional committees that review EDP students' progress and learning plans. More recently, top administrators at the college have moved more rapidly to incorporate EDP into the regular academic structure, taking control of academic decisions that were formerly in the hands of mentors and students.

From its inception, EDP has insisted that its program hold to an explicit and academically respectable rationale. But it has also espoused a commitment to student development. In the eyes of faculty members and administrators, this is a new, and somewhat heretical, doctrine—especially for a program whose students are older than those who typically attend Johnson State. Whether EDP will retain its emphasis on students' development and its character of openness and flexibility is still an open question. The politics of survival may exact a high price.

Fighting to Get Inside:
The Labor Institute of Applied Social Science

What is a school that is sometimes called "the Harvard of Long Island" doing with a program for union members, operated in conjunction with unions and held miles away from its campus? The program's student body averages age thirty-eight (compared to an average of twenty-one on campus), and has 73 percent Hispanics and blacks (versus 4 percent on campus). This is more than a bit out of character for an institution like Hofstra University and probably would not exist at all had it not been for a series of fortuitous circumstances.

In 1973, the dean of the College of Arts and Sciences at Hofstra asked Bertram Silverman, a tenured member of the economics department, to work on setting up a center for cultural or ethnic studies. At that time, the university was experiencing the beginning of an enrollment decline and was striking out in several new directions to redefine itself. Silverman proposed a research center focused on issues of work and leisure and was given time to develop it. At just about the same time, David Livingston, president of District 65 (formerly part of the Distributive Workers of America and now a United Automobile Workers affiliate) was trying to interest an academic institution in offering a program for union members being groomed for leadership positions; students would meet in or near the union's headquarters in Greenwich Village. Silverman heard about Livingston's efforts and approached him about working out a program with Hofstra. Both the union and the university were skeptical, not only because of the geographical distance between the union and the campus but also because of the philosophical differences between them. The union was worried about entrusting its most precious resources to a group of outsiders who lacked day-to-day experience of union life. The university found the idea of attracting adult students appealing but was nervous about union control over academic decisions.

Over a period of two years, the two institutions, with Silverman as go-between, forged an agreement that is unique in U.S. higher education. Although they were not involved in working out the details of the agreement, the president of the union and the president of the university, Robert Payton (later to become president of the Exxon Education Foundation), supported the idea in principle. Nevertheless, there was enough suspicion on both sides that very explicit and detailed agreements needed to be laid down. To ensure regular communication and accountability, each side appointed a liaison person to deal quickly with any problems that might arise. To involve the union in academic matters, District 65 appointed an education coordinator from its own staff to work with the program staff and serve on curriculum and personnel committees. Conversely, to bring the program staff closer to the union, the directors of the program and sometimes faculty members were to participate in the deliberations of all governing bodies in the union, including regular meetings of the top leadership. On its side, the university established a special ad hoc committee, with participants drawn from among the most respected members of the faculty, to work on curriculum and academic standards with the program's staff. Later, another program was established with District Council 37 (of the American Federation of State, County, and Municipal Employees), although it never developed the close university and union collaboration that the program with District 65 did.

The Labor Institute of Applied Social Science opened in 1976 with a three-year grant from the Fund for the Improvement of Postsecondary Education, a union scholarship fund, and arrangements for time off from work for students. After two years, the academic standards and curriculum committees of the College of Arts and Sciences reviewed the program and the faculty senate overwhelmingly endorsed it. The program was made organizationally equivalent to a department but without the power to make tenure appointments. About 60 percent of the teachers in the program are members of the regular Hofstra faculty; the remainder are on year-to-year adjunct appointments.

That is the formal side of the story. Informally, it is clear that the program derives its strength from the academic credibility of its directors, one of whom received a distinguished service award from the university for his work with the program. The dean of the College of Arts and Sciences is a quiet supporter who sees the benefits for the university from the relationships with the two unions involved in the program, both noted for their enlightened leadership and democratic structures. The directors of the program, with strong support from the union, have insisted that they do not want a separate program in spite of their physical distance from the Hofstra campus. They have actively sought integration with legitimate bodies within the university and access to the resources such legitimacy brings. One of the directors insists vehemently that the program does not "want to be a marginal part of the university. I want all the resources I can get to enrich the program. I feel the real tension of potential parochialism that can set in by not having the resources. So I fight to get as much of the larger university's resources integrated as much as possible into the program."

The program is hardly a secure operation. In a time of economic and political trouble for the labor movement, it is difficult for the unions to allocate tuition funds. (District 65 in 1983 was paying all of the tuition for its members. When federal student aid programs are taken into account, this amounts to $1,300 per student.) Strong support from the union ensures the program's acceptance from the university, as long as the program continues to remain economically viable and academically respectable. However, it may founder on another problem: insufficient enrollment. For whatever reason—the preference of blue-collar people for practical, vocational programs, or the difficulty of reaching rank-and-file workers through the usual union channels—not enough students have been enrolling.

Joining the Club: College of Liberal Studies

Lest we think that all programs for adults are fated to struggle constantly, let us turn to the venerable College of Liberal Studies (CLS), which has been around for more than twenty years.

The University of Oklahoma, the state's flagship campus, is a rather traditional institution. The faculty has been uncommonly stable over the years, and relationships among some of its senior people cross departments. It is this established group that helped found CLS and continues to give it support. A group of Oklahoma faculty began meeting in 1957 in a yearlong seminar to talk about what they saw as the central issues of the twentieth century. They turned their attention to the curricular implications of their discussions and came up with the idea of an integrated, interdisciplinary liberal studies curriculum for adults. With support from several top administrators, including the dean of continuing education, who was building a network of outreach activities at the time, a committee of faculty members from the original seminar group drew up a proposal for a degree in liberal studies. This took three years, but approval by the regents of the university followed quickly in 1960. The first students were enrolled in 1961 with a grant of seventy-five scholarships from the Carnegie Corporation.

CLS's approach to undergraduate education differs markedly from the more typical distribution and major system in the College of Arts and Sciences, yet it has been able to recruit about one quarter of the Arts and Sciences faculty over the years. CLS has no regular faculty lines and must draw all of its instructors and advisers from among the existing University of Oklahoma faculty. Some 100 are listed on the CLS roster, all senior members and some of the most respected people on the faculty. CLS is headed by an historian, who has twice been elected president of the faculty senate, and it is guided by a ten-member executive committee composed of instructors who teach in the program.

Faculty participants are paid on an overload basis that hardly compensates for the time many of them devote to it. Some of the departments have been downright hostile to their members' participation in CLS, although most are indifferent. Why, then, do some faculty members from the departments teach in CLS? The common answer to this question is: for my own education, for what I learn from my colleagues, for the sense of having an effect on adults.

The program was located originally in the continuing education department, which occupies a handsome set of buildings on a campus at the edge of the sprawling university. While CLS continues to house its staff, run its classes, and board its students on the continuing education campus, it has been located organizationally within the academic sector of the university since the early 1970s. It now stands as one college equal to the other colleges at the university, and it is funded like any other degree program. This shift has brought CLS its final security within the university.

Not all problems have been solved, by any means. Enrollments have been declining, as other programs around the country compete for adults (including those that have used CLS as a model) and as student interests shift away from the liberal arts. The recruitment of young instructors is a problem because of the pressure on them to publish. Closer supervision of student work and courses has been suggested from time to time, but this has run up against the laissez-faire attitude of a research university. The College of Arts and Sciences may have paid CLS the ultimate compliment: As it began examining its undergraduate curriculum under the pressure of declining graduate enrollments and pressure from the state, it turned to CLS for advice.

We look now at two programs for a regular student body in major research universities—the Program on Women at Northwestern University and the Federated Learning Communities at the State University of New York at Stony Brook.

Burrowing in: The Program on Women

Although it started officially in 1979, the certificate program in women's studies has its origins in the late 1960s, when women at Northwestern University began pressing for women's studies. The Program on Women (POW) was founded in 1974 with the intention of forming a curricular component. For its first five years, however, it operated as a center for research and a general support unit for women on campus. It was assigned comfortably appointed offices in two converted houses close to the heart of campus, but its status was a bit of an administrative anomaly: Its money came from a discretionary fund in the provost's office, but it was located organizationally in the office of the vice-president for research.

After proposals to foundations for outside funding were turned down, it became clear that women's studies at Northwestern would have to go through the usual channels for approval and eventual funding. Certificate programs at Northwestern, designed to supplement but not replace a major, must be approved at several levels in the College of Arts and Sciences. Despite its challenging view of the university and women's place in it, POW took the long road to respectability. In 1978, it approached the office of the dean of the College of Arts and Sciences with a proposal for a certificate program. The dean appointed a special ad hoc committee on women's studies curriculum to guide the enterprise. With the help of this committee, POW drew up a formal proposal for the curriculum committee of Arts and Sciences. The curriculum committee scrutinized the proposal closely and requested a series of revisions, several of which were incorporated into the final document—including the insistence that an introductory course in social sciences, behavioral sciences, or historical studies be required as a prerequisite for enrollment in the program. The final proposal, one of the longest submitted in the history of the college, was approved unanimously by its faculty.

By this act, POW was woven into the fabric of the university, although the fact that most of its students are women in a university where women number less than half of the student body means it will always be a visible thread. The ad hoc committee on women's studies, consisting of members from the College of Arts and Sciences faculty, has become a permanent committee. The director of POW teaches two of the required core courses in the program and keeps in regular touch with the women's studies committee. Her liaison duties bring her in contact with the college's faculty, since regular departmental courses fill out the program beyond the core courses. Courses offered as part of the certificate must be approved by the women's studies committee.

Although it has entered the mainstream of the university, POW's location within the domain of the vice-president for research gives it an additional measure of independence and legitimacy in the eyes of the research-oriented faculty at Northwestern. The nationally known sociologist, Arlene Kaplan Daniels, who was the founding director, the growing reputation of its second director, Bari Watkins, and a group of respected female and male supporters on the faculty ensure a strong measure of support. With the protection of the provost and the vice-president for research, who have consistently given the program most of what it has asked for, POW appears to be fairly secure.

Money problems persist, however. Although he has allocated some funds to the program, the dean of Arts and Sciences, pleading poverty, has been reluctant to cover the time and materials POW devotes to the certificate program, despite lobbying from a group of women on the faculty who regularly act in its behalf. Since it runs primarily on courses that are already being taught and on the donated time of the director, the certificate program can continue almost indefinitely under the umbrella of POW. After all, in the eyes of faculty members and administrators, this is the least Northwestern can do to keep up with other major universities around the country, many of which are doing considerably more ("Women's Studies . . .", 1981). For the majority of the faculty, the Program on Women has survived long enough to become part of the family or, more accurately, "part of the furniture" as one POW faculty member put it.

Playing the System: Federated Learning Communities

The story of the Federated Learning Communities (FLC) goes back to the early 1970s, when an institutional self-study at the State University of New York at Stony Brook turned up some serious problems with undergraduate education. There was, first, the problem of the "mismatched expectations" of students and faculty. Second, there was an absence of connection among the courses taught at Stony Brook. Related to this was the third problem of a lack of shared experience among students and faculty. And finally, there was little support and guidance for the intelligent use of the freedom Stony Brook offered (Hill, 1974).

The self-study committee commissioned one of its members, the philosopher Patrick Hill, to work up a response to these problems. As a first step, the administration paid for Hill to look into what was happening in undergraduate education at some innovative institutions on the West Coast. Hill returned especially impressed with the lower division program at the University of California at Los Angeles and the coordinated studies approach at Evergreen State in Washington. In general, however, he was critical of the isolation of many experiments he saw from the mainstream of higher education. If Stony Brook wished to revitalize itself, he argued, it would have to work with the dominant structure of disciplinary departments rather than setting up segregated experiments at the periphery, which indeed it had done in the 1960s. It would have to deal head on with the problems the self-study had identified.

The root of the problem at Stony Brook, what Hill termed "social atomism," resulted from specific structural arrangements. To be solved, new structural arrangements would have to be invented. The organization of the program that was eventually developed addresses each point in Hill's diagnosis in specific ways that brilliantly take advantage of how a university like Stony Brook works. By making use of a diverse set of existing courses taught by regular faculty members brought together voluntarily with a volunteer group of students, FLC does not question the value of individual freedom or departmental specialization. Nevertheless, through the devices of the core course and the program seminar, it does challenge the faculty to relate their courses to one another in the federation and to its overriding theme. It forces faculty members to relate to one another and to students in new ways as well.

FLC opened in 1976 with a grant from the Fund for the Improvement of Postsecondary Education, financial support from the academic vice-president, and the political backing of several influential faculty members. As one administrator put it, FLC has become both an influence and an irritant—a yearly one at that, since federations are composed anew each year. Why would the faculty bother to participate? Most were skeptical when it began and quite a few remain so. Hill had to marshal his persuasive powers to "seduce" the first group of faculty members into participating. With help from key administrators, he could offer the incentive that counts most with academic people: time to do their own work. The exchange was not the most generous, even at the beginning, and it has become even less so as FLC has expanded. For meeting once a week for four terms in a faculty seminar, meeting in the core course once a month in addition to teaching their regular class, dealing with more students as FLC doubled and even tripled its enrollments, and directing independent study projects in their federation's last term, faculty were given a two-course reduction in their teaching loads. Now, as FLC makes up in psychic rewards what it cannot offer materially, faculty participants must, in addition, teach two one-credit seminars or one three-credit seminar to incoming freshmen on the theme of their federation, as well as participate twice in the federation.

How has FLC been able to go so far with so little? Like Northwestern, Stony Brook is the kind of university that lets faculty members ride their own hobbyhorses; this is the positive side of the atomism Hill criticized. As a respected member of a respected department, Hill was able to capitalize on the freewheeling style of Stony Brook. Like the Program on Women, FLC was left to its own devices once it was established. And its devices are powerful indeed: The strengths of the research university are put to work against its weaknesses.

In universities, there will always be some volunteers for innovations, and there is no question that FLC drew in its share of such people. But it has also made inroads into the mainstream. As more faculty members gained experience in the program, word got around that it was not bad after all; in fact, it could be fun. Instructors enjoyed the gossip and the political intelligence that they picked up in their seminars, as well as the opportunity to argue with and learn something from their colleagues. Several admitted that they had gained a new respect for their students and changed the way they taught when they returned to their regular round of activities.

Although it continues to struggle for money, relying almost exclusively on discretionary funds from the administration, FLC has not become a separatist program. Students and instructors identify themselves as members of their particular federation—as "SEILS" (Social and Ethical Issues in the Life Sciences), for example, rather than "FLC." It has hardly taken over Stony Brook, but FLC has gone far since its inception: It

now runs several federations at the same time, in one term stag-
ing fifteen affiliated courses. Its students may live in one of the
dormitory houses on campus. It has even infiltrated the admissions office, which uses FLC to show parents and prospective
students how much Stony Brook cares about undergraduates.
Officials in the central administration of the State University of
New York system have given the program extra financial support from time to time. And it has received the ultimate compliment in higher education: Several other schools are copying it.

Let us now consider a cautionary tale from Brooklyn College.

Falling off the Edge: The New School of Liberal Arts

Things looked rosy when the New School of Liberal Arts
(NSLA) opened. In the wake of student protests, a special commission at Brooklyn College recommended in 1970 that the college be divided into six different divisions. Two of these divisions, both new, were to be nondepartmental. One was to focus
on contemporary studies, the other on the traditional liberal
arts. NSLA, which became the latter division, was to offer a
structured course of studies patterned after the great books
curricula of the University of Chicago and St. John's College.

Each division was given $1 million to get started. With
the support of several key faculty members at Brooklyn College, a respected physicist was selected as dean. The dean was a
veteran of several major committees and administrative posts
and close to the president of Brooklyn College, who had taken
office at the height of the student protests in 1970. The dean
hired a faculty, recruiting all but one instructor from outside of
Brooklyn College. The new members of the faculty were young
and, like the dean, dedicated to finding ways of improving the
quality of undergraduate education.

The college opened in 1972 in a renovated building in
downtown Brooklyn, six miles from the main campus. The curriculum, whose design had been set the year before by the dean
at the insistence of the faculty council of Brooklyn College,
placed heavy demands on the faculty. This was especially true

for those involved in the Preparatory Year Program, which was introduced after the college opened and was designed for the underprepared students who were being admitted under the newly instituted open admissions policy of the City University of New York. Physically isolated from the main campus, the faculty was socially and organizationally isolated as well. Few instructors had ties to the faculty in the disciplines in the large liberal arts college and hardly any served on the college committees or were connected to the informal faculty networks that are essential for those who are plugged in politically at Brooklyn College.

Then the first in a series of fiscal crises hit the City University in 1976. Over 1,000 faculty members were fired with less than a month's notice. Brooklyn College was hit hard, and NSLA was affected not only by losses of faculty positions but in less direct ways as well. When the Brooklyn faculty revolted against the president, forcing his departure soon after, the dean of NSLA, who was publicly associated with the president, lost his main supporter. An economy move brought NSLA into the basement of a building on campus, but this did not lessen its isolation.

NSLA became more and more vulnerable to attacks from faculty members from the rest of the institution, who looked on the school as taking money away from them. They pointed to the fact that NSLA was the only program allowed to recruit its own students. They looked with envy on what they thought was a lower teaching load. They questioned the quality of the faculty who had been given tenure without the involvement of the departments. Some raised questions about the elite bias of the program, saying that it only worked for the brightest students, while others raised the opposite objection that it only worked for underprepared students.

Without a credible leader in a situation where it was already isolated from the rest of the institution, it was only a matter of time before NSLA would be seriously threatened. That time came when a major reorganization of Brooklyn College was launched under a new president. NSLA was one of the first academic units to be reorganized—right out of existence.

The Politics of Small Worlds

How have the other programs managed to survive as long as they have? Are they, as Boyer and Levine (1981) say about general education, at the periphery of the institutions they occupy? It is clear that the newer programs are still in the earliest phases of being integrated into their institutions. Yet even the youngest—POW and EDP—have tried to incorporate themselves. They have done so in a variety of ways, depending on the kind of institution they inhabit.

The first problem they faced was simply to get a foothold. A group of faculty members or senior administrators, sometimes both, typically became interested in a subject or a project that led to the program. These "prime movers" (Kanter, 1983), if they were not senior administrators, needed start-up funds. Support from top administrators was especially important because they controlled access to resources within the institution and channels to outside funding. In three of the programs—Core, FLC, and the Labor Institute—senior administrators were also responsible for starting the chain of events that led to their founding. They provided seed money and release time to the program designers. Indeed, it is striking how many of the programs had external funding to get them going. POW, the one that did not, was supported with discretionary funds from the office of the provost.

External funding lasted typically two to three years, giving the program developers time to establish administrative procedures, design a curriculum, and enroll the first group of students. It is clear that, if the programs were to survive, they would have to get themselves a stable income. Even in the affluent 1960s, when the College of Liberal Studies was established and Core was getting under way, the program developers had their eyes on ways to "internalize" their creations.

In order to do so, they had to show that they brought something worthwhile to their institutions, that they were filling a "performance gap" (Zaltman, Duncan, and Holbek, 1973). In the case of the programs for adults, it is fairly clear that their institutions viewed adults as a market that might offset enrollment declines. Oklahoma's program began when enrollments were not a problem; rather, CLS served as one of several ways in which the University of Oklahoma could say it was serving the public. Programs that did not serve adults needed to show how they fulfilled some of the most important values held by their institutions. Core was a way for the faculty at Saint Joseph's to revive their commitment to a coherent liberal education that would express the changes going on in Catholic circles in the late 1960s. FLC was a way for Stony Brook to capitalize on its diverse and specialized faculty to improve undergraduate education. POW was a way for Northwestern to show that it could keep up with the best universities in the country by having its own rigorous program in women's studies.

Serving a need is something that must be articulated. Leaders are crucial in articulating the purposes and ideals of their programs in ways that others in the institution will find convincing. The founders of the Hofstra and Stony Brook programs were entrepreneurs who knew how to attract people and resources to their projects and who could speak eloquently about why their programs were important to their institutions. The first director of EDP took pains to describe herself as an academic traditionalist and insisted that the program have stringent distribution requirements, a point of some importance if the program was to achieve academic respectability within Johnson State College. The founding director of POW was a nationally visible researcher who could articulate the meaning of feminism in a way that was acceptable to Northwestern.

The development of a core group capable of carrying on the major tasks of the program also becomes important early, since it is impossible for the leader to take on all of the responsibilities of implementing the program while acting as its minister of foreign affairs as well. The core group is also an important source of future leadership when the original leader steps down (Gamson, 1979; Sarason, 1972). In some programs, the core group is a formal body—the women's studies committee at Northwestern, the sixteen-member executive board at CLS—and in some cases all those teaching in the program, as in Core at Saint Joseph's.

None of the programs we have reviewed in this chapter has departmental status. The programs are either separate colleges or are located within existing departments or colleges in the primary academic structure of their institutions. This means that they must constantly live at two levels—at the level of their own internal operations and at the level of the academic units they inhabit. Being part of a larger unit, especially if it is very different, puts great strains on a program (Levine, 1980; Gamson, 1979). There is sometimes an overwhelming temptation to go it alone, but this temptation must be resisted. One of the main lessons of NSLA and of many other innovations of the past fifteen years is the vulnerability of the enclave approach. With outside money or a social movement to support them, it was relatively easy in the late 1960s and the early 1970s to start new programs. Typically viewed as illegitimate and even deviant by the mainstream, such units quickly formed a counteridentity. But since they lacked ties to the mainstream, they were vulnerable as the competition for money increased later in the 1970s.

Curriculum reformers today are much more likely to work within the mainstream of their institutions (Gaff, 1983). More sophisticated than their predecessors about the "micropolitics" of organizations and strategies for planned change (Gaff, 1980; Lindquist, 1978), they have worked out a variety of ways to influence the mainstream: appointing "czars" to look after undergraduate education; forming new centralized structures; constituting college-wide committees to formulate criteria, review courses, and evaluate programs; and ensuring regular reviews of the undergraduate curriculum (Wittig, 1981; Wee, 1981). Starting special programs with formal links to the mainstream or forging such links with existing programs like women's studies and black studies is becoming more common (Gamson, 1978). Most of the programs in National Project IV take this tack.

How they do so varies. In research-oriented universities like Stony Brook, Oklahoma, and Northwestern, the programs have built ties to disciplinary departments—at FLC and Northwestern by actually incorporating regular departmental courses into their curricula and at Oklahoma by drawing on departmental faculty as advisers and instructors. Even the programs for adults, which tend to be located at the periphery of their institutions, employ the regular faculty to handle some of their teaching.

Arrangements of these sorts are especially helpful in building a network of supporters for the program, especially if the core group attracts "citizen" faculty—people found on most campuses who are seen by their colleagues as having a strong sense of responsibility to their institutions, are interested in new efforts that keep their schools alive, and are willing to actively support programs outside their own departments (Mills, 1982). With the help of such people and the word carried by students and teachers, programs within larger institutions develop a "climate of success" that indicates to outsiders that things are going well (Kanter, 1983).

Once this has happened, it is time for new programs to face the question of becoming regular, which means finding a reliable source of money, having regular procedures for admitting students and attracting teachers, offering more than psychic rewards to teachers, and locating themselves within the accepted academic structure. This is called "institutionalization" in the literature on innovation (Munson and Pelz, 1981), and it is dependent on the age of the program as well as when it was founded historically. Older programs and those founded in affluent circumstances are much more likely to become institutionalized than new programs, especially those that opened in times of economic insecurity. Core and CLS are the oldest programs among the seven that we have looked at in this chapter, and they also have the advantage of having been founded in prosperous times. They are accepted parts of their institutions with regular budgets, standardized procedures for getting their work done, and respected organizational locations. They can offer their faculties benefits like grants, extra pay, release time, national recognition, new lines of scholarship, and career development.

If a new program starts with support from top administrators, adequate start-up money, and a leader and a core group who command respect and then develops ties widely, it will probably gain a foothold within its institution. This is not to say that the present is effortless or that the future is guaranteed. Like alternative organizations, new approaches must struggle constantly within the context in which they operate. At the very least, they must fight against losing their distinctiveness in the struggle to survive (Mills, 1982). Thus, for example, Northwestern University's Program on Women must convince departments to offer more courses related to women's studies while resisting the assumptions and behaviors characteristic of an institution that it sees as not very hospitable to women. EDP must satisfy faculty members and administrators at Johnson State that it is academically respectable without giving up its vision of human development. The Labor Institute must reassure faculty colleagues at Hofstra that it is rigorous and, at the same time, show its union cosponsors that it respects their members.

There is a general climate of support for improvement in the undergraduate curriculum in the 1980s, but it comes at a time of severe financial constraints. Even institutions like Stony Brook and Northwestern, where sheer longevity has usually guaranteed survival, programs must justify themselves politically as well as educationally. The younger they are, the more vulnerable they are, as existing departments and programs fight over a smaller pie. To survive and, even more, to become regular parts of their institutions, programs like the ones we have been examining must learn to live with—better yet, exploit—this situation.

CHAPTER NINE

Evaluation
to Sustain Change

Educational research could well take as its central domain the study of the "experience of education." This would include the naturalistic study of classroom . . . practices and transactions; it would involve a holistic treatment rather than a fragmentary one; it would take the study of participants' concerns as a point of departure; and it would fulfill a practical function of certain value.

—Parlett and Dearden, 1977, p. 144

The purpose of National Project IV was to understand the nature of liberal education in the 1980s through the close scrutiny of different programs and institutions that claimed to be engaged in liberal education. The project drew on self-studies at these programs and institutions, in addition to the observations of outsiders. In reaching for a way to do evaluation that would be consonant with liberating education, these studies collectively illustrate an approach to evaluation that is more accurately termed *examination*. How is this approach different from most evaluations of educational programs? *To evaluate* means to fix the value of something. *To examine* is to inspect something in detail. Clearly, a close examination of what is to be studied is a first step in a proper evaluation. Evaluations, as they are carried out, however, often presuppose that what is to be assessed is clear enough to be measured. Educational concepts are notoriously difficult to pin down—especially ones with a variety of referents like liberal education. Indeed, most of the educational results and processes that matter cannot be measured in any simple way because they occur over time, are often delayed, and show themselves unexpectedly.

If the kind of education we are calling a liberating one is to be evaluated properly, it must first be analyzed with care. This book has done that. Rather than trying to fix the value of such education—a legitimate but premature question—this book has asked what a liberating education is and how it comes about. Evaluations of educational programs are focused on fixing worth without paying enough attention to careful observation and analysis of what is to be studied. They tend to bypass faculty members and students as participants in the evaluation process. They often make use of one-shot methods that wrench findings from their contexts instead of making a cumulative assessment. They are frequently naive about the effects of the research process on those involved in it and about their usefulness for improving practice.

Liberating Evaluation:
Collaborative, Cumulative, Contextual, and Critical

In contrast, evaluation conducted as examination must be a continuous activity, as regular as making budgets and scheduling courses. As an honored element in any educational program, evaluation becomes an important aspect of pedagogy and its improvement. The first step in such an evaluation is to convince those who are in a position to improve practice of its value—that is, the teachers. If faculty members are expected to act on the results of evaluation, they must believe in it. This is not an easy task, since many faculty members are unconscious of themselves as educators and resist educational talk with a vengeance. In any case, they do not like to participate in someone else's research, especially if it is in their own domain.

Professional evaluators and review committees know this, and understandably they tend to avoid too much contact with the faculty. But there is no way to bypass faculty members in evaluation as a process of examination; their resistance must be confronted head on and taken into account. Even some of the participants in National Project IV, people who had chosen to conduct evaluations on their campuses, raised objections to certain approaches to evaluation. A chemist, for example, said that she found "quantitative evaluation studies boring to read," not because she was against such research—her own work as a chemist made use of quantitative methods—but because they are "covered with a veneer of objectivity and reality which isn't really present."

Similarly, teachers in the New School of Liberal Arts (NSLA) at Brooklyn College fiercely resisted filling out a questionnaire distributed by their three colleagues participating in National Project IV. "They rarely use terms such as *goals* and *objectives. Critical thinking skills, value orientation, location of self in time and place, self-actualization*—these terms were virtually never heard when NSLA faculty talked about their program and what they were doing in it. . . . One faculty member protested that 'liberal arts skills' was a 'horrible expression' and thus wouldn't answer a questionnaire item on the subject" (Black, Hey, and Margon, 1981, p. 11).

Yet despite their distaste for educational jargon, when given the chance to describe what they did in the classroom, NSLA instructors talked about many of the issues the questionnaire tried to raise. They may have disliked the wording of a question that asked whether changes in personal values were the goal of their classrooms, but two thirds answered yes anyway. ("Who in hell is a teacher to change or challenge anybody's values?" one wrote.) Answering yes meant little; their explanations told the story: "I try to get them to be self-conscious, aware of their values—rather than to change them," and "I emphasize that music is made by people whose expectations about life, participation in society, experiences and manifestations of religious beliefs . . . take form in ways that challenge us and force us to deal with concepts such as primitive, uncivilized, culture, ethnocentricity, prejudices, and so on" (Black, Hey, and Margon, 1981, p. 11).

When they were asked about whether they wanted their students to think "critically" or "analytically" or "abstractly," NSLA faculty members just said they wanted to teach their students to "think," period. What did they mean by *think*? The very things the terms *critical, analytic,* and *abstract* compress: To formulate stimulating questions, to develop clear and logically consistent arguments, to work out standards of proof, to use evidence in support of or to test arguments, and to synthesize information from several disciplinary perspectives into a coherent whole. The NSLA faculty apparently was not against quantitative methods or surveys in principle. Rather, the instructors opposed the analytic simplifications of certain methods—in particular, those that assume education consists solely of its outcomes. They wanted to talk about how students saw and experienced classes. They were interested not only in what students and faculty members thought but also in how they came to think as they did.

Reactions like those of the NSLA faculty must become part of the examination process, for they tell us how participants in the program preferred to describe what they thought they were doing. Indeed, systematic description is a necessary part of any study. Although it has only recently begun to receive serious attention in evaluation studies and educational research (Parlett and Dearden, 1977; Grant and others, 1979), description has been central in some of the most thoughtful writing on methodology in the social sciences (Geertz, 1973; Glaser and Strauss, 1967; Reinharz, 1979). Context comes to the forefront in good descriptions. Glaser and Strauss (1967), the preeminent writers on qualitative research, call this grounded research. Rather than removing people from their natural contexts, grounded research allows people to speak their usual language as they play their normal roles in their natural settings (Mishler, 1979). As we have seen throughout this book, the meaning of liberating education and of particular practices is conditioned by the contexts in which they occur. Writing, for instance, as it is taught in the developmental English program at Northern Virginia Community College, reflects the values of a community college dedicated to responding to the interests

of students, while writing as it was taught in the Preparatory
Year Program in the New School of Liberal Arts, was shaped
by a classical curriculum and the academic culture of Brooklyn
College. Both succeeded in teaching their students to write and
think better, yet they went about it in opposite ways. Only an
understanding of their particular contexts could reveal how
they did so and why.

Contextual studies of the college environment are rare,
as are studies that systematically attempt to relate student outcomes to a detailed, holistic understanding of the settings in
which they are supposed to be produced. Although it is far
from ideal, National Project IV offers several examples of how
to conduct such studies. Resource B summarizes the topics,
methods, and samples used in the on-campus evaluation studies. It shows that the projects investigated questions in several
domains: students' reactions to various aspects of the curriculum, teaching practices and assumptions, the curriculum, and
the larger institutional environment. Research on students' reactions was especially rich and diverse. Current students, and
sometimes graduates, were probed for their attitudes toward
their programs and institutions, their mastery of basic as well as
complex cognitive competences, career plans, developmental
levels, cognitive styles, personality traits, and relationships with
family, work, community, and friends.

In spite of some of their criticisms of standardized tests
and quantitative measures, all of the projects used tests like the
American College Testing Program's College Outcomes Measures
Project, the Group Embedded Figures Test, the Omnibus Personality Inventory, the California Personality Inventory, the
Rotter Locus of Control Scale, the Defining Issues Test, and
fixed-response questionnaires. The qualitative methods ran an
even wider gamut. The African-American Music Program invited
three music educators to observe classes and write a critical description of what they saw. The National Project IV participants
at Brooklyn College became participant observers in selected
classes and wrote field notes and reports on their observations
of critical incidents. The Radcliffe College study asked students
to write about critical incidents illustrating a vivid moment in

their educational experience. Researchers in the Program on Women dug into the history of women at Northwestern University to provide a context for their research on the effects of a women's studies course.

The on-campus evaluators in National Project IV were, on the whole, new to empirical research in the social sciences; more than half were in the humanities and the arts and only three or four had any experience doing systematic evaluation research. Perhaps because of this, the research on some campuses was carried out by several people, not just the person directly involved in National Project IV. Students, faculty members, and administrators helped to collect the data in several of the projects, guided and prodded occasionally by experienced researchers on their own campuses, outside consultants, and advisers on the staff of National Project IV. For example, Saint Joseph's College asked a specialist in qualitative approaches to educational evaluation to clarify what they were doing from time to time at different stages in its large institutional self-study—and then pressed students and the faculty into service. With the help of an outside consultant and members of the National Project IV staff, the Hampshire College researcher designed a study that made use of a survey questionnaire as well as interviews with students and the faculty about teaching in the natural sciences.

There is a danger in relying exclusively on participants, since it may be especially difficult for them to see what they take for granted. Therefore, evaluators, especially if they are long-time participants in the setting under scrutiny, must think of ways to bring unexamined assumptions to awareness. A running dialogue with representatives from other programs and the staff of National Project IV, combined with the requirement that they produce final reports according to a common outline, forced the on-campus researchers to ask questions that they would not have been likely to ask had they been operating on their own. Conscious of having to play this role, National Project IV staff members pressed faculty members, administrators, and students during site visits to explain why they held certain educational beliefs and engaged in given educational practices. Following a common protocol (see Resource C), they concentrated especially on collecting concrete instances—stories, observations, and critical incidents—that illustrated the programs in action.

How can observers be incorporated in a situation lacking the benefit of an outside grant—a program without funds to pay observers? First, diversity and criticism must be embraced as part of the evaluation process. Once this principle is accepted, a variety of inexpensive devices can work. Different programs, departments, or schools could agree to be observers of one another. For colleges and universities where competition among units is likely to interfere with candor, units could be paired with other institutions, preferably in the same geographical area to minimize costs. Members of the faculty could be given release time and students could be given course credit for working on evaluations. Arrangements could be rotated among a group of faculty members so that instructors could all learn how to do educational research—and, not incidentally, spread commitment to acting on the results more widely. If release time is difficult to arrange, giving a graduate student the opportunity to collect data for a dissertation is a time-honored way to get free help in research. One school, the College of Public and Community Service at the University of Massachusetts in Boston, may write a request for proposals, much as federal agencies do, for an evaluation of their curriculum in exchange for access and publication rights. Another idea would be to invite a team of people from within the institution or from nearby colleges, universities, and nonacademic organizations, to constitute a visiting committee that would conduct interviews and review documents for a day or two on several occasions. The expense of bringing such a regional group together should be fairly low.

Although criticism is part of evaluation conducted as an examination, it is not antithetical to a cooperative spirit. Indeed, it requires and assumes collaboration between the researchers and the participants in programs. Collaboration is the most important way to build commitment to the procedures and findings of an evaluation. It also serves as a check on idiosyncrasy and bias; a group of people (students included) is more likely to come up with an accurate and useful evaluation than is a single person. Whatever the specific collaborative arrangement, it is crucial that the faculty has a say in the questions to be addressed and even some of the methods to be used. This does not require an inordinate amount of time, just a commitment on the part of those involved to take responsibility for checking in from time to time after determining the basic direction of the research.

This discussion assumes that evaluation is not a one-shot affair but a cumulative effort. Certainly, this is an ideal held in the literature on evaluation, but it is rarely carried out in practice. A few of the programs in National Project IV—most notably Saint Joseph's College and the Federated Learning Communities at the State University of New York at Stony Brook—were engaged in self-studies spread over a number of years. In those schools and, we suspect, more generally, the key to making evaluation cumulative is to use multiple sources of data collected at different times. Several of the programs in National Project IV used a variety of qualitative and quantitative methods and drew on information not only from students but also from the faculty and occasionally graduates by administering questionnaires, interviewing, looking at documents, and observing.

The use of multiple methods and sources is called *triangulation* in the research literature (Patton, 1980; Parlett and Deardon, 1977). One of the most important ways to verify and validate findings, triangulation also helps overcome participant bias, since it compels the researcher to look at a topic of investigation in several ways. A less obvious effect of triangulation is the requirement for reflection during the process, since data collected several ways or at different times must be self-consciously compared and integrated. Thus, for example, the evaluation of Core at Saint Joseph's College consisted of a complex of interconnected observations and measures on a variety of student samples based on standardized instruments, locally developed surveys, in-depth interviews, and site visits by outsiders. Each step in the research process could be focused more sharply because of the findings from previous steps. Conflicts among several sources of data raised questions that needed to be tracked down; convergences meant that the researchers could proceed to make recommendations.

It is a good idea to formalize reflection in evaluations by providing structured opportunities for discussions of findings, their implications for practice, and reactions to the research process. We can turn to few guidelines for models of this kind of reflection about evaluation. We can, however, make use of some of the questions participants in National Project IV tried to address, such as the following:

- What assumptions and biases underlie the questions you are asking?
- Why are those questions important to you?
- Do your methods and research design accurately tap the questions that are important to you?
- How did the researchers react to doing the research?
- How did the subjects of the research react to participating?
- How might their reactions affect your findings?
- Which techniques and instruments were most effective? Which were not? Why?
- Which findings did you expect? Which did you not expect?
- How consistent are your findings across different questions, samples, and times?
- What further questions does your study provoke?
- How will you address those questions systematically now or in the future?
- What conclusions and implications for change follow from your study?
- How will you present those conclusions and recommendations?
- How did your audience respond to your findings, conclusions, and recommendations?

If researchers take the time to ask themselves questions like these, they are much more likely to detect problems—as the researchers at the Institute of Study for Older Adults did when they discovered that they had no way of explaining why their students were less satisfied with their lives than people who were not students. Since their study had not been designed to uncover the reasons students gave for their answers, people in the program made plans for a study that relied more on personal interviews. The finding also provoked much discussion of how the program ought to act. Did it attract students who were already more dissatisfied than other people or did it make them more dissatisfied? The design of the study could not answer this question because it was not longitudinal. Was being dissatisfied with life necessarily bad? If education were to help students understand their lives and the conditions that affected them, did the program have some responsibility to help students become more able to act in their own behalf?

The important point here is that reflection on the evaluation itself, combined with an unexpected finding, led to a reexamination of the program's values and activities, which laid the groundwork for research that would be more valuable for practice. This reflectiveness follows a developmental path; each new effort for understanding builds on what was learned earlier in increasingly complex and differentiated ways (Rogers and Gamson, 1982; Sanders, 1981). This is as true for the individuals doing the evaluations as for what they were evaluating. Since most of the evaluators also taught or carried administrative duties, what they learned could be translated into proposals for change in their programs. Several of the National Project IV participants specifically spoke to the question of the ambiguities of being participants in the programs they were also evaluating. Nancy Black, the literature instructor who directed the National Project IV research at the New School of Liberal Arts with two colleagues, described their early worries about being teachers in the program they were studying and their growing realization that this might be an advantage:

> One of the most exciting realizations we made was that we, the project directors, could adopt the role of "field researchers." Instead of worrying about our biases, as we had been doing, we came to see our involvement in the program as a great advantage. No one from outside, in a short

span of time, could know the program as intimately as we. All the data we needed were at hand; we had only to look at them more objectively: collect them, record them, and analyze them systematically.

Similarly, Laurent Daloz, the National Project IV researcher at the External Degree Program at Johnson State, said he was "not just gathering data; I was trying to see better what was right there." Continuing, he observed:

> Without question, the most valuable aspect of the entire study has been my dual role as participant and observer, mentor and evaluator. As a mentor I have learned about how my students are changing, how to listen to their words, how to see their development, how to sense their pain. As evaluator, I have been able constantly to practice my skill as interviewer. With every meeting with a student, I am listening for common patterns, looking for unique insights. I've learned to watch myself at work better. The study forced me to wear an "observer" hat. Not only can I now hear myself better as I work with students, but I have found few better training materials than a good tape of a student and me talking.

Other participants talked of how they became less fearful of making mistakes and of their own empowerment as educational researchers. Roland Braithwaite of Talladega College, a music professor who was then dean of the college, worked closely with a young psychometrician in designing, executing, and analyzing the Talladega study. Braithwaite spoke of learning gradually to trust his own judgment:

> My understanding of evaluation evolved from a dependence on highly sophisticated, psychometric evaluations to an understanding of nar-

rative evaluations in which comments and observations are allowed to speak descriptively. Later, I gained a perception of the worth of nationally standardized tests and the need to have a clear understanding of the populations being compared.

Nancy Lowry, the chemist at Hampshire College who collected much of the research material herself, also described her growing sense of confidence:

> I had one of those eye-opening revelations the first few minutes I talked to our consultant at the beginning of my examination of science at Hampshire. I was worried about my bias; worried about my preference for qualitative evaluation; worried about what I was going to do and how I was going to hold my head up in a world devoted to statistics and averages and p values. He sat back and told me that you cannot avoid biases and you cannot be totally objective. He underlined my own sense that in this kind of evaluation you must trust your intuitions.

Maria Burgio, the researcher at the Institute of Study for Older Adults, was forced to come to terms with the surprising findings we have just discussed. An experienced evaluation researcher, she explained her disappointment with her original approach to the project:

> I approached the project, first of all, with a sense that I would measure some very neat parameters within the elderly population. As it turned out, evaluation of educational processes and operations now seems a much harder task. At first, changes in people due to being part of an educational process seemed easy to measure. However, after trying to define my program and trying to pinpoint *exactly* what the program did and how it

did it, evaluation seems a mere beginning in a series
of questions.

As a process of examination, evaluation is, precisely, the
growing awareness that is "a mere beginning in a series of questions." Indeed, this awareness is very much like a liberating education for evaluators. It is critical and it is informed by and increases the potential for useful application. It grows from
inquiries that are active, articulated, and demanding and draws
on a "curriculum" of methods that are diverse, critical, experiential, and integrated. When this is true, evaluators and those
who are affected by them are likely to feel that they can do
something about what they learn.

CHAPTER TEN

Implications
for Society
and Higher Education

He was already dead, he reflected. It seemed to him that it was only now, when he had begun to be able to formulate his thoughts, that he had taken the decisive step.
　　　　　　　　　　　　　　　　　　　　—Orwell, 1949, p. 27

　　If a liberating education existed only to reclaim the lost territory of liberal education, it might be interesting, but it would be ultimately irrelevant. For colleges and universities, it must stake a larger claim: the preservation of the spirit of ordinary Americans. We have seen that education of the highest quality is possible not only for those who are typically thought to be college material but also for people considered incapable of it in times past: those in the midst of the full responsibilities of adulthood, members of minority groups, people with few financial means, those whose preparation for academic work has been minimal. To them, a liberating education offers a vision of life. In many ways, this vision stands in opposition to the world of Orwell's *1984*—and aspects of the world today. Against loneliness, liberating education offers community. Against fragmentation, it brings a sense of wholeness. Against helplessness, it offers understanding and a certain power. Most of all, a liberating education means vitality. Instead of the many stupefactions of modern life, it brings awakeness.

There is no question that people are the better for an education like this. Their sense of themselves and of their place in the world and their capacity to apply what they learn to their lives are considerably enhanced. This education enables students to see that they have more control over their lives than they thought they had.

But does personal education have social implications? Americans have few vital collective identifications on which they can act (Gurin, Miller, and Gurin, 1980). While some black students at Talladega and some women students at Radcliffe, for example, identify themselves with blacks and women, they do not explicitly link their own sense of empowerment with the need to act with or on behalf of other blacks or women. Students at Saint Joseph's College talk about "opening up" to other people, but this feeling does not seem to be connected with an enduring sense of social responsibility to a community of other people. Even students in the External Degree Program at Johnson State, who have lived in stable communities for most of their lives, do not necessarily see their communities as arenas in which they can apply their new-found sense of themselves. In sum, we can say that a liberating education has profound effects on students as individuals. Whether it also has an impact on what they do on behalf of others in their places of work, communities, and in society at large is not entirely clear.

I raise these points because of the place that education has traditionally been thought to hold in a democracy. Schools are the few remaining places where people are expected to learn about democracy, but rarely are they given the opportunity to experience it or to develop the skills that are required for democratic participation. Schools, and higher education even more, must recognize that they should be engaged in a mammoth reclamation project: the teaching of the arts and skills of democracy and community. How do people learn these things? By participating in communities that require them to cooperate with others and make decisions that matter. The key to the social implications of a liberating education lies in what Brann (1979), writing about the ideal of liberal education in a republic, calls small republics of the intellect, what we have been calling learning communities. In them, students and faculty members experience the meaning of community, often for the first time in their lives. They learn what it means to take into account people who are not close friends or members of their families. In practicing the arts of discourse and the application of the mind in everyday life, they come to understand these people and cooperate with them in the common tasks of learning.

Without communities and structures to support the learning of democracy, liberating education or any other scheme for reviving the civic tradition (Boyer and Hechinger, 1981) or bringing morality back into the curriculum (Hesburgh, 1981) will be empty. For arrayed against such schemes are powerful forces, some of them within higher education itself. In a society in which a national commission on excellence in education must invoke the fear of foreign powers to get attention, it is not surprising that universities and even some colleges might have become preoccupied with big-time research and politics—and have forgotten about education. It will take more than pious words to change the scenario.

There are severe limits on the extent to which educational institutions can redirect major social forces, even if they were inclined to do so—and they generally are not (Bowles and Gintis, 1976; Carnoy and Levin, 1976; Katz, 1971). Yet in an age that is becoming more dependent on information and an educated work force, universities and colleges may have more power than they have had in the past. They may not have exercised this power intentionally or even very responsibly, but some are beginning to take their responsibilities and powers more seriously by turning to the task of improving undergraduate education. This presents a great opportunity to reform the purposes and the structures of higher education as well.

It will be a difficult struggle. Any change in the curriculum must face the fact that the distribution system has survived for good reason: It does not require much administration or coordination, does not threaten departments, and does not ask that money or faculty energies be shifted around much. The current discontent with the undergraduate curriculum is unlikely to lead to any fundamental change unless it can find an expression. Such an expression is both sociological and philosophical, structural as well as conceptual. If new curricular patterns cannot find expressions equal to, or better than, a distribution system, we are likely to end up with a somewhat more rigorous distribution, less of a range in what can meet requirements, and an occasional integrative course—essentially, versions of Harvard's core curriculum (Keller, 1982). These alternative patterns will eventually degenerate into the free distribution systems of the early 1970s (Blackburn and others, 1976). Is this so bad? Yes, because the strength of the distribution system is also its weakness. Unlike the programs we have analyzed in this book, distribution structures cannot be centers of activity. By their nature, they have no center—no place, vision, or identity.

A program with a structure that embodies its ideal is critical to efforts to reform the undergraduate curriculum. This structure must, at the same time, live within the larger academic system in order to survive. Unlike general education distribution requirements which, as Boyer and Levine (1981) point out, have been treated as a shabby guest relegated to the spare room in the house of academe, a program of liberating education must not be treated as a guest at all. It must have a proper room in the center of the house with the amenities, and the responsibilities, of any member of the family.

How is this change to come about in the face of the fractionalization of most colleges and universities? Again, through the creation of learning communities. Some small colleges still retain a strong sense of their purposes and can build on this to create a single expression of their educational vision (Martin, 1982). Saint Joseph's Core, Talladega's curriculum based on that of the University of Chicago, and Hampshire's divisional structure are three examples of what small colleges can do. Larger schools cannot be expected to reach fundamental agreement about educational purposes and curriculum. Therefore, it makes more sense for universities, and many colleges as well, to face the fact that there cannot be a single curriculum for a liberating education. This does not mean, however, giving up on the creation of learning communities centered on the study of particular subjects. Rather than settling for a distribution system, colleges and universities should embrace pluralism and encourage groups of faculty members and students to create strong intellectual communities with their own requirements and structures. These communities could be designed with an eye to longevity, as the cluster colleges of the 1960s were (Gaff and Associates, 1970), or they could be temporary ones, as are each of the clusters in the Federated Learning Communities at Stony Brook. They could offer general education, as did the New School of Liberal Arts at Brooklyn College, or they could be studies within a field of concentration, as with the African-American Music Program at Old Westbury. They could be completely prescribed in a series of core curricula from which all undergraduates would choose, or they could be completely open. They could be based on the study of contemporary problems; historical periods; the concerns of special groups like workers, minorities, women, or older people; the classics; or contemporary disciplines.

Certain things, however, would not vary. Ideally, all undergraduates in the institution would be associated with at least one learning community and so would faculty members for a given period of time. The different communities would be expected to articulate their educational purposes publicly. They would express their purposes explicitly in their structures, their curricula, and their teaching. They would select content that is diverse, integrative, experiential, and critical. And they would engage in systematic and regular self-assessment.

Would this approach fragment institutions even more than they are already? From the point of view of the student, the creation of a series of learning communities provides more, rather than less, coherence than the typical distribution system. By substituting programmatic for individual choice, they give students a more coherent education and challenge faculty in new ways. Furthermore, these communities need not undermine or challenge departments; they can be integrated with and offer benefits to people in departments in many ways: new students, a sense that they are educators as well as specialists, collaboration with people from other fields, and openings to new scholarly terrains.

The faculty is essential to the reform of undergraduate education. There is strong evidence that most faculty members in U.S. colleges and universities think of themselves first as teachers and secondly as researchers (Finkelstein, 1978; Ladd, 1979). Yet many are trapped in institutions and structures that do not reward them for teaching well. Many yearn for an intellectual community, and this may be a favorable time for colleges and universities to encourage instructors to create communities for undergraduate education. In order for this to happen, however, faculty members must receive recognition for collective as well as individual accomplishments. For economic reasons, more collaboration is being promoted in some small colleges where tiny departments are being combined to form multidisciplinary divisions and in larger institutions in which joint appointments and cross-listed courses are being used to reduce proliferation. These are rather mechanical responses to scarcity. How much more imaginative it would be to say that faculty members will be expected to create or participate in at least some learning community with undergraduates and that they will be evaluated according to how well those communities succeed in educating students according to the purposes they have articulated.

Does all this sound farfetched? Those who would answer yes should look beyond the groves of academe. While some colleges and universities have become more anxious, centralized, and competitive in recent years (Austin and Gamson, 1983), other sectors of society have been moving toward new forms of association and organization. In towns and cities, there is a resurgence of local participation (Boyte, 1980). Across the country, networks of people have been joined together by common interests and, increasingly, by microcomputers (Ferguson, 1980). Cooperatives and worker-owned enterprises have come into their own in the past decade (Carnoy and Shearer, 1980; Zwerdling, 1980). Corporations, government agencies, and nonprofit organizations are experimenting with ways of increasing the participation of employees in planning their work and making organizational decisions (Simmons and Mares, 1983; Kanter, 1983).

Like many of the students in the programs described in this book, people involved in these efforts often speak with great feeling about what happens to them when they join with other people in new ways. Indeed, many of these activities in places of work and in communities seem to operate like learning communities much like the programs we have come to know. People in them, working together, feel that they develop a broad understanding of their work and their communities. They learn to apply that understanding to their everyday lives and exercise greater power as a result. Indeed, these communities could be viewed as graduate schools for programs in liberating education, since they could provide alumni with the opportunity to apply what they have learned to a public realm. That, of course, is the significance of liberal education in a democracy. Just as important is the recognition that a liberating education need not be limited to those who go to colleges and universities. Lest any more people go to sleep in the middle of the show, Americans must see that a liberating education is possible for all of them.

RESOURCE A

Basic Characteristics
of the Programs

	Year Program Began	Organizational Location of Program	Special Student Characteristics	Areas or Subject(s) Taught	Scope of the Curriculum
Brooklyn College, New School of Liberal Arts	1972 (closed in 1980)	Separate college	Underprepared students in Preparatory Year Program	Sciences, social institutions, literature, arts	Whole general education curriculum for subset of students (48 credit hours)
Hampshire College	1970		None	All subjects taught at Hampshire; classes available from 5-college consortium	Whole undergraduate curriculum (divisional organization)
Hofstra University, Labor Institute of Applied Social Science	1976	Program in arts and sciences	Union members	Applied social sciences, humanities, mathematics (50% liberal arts subjects)	Whole undergraduate curriculum for subset of students
Johnson State College, External Degree Program	1977	Program in continuing education	Adults	Subjects taught in the Vermont State College system	Whole undergraduate curriculum for subset of students (upper division only)
University of Nebraska at Lincoln, University Studies Program	1971	Program in arts and sciences	Adults and students of traditional age who are highly motivated	Undergraduate courses taught at Lincoln	Whole undergraduate curriculum for subset of students

Special Content	Curriculum Arrangements, Structures, and Requirements	Primary Instructors
Curriculum formed from simultaneous study of 5 historical periods (ancient world, medieval world, early modern period, age of revolutions, and twentieth century) from the 4 subject areas	Specific courses required in first 2 years. Courses met in 4-hour blocks. Students required to take courses in same historical period.	Separate faculty
Interdisciplinary focus and student research encouraged	Progress through 3 divisional levels by successful completion of individually designed projects. Division I: learning contract and comprehensive examination in natural sciences, social sciences, humanities and arts, language and communication. Division II: learning contract, comprehensive examination in a concentration project. Division III: major research paper, integrative seminar, and community action project.	Entire faculty
Special emphasis on trade unions	Liberal arts required in first 2 years in writing, mathematics, and social sciences. Concentrations in trade-union administration or in administration and delivery of human services. Courses taught in union hall late afternoons and evenings. Joint university-union sponsorship.	Separate adjunct and regular faculty in arts and sciences
None	Individualized contracts worked out with faculty mentor include goals, capacities, needs, learning style, and plan of study. Plan must have minimum of 60 liberal learning credits and 30 concentration credits. Students must demonstrate proficiency in critical analysis, comparative study, advocacy, observation, and reflection. Courses can be taken anywhere; students assigned to geographical clusters with a mentor. Some credit for prior learning possible.	Separate and regular faculty in arts and sciences
None	Students must apply to the program with personal profile, summary of academic experiences, educational and career objectives, and proposed course of study. Individualized study plans worked out with faculty adviser. Distribution and coherence required.	Regular faculty in arts and sciences

	Year Program Began	Organizational Location of Program	Special Student Characteristics	Areas or Subject(s) Taught	Scope of the Curriculum
New York City Technical College, Institute of Study for Older Adults	1969	Program in continuing education	Elderly students	Selected liberal arts subjects	150 courses for subset of students (noncredit, nondegree)
Northern Virginia Community College at Manassas, Project Intertwine	1977	Program in student affairs office	Underprepared students	English, mathematics	2 courses for subset of students
Northwestern University, Program on Women, Certificate Program in Women's Studies	1979	Certificate program in arts and sciences; Program on Women under vice-president for research	Women	History, sociology, literature, arts	Certificate program (like a minor) for subset of students
University of Oklahoma, College of Liberal Studies	1961	Separate college	Adults	Humanities, social sciences, natural sciences	Whole undergraduate curriculum for subset of students
Radcliffe College, Radcliffe Seminars	1950	One of four major divisions at Radcliffe	Women, adults	Humanities, arts, social sciences, mathematics, plus special career-oriented programs	Approximately 70 courses (nondegree; certificates in career areas)
Saint Joseph's College, Core	1969	Program in arts and sciences	None	Humanities, natural sciences, social sciences	Whole general education curriculum (45 credit hours— 40% of coursework for B.A. degree)

Special Content	Curriculum Arrangements, Structures, and Requirements	Primary Instructors
None	Classes meet in centers for the elderly. Potential students at centers vote on courses to be taught.	Adjunct faculty
Developmental	Regular faculty and counselors team teach. Students learn to set goals, examine their lives, and listen to others in the context of English and mathematics.	Regular faculty and counselors
Special emphasis on women and sex roles	Basic introductory courses. Approved electives in social sciences and humanities. 4 courses focused on women.	Regular faculty in arts and sciences
None	Readings and examinations in 3 core interdisciplinary areas completed at home. Team-taught seminars on campus for 3 weeks on completion of core requirements in each of the 3 areas. Integrative area studies after completion of all core requirements: independent study designed by faculty adviser; research paper; and 4-week, multidisciplinary, team-taught seminar.	Regular faculty in arts and sciences
None	All classes seminar style and often cross-disciplinary.	Adjunct faculty
Interdisciplinary curriculum	Ten specific courses required over 4 years. Lecture/discussion format. Faculty as "colearners" often teach discussion session outside their areas of expertise.	Regular faculty in arts and sciences

	Year Program Began	Organizational Location of Program	Special Student Characteristics	Areas or Subject(s) Taught	Scope of the Curriculum
State University of New York at Old Westbury, African-American Music Program	1971	Program in regular department	None	Music, related courses in humanities and social sciences	Music major
State University of New York at Stony Brook, Federated Learning Communities	1976	Program in arts and sciences	None	Subjects taught in undergraduate courses at Stony Brook	3 to 15 courses for subset of students (elective or minor)
Talladega College	1850s		Black students	All subjects taught at Talladega	Whole undergraduate curriculum

Special Content	Curriculum Arrangements, Structures, and Requirements	Primary Instructors
African-American music, interdisciplinary	Improvisation emphasized. Courses in African-American music required. One third of credits in ensemble performance. Senior project is a concert performance of original compositions and arrangements with elements from at least 3 different African-American music forms on instruments from at least 2 of the standard classifications. Students also coordinate arrangements for concert.	Regular faculty in arts and sciences
Courses from different departments grouped over 1 to 3 semesters according to a contemporary theme	Faculty meet weekly for 2 years to plan federation. Program seminar led by "master learner" and a graduate student, who take federated courses with students, meets weekly. Faculty members team teach program core course, which meets once a week. Optional interdisciplinary projects in term following federation.	Regular faculty in arts and sciences
None	General education requirements in communications, general humanities, social sciences, natural sciences, mathematics, and physical education.	Entire faculty

Topics, Methods, and Samples Used in the Self-Assessments

Program	Topics	Methods	Samples
Brooklyn College, New School of Liberal Arts	1. *Faculty's educational attitudes and values* Attitudes toward the curriculum Liberal arts goals and values Classroom approaches Effects of institutional change	Questionnaire, with follow-up faculty conference to discuss questionnaire findings	Tenured faculty
	2. *Students' attitudes toward NSLA* Classroom experiences Student-faculty relationships Integration of courses	Questionnaire	Regular-entry students
	3. *The curriculum in action* Faculty collaboration in teaching Classroom approaches	Case study of 2 courses taught for 2 historical periods, drawing on participant observation, meeting notes, critical incident reports, videotapes of classes, and faculty interviews	Preparatory Year freshmen, regular entry students, faculty
	4. *Preparatory Year Program* Demographic and family information Students' satisfaction with the program Changes in students' attitudes toward learning Activities of former students	Telephone survey	Former Preparatory Year students
		Questionnaire modification of telephone survey	Current Preparatory Year students
Hampshire College, School of Natural Science	1. *Identifying science concentrators and their advisers*	File reviews Division I Division II Division III	
	2. *Faculty teaching approaches, attitudes and experiences in natural science*	Interviews	Natural science faculty
	3. *Student experiences in science courses and with science faculty*	Interviews	Science concentrators
	4. *Students' attitudes toward the School of Natural Science*	Mail questionnaire	Current students and graduates

Hofstra University, Labor Institute of Applied Social Science	1. *Impact of the college program on students' attitudes and values* School experience Personal life Family Work Union Community	Questionnaire	Current students
Johnson State College, External Degree Program	1. *Students' cognitive and moral development*	Two questionnaires mailed one year apart; including Loevinger sentence stems, Perry protocol, and Rotter Locus of Control Test	Current students and graduates
	2. *Role of education in students' lives*	Two taped interviews at different times of the year Critical incident questionnaires	
	3. *Program strengths for development*	Group interviews with students and mentors	
	4. *Students' activities in and attitudes toward the program*	Taped student-mentor sessions	
University of Nebraska, Lincoln, University Studies Program	1. *Students' cognitive competencies* Functioning within social institutions Understanding science Understanding art Communicating Solving problems Clarifying values	American College Testing Program/College Outcomes Measures Project	Freshmen, seniors, and graduates
	2. *Students' evaluation of the program*	Mail questionnaire	Graduates

Program	Topics	Methods	Samples
University of Nebraska, Lincoln, University Studies Program	3. *Students' perceptions of impact of the program* Intellectual and moral development Graduate study Employment	Interview	Faculty
	4. *Description of program goals and practices*	Interview	Faculty
New York City Technical College, Institute of Study for Older Adults	1. *Program growth rates*	Records analysis	
	2. *Effects of educational experience on students' quality of life* Social networks Social interaction Community involvement Life satisfaction Perceived well-being Self-determination	Questionnaire	Students who completed 3 or more courses, non-students active in center where courses taught, nonstudents inactive in center
	3. *Students' evaluation of ISOA Program* Assessment of ISOA courses Effects of course involvement on self and relationships with others Teachers and teaching approaches	Questionnaire	Students who completed 3 or more courses, non-students active in center where courses taught, nonstudents inactive in center
Northern Virginia Community College at Manassas, Project Intertwine	1. *Demographic characteristics of developmental math students*	Questionnaire	Current students
	2. *Assessment of program effectiveness*	Computerized analysis of records on retention and success rates Comparisons of syllabi and assignments in developmental and beginning regular courses in English and math	
	3. *Attitudes toward Project Intertwine*	Interviews	Current students

Institution	Variables	Method	Sample
Northwestern University, Program on Women	1. *Self-descriptions* Educational experiences and aspirations Familial and other interpersonal relationships Work experiences and aspirations Beliefs and values about women's roles	Interviews, conducted before and after the course	Students taking women's studies core course
	2. *Impact of women's studies core course* Rotter Locus of Control Test, Spencer and Helmreich Attitudes Toward Women Scale, social desirability scale Rotter Locus of Control Test, Spence and Helmreich Attitudes Toward Women Scale, social desirability scale	Questionnaires administered at the beginning and end of the course	Course takers, course applicants but non-takers, English course students
University of Oklahoma, College of Liberal Studies	1. *Cognitive competencies* (See University of Nebraska)	American College Testing Program/College Outcomes Measures Project	Current students
	2. *Cognitive styles:* Field dependence and field independence	Group Embedded Figures Test	Current students
	3. *Program evaluation learning preferences*	Questionnaire	Current students
Radcliffe College, Radcliffe Seminars	1. *Student characteristics and responses* Personal background Decision to enroll in seminars Effects of participation on: • perception of self • attitudes toward work • cognitive development • new awareness	Mail survey	Alumnae

Program	Topics	Methods	Samples
Saint Joseph's College, Core	1. *Experiences in and attitudes toward Core*	Interviews	Current students, faculty
	2. *Curriculum and teaching*	Course ratings questionnaire "Discussion benchmark" (rating of role of discussion in Core)	Current students, distributed over all years
	3. *Impacts on students* Intellectual interests and values Achievement orientation Well-being—California Psychological Inventory Tolerance Responsibility Cognitive and moral development	Omnibus Personality Inventory Defining Issues Test	
State University of New York at Old Westbury, African-American Music Program	1. *Effects of beginning instrumental music class* Collective responsibility Self-generating creativity and learning skills Self-image Consciousness of other cultures	Questionnaire Analysis of end-of-term compositions	Beginning instrumental students
	2. *Teaching methods and philosophy*	Observations by music educators	
State University of New York at Stony Brook, Federated Learning Communities (FLC)	1. *Experiences in and attitudes toward FLC* Community Relationships with faculty Relationships with students	Questionnaire	Current FLC students, non-FLC students
	Tolerance Self-esteem Performance in courses	Open-ended questionnaire	Current FLC students

2. *The program in action*	Participant observation Interviews Questionnaire	Faculty, current students
3. *Impacts on students*	Interviews, including Kohlberg Moral Judgment interview, Erikson play interview, cognitive style questions, attitudes toward program	
Talladega College	1. *College activities and personal experiences*	Questionnaire	Current students
	2. *Cognitive competencies* (See University of Nebraska)	American College Testing Program/College Outcomes Measures Project	

RESOURCE C

Site Visit Protocol

The staff of National Project IV used the instructions and questions presented here for conducting interviews and observing classes in the fourteen programs. These site visits provided most of the material for the narratives and quotations in this book. Others may find the protocol useful for inquiring into liberal education and other aspects of undergraduate education.

Conceptions of Liberal Education

Throughout discussion, make separate notes about the language used to describe education in this school. At the end of this section of the interview, ask for the interviewee's interpretation of the meaning of each term you have listed *as it is used in his/her institution.* Probe for clarity of meaning and ask for specific examples. As individual speaks, listen for other "technical terms" and add them to your list.

Ask: Are there any other key terms that members of your program use in discussing the processes or outcomes of liberal education? Define.

1. In what sense do you consider your program engaged in liberal education? By what definition of liberal education? (*Probe for specific language.* "Ability to analyze a problem" is better than "think critically." "Ability to make decisions for themselves" is better than "develop maturity." "Organize powerless groups" is better than "empower." Constantly ask "What do you mean?" until you are satisfied that you understand what the person means by liberal education.)

2. Could you give a concrete example from a classroom experience or from things that have happened to your students that you would call a liberal education? (*Encourage* anecdotes, stories, concrete instances.)

3. How did your program come to this conception of what it is doing? Was it intentionally directed to finding a way to provide a liberal education, or was the liberal education aspect of it accidental, or unintended, or more of an afterthought?

4. What are the major goals of your program for students? How do you relate what you teach to these goals?
5. Which two general types of goals are most characteristic of your program?
    *   Acquisition of *intellectual skills* (ability to analyze problems, synthesize evidence, argue logically, write coherently)
    *   Acquisition of *intellectual attitudes* (open-mindedness, skepticism, rationality, reflectiveness)
    *   Acquisition of certain *bodies of knowledge*
    *   Acquisition of certain *values* (commitment to justice, equality, democracy, individuality, spirituality)
    *   *Psychological growth* (increased self-awareness, ability to make decisions for themselves, maturity of relationships with others, self-confidence)
    *   Capacity to *act* in the world (exercise democratic citizenship, ameliorate suffering, exercise leadership, perform professionally)
6. How much agreement is there among the faculty, students, and administrators about the goals of liberal education? What disagreements or problems come up that seem to indicate lack of agreement? (*Probe* for a specific, recent example.)

For Instructors Only

1. What criteria do you use to evaluate students' accomplishments in your class? How do these criteria fit in with your program's definition of a liberal education?
2. What was your most successful class this term/year in this program? Why?

Context

Organizational Context

1. The institution/characteristics
    *   What are the philosophy and purposes of the institution?
    *   Have there been recent changes? Specify.

- How do they relate to or affect the program?
- What are the major decision-making groups in this institution and how does this program fit into their priorities and values? (*Probe*—board, faculty bodies, executive officers, union, student government.)
- Have there been any recent shifts in institutional support?
  —student enrollments
  —state support
  —gifts and donations
  —soft money
  How does this affect the program?
- What is the institution doing now and in the near future to deal with these changes? How is this likely to affect the program?
- Has there been recent administrative turnover? Where? If yes: effect of turnover on program
          —general outlook
          —specific attitude toward this program

2. Program focus
- Faculty in program: How do they differ from those in other parts of the institution? (Get *vitas* of faculty where possible.)
  —number, total associated with program
  —full-time appointment in program
  —part-time, *without* joint appointment in another department
  —part-time, *with* joint appointment in another department
  —tenure status
  —average age, years of service, academic degrees and training
- What is the organizational location of this program?
- Which administrator has charge of its budget? Is the program budget linked to or embedded in another? How do the size and breakdown of the program's budget compare to others?
- How is this program coordinated with others? What linkages exist with other programs?

3. Dynamics of introduction of program
    - Why was the program introduced? By whom? When?
      —Was the cause primarily internal or was it in some way(s) related to events or persons external to the institution? Specify. (*Probe.*)
      —What were the key issues of discussion/concern through the introduction phase? (*Probe.*)
      —What institutional, faculty, and administrative characteristics, values, conditions, and so on, eased the entry of the program? (*Probe.*)
4. Development
    - What major changes have occurred in the program since its inception?
      —list major changes
      —when they happened
      —how long they took
      —Who initiated them?
      —Who planned?
      —Who carried out?
    - Were the changes made intentionally, that is, were they planned? (If so, state the cause or reason for the change.)
    - Or did change just come with time? If so, describe carefully the nature of the change.
5. Projections
    - What major changes do you project for the program? Definite changes, possible changes.
    - What do you now see as the greatest hindrances to and support of the program's survival and continued growth? How serious are the hindrances? What can be done or what are you now doing to alleviate these? What factors do you see as the greatest assurances of continued program development?

Teaching-Learning Context

To be asked of students:

1. What about this program attracted you to enroll in it?
2. Describe a highlight of the term in this class.

3. Are you finding any significant differences in the way you look at, deal with, or act in your everyday life since you entered this program? If yes, specify. Can you account for these changes?
4. What is the most meaningful thing you have learned in this program—whether or not it relates to your studies, whether or not it relates to a classroom experience? Can you describe the instance of your learning it?
5. What do you dislike most about your learning experiences here? Have you done anything about these?

To be answered while observing a class in session: Describe fully and carefully the classroom activities. The following questions are guides:

1. Describe the room and the setup for the class.
2. What is the composition of the class? How do people look?
3. What is the subject under discussion? Is it related to life or world events? Do students relate it to occurrences in their own lives?
4. What is the main instructional mode—lecture, question-answer, general discussion?
5. What is the interplay of question-answer-exploration—ordered response patterns—versus spontaneous responses and interruptions? Who asks questions, gives answers, mediates, summarizes?
6. Is there an atmosphere of general agreement? Or is there controversy? Controversy: Describe sequence of events including instigation, positions, arguments, evidence for stands, level of involvement, teacher role, response/listening patterns, resolution efforts.
7. Are patterns static? Do they change? What role does the instructor play at different points?

Students

1. In general, how would you describe the students who enroll in this program? How are they similar to or different from

other students in this academic division? How are they recruited?
2. What about this program particularly attracts these students?
3. What skills and qualities does this program especially work
    to develop in students?
4. Student impact
    - How does the program evaluate educational outcomes in
      students?
    - What effect do you think the program has on student
      learning? Is there evidence that students are learning
      better or performing better? Explain.
    - Is there evidence of impacts on students in noncognitive
      areas such as self-image, relational skills, attitudes toward
      education, and so on? What are these? Explain nature of
      the evidence.
5. What do you consider to be the primary characteristics of
    the program which develop these skills and qualities?
6. What, if any, groups or activities are sponsored by this insti-
    tution to bring students together outside the classroom?
    Are these student initiated? What role do these play in in-
    stitutional policy making?
7. Are there issues or concerns about the program which stu-
    dents have expressed? What are they?
8. Collect available documents to supply the following data:
    - age range and mean
    - urban/rural
    - ethnic breakdown
    - male/female
    - attrition and completion rates
    - information on job placement rates
    - rates on continued education
    - admissions criteria
      —average Scholastic Aptitude Test score
      —screening procedures
      —grade point average
      —other tests

    Ask: Have these characteristics of students in the program

changed over time? Are these statistical breakdowns different from those of the institution as a whole?

Evaluation

The Evaluation Plan: Intents and Politics of Beginning

1. Looking at the plan as a whole, what program dimensions are you trying to evaluate? Using what types of methods for each dimension?
2. Why are you doing the evaluation? What questions do you want to be able to answer with your evaluation? Are they all equally important or do some stand out as being more important than others? State how.
3. What populations are you evaluating? From what populations are you gathering data?
4. Obtain copies of all instruments, guides, designs, and so on, that are being used. (This should be accomplished before the visit.) Probe for:
   - The specific purpose of using each questionnaire, interview guide, and so on. What information are you trying to get? What question(s) will this help you answer?
   - The interrelationships among various instruments. Are they purposefully repetitive (overlapping) of each other in some respects? Why? Are they discrete in that each instrument seeks a different kind of information?
   - Describe the plan in full.
5. Are you satisfied that you are gathering the data you need to answer your questions? If not, probe for the discrepancy that is perceived.
6. Who was involved in your examination plan? How extensively? Who selected the people involved? Did someone give approval to the final plan? Who? Did controversy arise over the issue of approval? Describe.

Process of the Evaluation

1. What is your time schedule? Is it working?
2. Who is doing the evaluation work? If more than one person, specify division of labor and coordinating functions.

3. Do you have an adequate budget for this evaluation? What are the funding sources for the evaluation? What will happen when funds run out? Will you complete the evaluation, as you have planned it, within this budget period?
4. What are the attitudes of key administrators toward this evaluation?
   - Supportive of it. Reasons:
   - Actively oppose it. Reasons:
   - Oppose it in silence. Reasons:
   - Indifferent. Comment:
   What effect has this attitude had on the carrying out of the evaluation?
5. What major issues have come up for decision making in the process of evaluation? Who is involved in the decision making?
6. What problems or obstacles have you encountered in doing the evaluation? Were they solved? How? (If not solved, look for ways in which we may assist.)

Analysis and Reporting

1. How will you analyze your data? Do you need help in doing your analysis?
2. How will the data be reported? Do you have a format in mind?
3. Has it been established who will be able to use the data and what purposes they might be used for?

Outcomes, Decisions, and Assessment of Evaluation

1. Who are the projected audiences of the final evaluation report?
2. What do you hope will be the outcomes?
3. Do you think that the evaluation outcomes will affect the program? How and to what extent?
4. Who will make decisions on the basis of the data?
5. Who will be responsible for carrying out the decisions?
6. As you are carrying out the evaluation:
   - What strategies and techniques are you finding to be

successful for the purpose of evaluating aspects of liberal education?

- Are you stumbling on any new (or previously unexamined) aspects of liberal education that you think would
  be worth examining?
- Are you discovering any new or different strategies or
  techniques of evaluation?

References

Astin, A. W. "Undergraduate Achievement and Institutional 'Excellence'." *Science,* 1968, *161,* 661-668.

Astin, A. W. *Four Critical Years: Effects of College on Beliefs, Attitudes, and Knowledge.* San Francisco: Jossey-Bass, 1977.

Astin, A. W., and Lee, B. T. *The Invisible Colleges.* New York: McGraw-Hill, 1972.

Austin, A. E., and Gamson, Z. F. "Colleges and Universities as Workplaces." Ann Arbor: Center for the Study of Higher Education, University of Michigan, 1983.

Barzun, J. *The House of Intellect.* New York: Harper & Row, 1959.

Bateson, G. "The Logical Categories of Learning and Communication." In G. Bateson, *Steps to an Ecology of Mind.* New York: Ballantine, 1974.

Bayer, A. *Teaching Faculty in Academe: 72-73.* Research Report No. 8. Washington, D.C.: American Council on Education, 1973.

Beck, R. E. *Career Patterns: The Liberal Arts Major in Bell System Management.* Washington, D.C.: Association of American Colleges, 1981.

Bell, D. *The Reforming of General Education: The Columbia College Experience in the National Setting.* New York: Anchor, 1968.

Bennett, W. "The Shattered Humanities." *American Association of Higher Education Bulletin,* February 1983, pp. 3–5.

Bird, C. *The Case Against College.* New York: McKay, 1975.

Birnbaum, N. "Students, Professors, and Philosopher Kings." In C. Kaysen (Ed.), *Content and Context: Essays on College Education.* New York: McGraw-Hill, 1973.

Bizzaro, P. "Intertwine and Developmental Writing." In *Faculty-Counselor Collaboration in the Developmental Classroom: A How-To Manual.* Final Report on National Project IV for the Fund for the Improvement of Postsecondary Education. Manassas: Project Intertwine, Northern Virginia Community College, 1981.

Black, N., Hey, K., and Margon, A. *An Experiment in Liberal Education at Brooklyn College: The New School of Liberal Arts (1972–1980).* Final Report on National Project IV for the Fund for the Improvement of Postsecondary Education. Brooklyn, N.Y.: New School of Liberal Arts, Brooklyn College, 1981.

Blackburn, R. T. "Liberal Education's Multifarious History: Some Observations." Ann Arbor: Center for the Study of Higher Education, University of Michigan, 1981.

Blackburn, R. T., and others. *Changing Practices in Undergraduate Education.* Berkeley, Calif.: Carnegie Council on Policy Studies in Higher Education, 1976.

Borden, E. B. "The Radcliffe Seminars." *Radcliffe Quarterly,* 1950, *34,* 9.

Bordo, S. "FLC: Reflections of a Participant Observer." Stony Brook: Federated Learning Communities, State University of New York, 1979.

Bouton, C., and Garth, R. Y. "The Learning Group: What It Is and Why It May Be Better." *American Association of Higher Education Bulletin,* June 1982, pp. 7–9.

Bouton, C., and Garth, R. Y. (Eds.). *New Directions for Teaching and Learning: Learning in Groups,* no. 14. San Francisco: Jossey-Bass, 1983.

Bowen, H. R. *Investment in Learning: The Individual and Social Value of American Higher Education.* San Francisco: Jossey-Bass, 1977.

Bowles, F., and DeCosta, F. *Between Two Worlds.* New York: McGraw-Hill, 1971.

Bowles, S., and Gintis, H. *Schooling in Capitalist America.* New York: Basic Books, 1976.

Boyer, E. L., and Hechinger, F. M. *Higher Learning in the Nation's Service.* Washington, D.C.: The Carnegie Foundation for the Advancement of Teaching, 1981.

Boyer, E. L., and Levine, A. *A Quest for Common Learning: The Aims of General Education.* Washington, D.C.: The Carnegie Foundation for the Advancement of Teaching, 1981.

Boyte, H. C. *The Backyard Revolution: Understanding the New Citizen Movement.* Philadelphia: Temple University Press, 1980.

Braithwaite, R. *The Effect of Liberal Education on Minority Students in Talladega College: The Perception of and Accomplishments of Minority Students in a Liberal Education Curriculum.* Final Report on National Project IV for the Fund for the Improvement of Postsecondary Education. Talladega, Ala.: Talladega College, 1981.

Brann, E. T. H. *Paradoxes of Education in a Republic.* Chicago: University of Chicago Press, 1979.

Brinley, D. "On Rethinking One's Philosophy of Education." Paper presented at annual meeting of the Midwest Region of the National Catholic Educational Association, Chicago, March 1974.

Brubacher, J. S. *On the Philosophy of Higher Education.* San Francisco: Jossey-Bass, 1977.

Bruffee, K. A. *A Short Course in Writing.* Cambridge, Mass.: Winthrop, 1980.

Bruffee, K. A. "Teaching Writing Through Collaboration." In C. Bouton and R. Y. Garth (Eds.), *New Directions for Teaching and Learning: Learning in Groups,* no. 14. San Francisco: Jossey-Bass, 1983.

Bruner, J. S. *The Process of Education.* New York: Vintage, 1960.

Burgio, M. *The Liberal Arts Program of the Institute of Study for Older Adults.* Final Report on National Project IV for the Fund for the Improvement of Postsecondary Education. Brooklyn: Institute of Study for Older Adults, New York City Technical College, 1981.

Burke, C. B. *American Collegiate Populations: A Test of the Traditional View.* New York: New York University Press, 1982.

Carlson, E. A. "Biology for Nonmajors." In A. W. Chickering and Associates, *The Modern American College: Responding to the New Realities of Diverse Students and a Changing Society.* San Francisco: Jossey-Bass, 1981.

Carnegie Council on Policy Studies in Higher Education. *Three Thousand Futures: The Next Twenty Years for Higher Education.* San Francisco: Jossey-Bass, 1980.

Carnegie Council on Policy Studies in Higher Education. *The Carnegie Council on Policy Studies in Higher Education: A Summary of Reports and Recommendations.* San Francisco: Jossey-Bass, 1981.

Carnegie Foundation for the Advancement of Teaching, The. *Missions of the College Curriculum: A Contemporary Review with Suggestions.* San Francisco: Jossey-Bass, 1977.

Carnoy, M., and Levin, H. M. *The Limits of Educational Reform.* New York: McKay, 1976.

Carnoy, M., and Shearer, D. *Economic Democracy: The Challenge for the 1980's.* White Plains, N.Y.: M. E. Sharpe, 1980.

Change Magazine Editors. *The Great Core Curriculum Debate.* New Rochelle, N.Y.: Change Magazine Press, 1979.

Cheit, E. F. *The New Depression in Higher Education: A Study of Financial Conditions at 41 Colleges and Universities.* New York: McGraw-Hill, 1971.

Cheit, E. F. *The New Depression in Higher Education: Two Years Later.* Berkeley, Calif.: Carnegie Commission on Higher Education, 1973.

Chickering, A. W. "The Best Colleges Have the Least Effect." *Saturday Review,* January 16, 1971, pp. 48–50, 54.

Chickering, A. W., and Associates. *The Modern American College: Responding to the New Realities of Diverse Students and a Changing Society.* San Francisco: Jossey-Bass, 1981.

Cohen, A. "Human Services." In A. W. Chickering and Associates, *The Modern American College: Responding to the New Realities of Diverse Students and a Changing Society.* San Francisco: Jossey-Bass, 1981.

Collier, G. *The Management of Peer-Group Learning: Syndicate Methods in Higher Education.* Guildford, England: Society for Research into Higher Education, University of Guildford, 1983.

Collins, R. *The Credential Society.* New York: Academic Press, 1979.

Commission on Non-Traditional Study. *Diversity by Design.* San Francisco: Jossey-Bass, 1973.

Commission on the Humanities. *The Humanities in American Life.* Berkeley: University of California Press, 1980.

Conrad, C. F. *The Undergraduate Curriculum: A Guide to Innovating and Reform.* Boulder, Colo.: Westview, 1978.

Conrad, C. F., and Wyer, J. C. *Liberal Education in Transition.* ERIC/Higher Education Research Report No. 3. Washington, D.C.: American Association for Higher Education, 1980.

Cowan, K. D., Saufley, R. W., and Blake, J. "Through the Hourglass (Darkly), Summary of an Exploratory Analysis of the 'New Student' at a Traditional University." Santa Cruz: Oakes College, University of California, 1980.

Cross, K. P. *Beyond the Open Door: New Students to Higher Education.* San Francisco: Jossey-Bass, 1971.

Dabney, J., and Chaiken, M. "The College in Long-Term Care." Unpublished manuscript, Kingsbrook Jewish Medical Center, Brooklyn, N.Y., n.d.

Daloz, L. A. *When the Thunder Comes: Liberal Learning for Rural Adults.* Final Report on National Project IV to the Fund for the Improvement of Postsecondary Education. Montpelier: Office of External Programs, Vermont State Colleges, 1981.

Daloz, L. A. "Notes Toward a Simple-Minded Mentor's Guide." Montpelier: Office of External Programs, Vermont State Colleges, n.d.

Dewey, J. *Democracy and Education.* New York: Free Press, 1966. (Originally published 1916, Macmillan.)

Downey, N., and Ware, N. *National Project IV at Radcliffe Col-

lege. Final Report on National Project IV for the Fund for the Improvement of Postsecondary Education. Cambridge, Mass.: Radcliffe College, 1981.

Drake, J. *Teaching Critical Thinking.* Danville, Ill.: Interstate, 1976.

Eble, K. *Professors as Teachers.* San Francisco: Jossey-Bass, 1972.

Elbow, P. *Writing Without Teachers.* New York: Oxford University Press, 1973.

Elbow, P. "Trying to Teach While Thinking About the End." In G. Grant and others, *On Competence: A Critical Analysis of Competence-Based Reforms in Higher Education.* San Francisco: Jossey-Bass, 1979.

Epstein, J. "Bring Back the Elitist Universities." *New York Times Magazine,* February 6, 1977, pp. 87–89, 102.

Feldman, K. A., and Newcomb, T. M. *The Impact of College on Students.* San Francisco: Jossey-Bass, 1969.

Ferguson, M. *The Aquarian Conspiracy: Personal and Social Transformation in the 1980s.* Los Angeles: Tarcher/St. Martin's Press, 1980.

Finkel, D. N., and Monk, G. S. "Teachers and Learning Groups: Dissolution of the Atlas Complex." In C. Bouton and R. Y. Garth (Eds.), *New Directions for Teaching and Learning: Learning in Groups,* no. 14. San Francisco: Jossey-Bass, 1983.

Finkelstein, M. J. "Three Decades of Research on American Academics: A Descriptive Portrait and Synthesis of Findings." Unpublished doctoral dissertation, Department of Higher Education, State University of New York at Buffalo, 1978.

Forrest, A. *COMP-ACT: Increasing Student Competence and Persistence. The Best Case for General Education.* Iowa City, Iowa: American College Testing Program, 1981.

Freeman, R. *The Over-Educated American.* New York: Academic Press, 1976.

Freire, P. *Pedagogy of the Oppressed.* New York: Herder and Herder, 1970.

Freire, P. *Education for Critical Consciousness.* New York: Seabury, 1973.

Fulton, O., and Trow, M. "Students and Teachers: Some General Findings in the 1969 Faculty Survey." In M. Trow (Ed.), *Teachers and Students*. New York: McGraw-Hill, 1975.

Gaff, J. G. "Avoiding the Potholes: Strategies for Reforming General Education." *Educational Record*, 1980, *61*, 50-59.

Gaff, J. G. *General Education Today: A Critical Analysis of Controversies, Practices, and Reforms*. San Francisco: Jossey-Bass, 1983.

Gaff, J. G., and Associates. *The Cluster College*. San Francisco: Jossey-Bass, 1970.

Gaff, J. G., and others. *General Education: Issues and Resources*. Washington, D.C.: Association of American Colleges, 1980.

Gamson, Z. F. "Performance and Personalism in Student-Faculty Relations." *Sociology of Education*, 1967, *40*, 279-301.

Gamson, Z. F. "Michigan Muddles Through: Luck, Nimbleness and Resilience in Crisis." In D. Riesman and V. A. Stadtman (Eds.), *Academic Transformation: Seventeen Institutions Under Pressure*. New York: McGraw-Hill, 1973.

Gamson, Z. F. "Programs for Black Students, 1968-1974." In M. Peterson and others, *Black Students on White Campuses: The Impacts of Increased Black Enrollments*. Ann Arbor: Survey Research Center, Institute for Social Research, University of Michigan, 1978.

Gamson, Z. F. "Understanding the Difficulties of Implementing a Competence-Based Curriculum." In G. Grant and others, *On Competence: A Critical Analysis of Competence-Based Reforms in Higher Education*. San Francisco: Jossey-Bass, 1979.

Gamson, Z. F. "The New Vitality in Undergraduate Teaching." *Journal of the National Association for Women Deans, Administrators, & Counselors*, 1982, *46* (1), 32-35.

Geertz, C. G. *The Interpretation of Culture*. New York: Basic Books, 1973.

Geertz, C. G. "Blurred Genres." *The American Scholar*, 1980, *49*, 165-179.

Geiger, R. "The College Curriculum and the Market Place." *Change*, November/December 1980, pp. 17-23, 53-54.

Glaser, B. G., and Strauss, A. L. *The Discovery of Grounded Theory: Strategies for Qualitative Research.* Chicago: Aldine, 1967.

Grant, G., and others. *On Competence: A Critical Analysis of Competence-Based Reforms in Higher Education.* San Francisco: Jossey-Bass, 1979.

Grant, G., and Riesman, D. *The Perpetual Dream: Reform and Experiment in the American College.* Chicago: University of Chicago Press, 1978.

Griffin, C. W. (Ed.). *New Directions for Teaching and Learning: Teaching Writing in All Disciplines,* no. 12. San Francisco: Jossey-Bass, 1982.

Grizzard, E. S. "Creating the Climate for Collaboration." In *Faculty-Counselor Collaboration in the Developmental Classroom: A How-To Manual.* Final Report on National Project IV for the Fund for the Improvement of Postsecondary Education. Manassas: Project Intertwine, Northern Virginia Community College, 1981.

Groppe, J. "Development of Study Skills through Core." Paper presented at annual meeting of the Midwest Region of the National Catholic Educational Association, Chicago, March 1974.

Gurin, P., and Epps, E. *Black Consciousness, Identity, and Achievement.* New York: Wiley, 1975.

Gurin, P., Miller, A. H., and Gurin, G. "Stratum Identification and Consciousness." *Social Psychology Quarterly,* 1980, *43,* 30–47.

Halliburton, D. "Curriculum Design." In A. W. Chickering and others, *Developing the College Curriculum: A Handbook for Faculty and Administrators.* Washington, D.C.: Council for Independent Colleges, 1977.

Harvard Committee. *General Education in a Free Society.* Cambridge, Mass.: Harvard University Press, 1945.

Hazzard, G. W. "Knowledge Integration in Undergraduate Liberal Learning." *The Forum for Liberal Education,* May 1979, *2,* 1–3.

Heath, D. A. *Growing Up in College: Liberal Education and Maturity.* San Francisco: Jossey-Bass, 1968.

Heiss, A. *An Inventory of Academic Innovation and Reform.* New York: McGraw-Hill, 1973.

Hendrix, R., and Stoel, C. "Improving Liberal Education: A Report on Fund Projects, 1973–81." *Liberal Education,* 1982, *68*(2), 139–159.

Hesburgh, T. M. "The Future of Liberal Education." *Change,* April 1981, pp. 36–40.

Hill, P. J. *Final Report on the Institutional Self-Study on Undergraduate Education in the College of Arts and Sciences at Stony Brook.* Stony Brook: State University of New York, 1974.

Hirst, P. H. *Knowledge and the Curriculum: A Collection of Philosophical Papers.* London: Routledge & Kegan Paul, 1974.

Hofstadter, R., and Smith, W. *American Higher Education: A Documentary History.* 2 Vols. Chicago: University of Chicago Press, 1961.

Honigman, R. D. *The Destruction of the Student Community in Ann Arbor: An Indictment of Higher Education in America.* Fraser, Mich.: Green Valley, Blue Water, White Cloud Press, 1982.

Hutchins, R. *The Higher Learning in America.* New Haven, Conn.: Yale University Press, 1967.

Hyman, H. H., and Wright, C. R. *Education's Lasting Influence on Values.* Chicago: University of Chicago Press, 1979.

Hyman, H. H., Wright, C. R., and Reed, J. S. *The Enduring Effects of Education.* Chicago: University of Chicago Press, 1975.

The I Ching or *Book of Changes.* (R. Wilhelm, Trans.; C. F. Baynes, English version.) Princeton, N.J.: Princeton University Press, 1976.

Jencks, C., and Riesman, D. *The Academic Revolution.* New York: Doubleday, 1968.

Kanter, R. M. *The Change Masters: Innovation for Productivity in the American Corporation.* New York: Simon & Schuster, 1983.

Katz, J. "A Day in the Life of FLC." Stony Brook: Federated Learning Communities, State University of New York, n.d.

Katz, M. *Class, Bureaucracy and Schools: The Illusion of Educational Change in America.* New York: Praeger, 1971.

Keller, P. *Getting at the Core: Curricular Reform at Harvard.* Cambridge, Mass.: Harvard University Press, 1982.

Kinneavy, J. *A Theory of Discourse.* Englewood Cliffs, N.J.: Prentice-Hall, 1971.

Kuhn, T. S. *The Structure of Scientific Revolutions.* Chicago: University of Chicago Press, 1962.

Ladd, E. C., Jr. "The Work Experience of American College Professors: Some Data and an Argument." In American Association of Higher Education, *Current Issues in Higher Education.* Washington, D.C.: American Association of Higher Education, 1979.

Landa, A. "Significant Changes: Analysis and Discussion of Fifty-Seven Responses to the Invitation: Describe the Most Significant Changes You See in Yourself as a Result of the FLC Experience." Stony Brook: Federated Learning Communities, State University of New York, 1981.

Lawrence, C. *An Alternative Approach to Education in Music.* Final Report on National Project IV for the Fund for the Improvement of Postsecondary Education. Old Westbury: State University of New York, 1981.

Leestma, R. "Global Education." *The Forum for Liberal Education,* January 1979, *2,* 1-3.

Levine, A. *Handbook on Undergraduate Curriculum: Prepared for the Carnegie Council on Policy Studies in Higher Education.* San Francisco: Jossey-Bass, 1978.

Levine, A. *Why Innovation Fails: The Institutionalization and Termination of Innovation in Higher Education.* Albany: State University of New York Press, 1980.

Levine, A., and Weingart, J. *Reform of Undergraduate Education.* San Francisco: Jossey-Bass, 1973.

Lin, L. "Can We Understand the Universe?" *The Research News* (University of Michigan), 1981, *32,* (6/7, entire issue).

Lindquist, J. *Strategies for Change.* Berkeley, Calif.: Pacific Soundings Press, 1979.

Little, J. W. "Norms of Collegiality and Experimentation: Workplace Conditions of School Success." *American Educational Research Journal,* 1982, *19,* 325-340.

Loevinger, J. *Ego Development: Conceptions and Theories.* San Francisco: Jossey-Bass, 1976.

Lowry, N. *Science Education at Hampshire College with Special Emphasis on Women and Science.* Final Report on National Project IV for the Fund for the Improvement of Postsecondary Education. Amherst, Mass.: Hampshire College, 1981.

McDermott, J. "The Laying on of Culture." *The Nation,* March 10, 1969, *208.*

McKeachie, W. J. "Implications of Cognitive Psychology for College Teaching." In W. J. McKeachie (Ed.), *New Directions for Teaching and Learning: Learning, Cognition, and College Teaching,* no. 2. San Francisco: Jossey-Bass, 1980.

Manuel, W., and Altendorfer, M. E. *Baccalaureate Origins of 1950–59 Medical Graduates.* Public Health Monograph No. 66, Public Health Service Publications No. 845. Washington, D.C.: U.S. Government Printing Office, 1961.

Margon, A. "Click #1." Unpublished report, New School of Liberal Arts, Brooklyn College, N.Y., November 1979.

Martin, J. R. "Excluding Women from the Educational Realm." *Harvard Educational Review,* May 1982, *52,* 133-148.

Martin, W. B. *A College of Character: Renewing the Purpose and Content of College Education.* San Francisco: Jossey-Bass, 1982.

Meiklejohn, A. *The Experimental College.* Washington, D.C.: Seven Locks Press, 1981. (Originally published 1932, Harper & Row.)

Meisler, R. *Trying Freedom.* New York: Harcourt Brace Jovanovich, forthcoming.

Mezirow, I. "Perspective Transformation." *Adult Education,* 1978, *28,* 100-110.

Mills, M. R. "The Stability of Interdisciplinary Programs: Lessons from Ten Cases." *Interdisciplinary Perspectives,* 1982, *11,* 4-12.

Minnich, E. K. "A Feminist Critique of the Liberal Arts." In Association of American Colleges, *Liberal Education and the New Scholarship on Women.* Washington, D.C.: Association of American Colleges, 1981.

Mishler, E. G. "Meaning in Context: Is There Any Other Kind?" *Harvard Educational Review,* 1979, *49,* 1-19.

Mlynarczyk, R. "Critical Incidents from the Ancient Prep Row, 1979–80." Brooklyn, N.Y.: New School of Liberal Arts, Brooklyn College, 1979.

Moffett, J. *Teaching the Universe of Discourse.* Boston: Houghton Mifflin, 1968.

Moffett, J., and Wagner, B. J. *Student-Centered Language Arts Curriculum and Reading, K-13: A Handbook for Teachers.* Boston: Houghton Mifflin, 1976.

Munson, F. F., and Pelz, D. C. *Innovating in Organizations: A Conceptual Framework.* Ann Arbor: Institute for Social Research, University of Michigan, 1981.

National Assembly on Foreign Language and International Studies. *Toward Education with a Global Perspective.* Washington, D.C.: Association of American Colleges, 1980.

National Catholic Educational Association. "The Danforth Report and Catholic Higher Education." *Bulletin,* Spring 1966.

Newman, J. C. *The Idea of a University.* New York: Doubleday, 1959. (Originally published 1852.)

Nichols, J. *A Study of the Core Curriculum at Saint Joseph's College.* Rensselaer, Ind.: Saint Joseph's College, 1980.

Nichols, J. "Interdisciplinary Skills, Core Curriculum and Faculty Development." *Interdisciplinary Perspectives,* 1981a, *11* (1), 24–31.

Nichols, J. *A Study of the Core Curriculum at Saint Joseph's College.* Final Report on National Project IV for the Fund for the Improvement of Postsecondary Education. Rensselaer, Ind.: Saint Joseph's College, 1981b.

Nisbet, R. *The Degradation of the Academic Dogma.* New York: Basic Books, 1971.

Orwell, G. *1984.* New York: New American Library, 1983. (Originally published 1949, Harcourt Brace Jovanovich.)

Parlett, M., and Dearden, G. (Eds.). *Introduction to Illuminative Evaluation: Studies in Higher Education.* Berkeley, Calif.: Pacific Soundings Press, 1977.

Parry, M. "From Rusty Minds to New Careers." *Radcliffe Quarterly,* 1981, *67*(1), 7–12.

"Pastoral Constitution on the Church in the Modern World." In

W. Abbott and J. Gallagher (Eds.), *The Documents of Vatican II*. New York: America Press, 1966.

Patterson, F. K., and Longsworth, C. R. *The Making of a College: Plans for a New Departure in Higher Education*. Cambridge, Mass.: M.I.T. Press, 1966.

Patton, M. Q. *Qualitative Evaluation Methods*. Beverly Hills, Calif.: Sage Publications, 1980.

Perry, W. G., Jr. *Forms of Intellectual and Ethical Development in the College Years: A Scheme*. New York: Holt, Rinehart and Winston, 1970.

Perry, W. G., Jr. "Cognitive and Ethical Growth: The Making of Meaning." In A. W. Chickering and Associates. *The Modern American College: Responding to the New Realities of Diverse Students and a Changing Society*. San Francisco: Jossey-Bass, 1981.

Peterson, M. W., and others. *Black Students on White Campuses: The Impact of Increased Black Enrollments*. Ann Arbor: Survey Research Center, Institute for Social Research, University of Michigan, 1979.

Peterson, R. E., and Associates. *Lifelong Learning in America: An Overview of Current Practices, Available Resources, and Future Prospects*. San Francisco: Jossey-Bass, 1979.

Piaget, J., and Inhelder, B. *The Psychology of the Child*. (H. Weaver, Trans.) New York: Basic Books, 1969.

Postman, N., and Weingartner, C. *Teaching as a Subversive Activity*. New York: Dell, 1969.

Radzialowski, T. "The Future of Ethnic Studies." *The Forum for Liberal Education*, March 1981, *3*(5), 1-3.

Reinharz, S. *On Becoming a Social Scientist: From Survey Research and Participant Observation to Experiential Analysis*. San Francisco: Jossey-Bass, 1979.

Richards, M. C. *Centering in Pottery, Poetry, and the Person*. Middletown, Conn.: Wesleyan University Press, 1964.

Richardson, C., Jr., Martens, K. J., and Fisk, E. C. *Functional Literacy in the College Setting*. AAHE-ERIC Higher Education Research Report No. 3. Washington, D.C.: American Association for Higher Education, 1981.

Riesman, D. *On Higher Education: The Academic Enterprise in an Era of Rising Student Consumerism.* San Francisco: Jossey-Bass, 1981.

Riesman, D., Gusfield, J., and Gamson, Z. *Academic Values and Mass Education.* New York: McGraw-Hill, 1975.

Rogers, C. *Freedom To Learn.* Columbus, Ohio: Merrill, 1969.

Rogers, J. R., and Gamson, Z. F. "Evaluation as a Developmental Process: The Case of Liberal Education." *Review of Higher Education,* 1982, *5,* 225–238.

Rudolph, F. *Curriculum: A History of the American Undergraduate Course of Study Since 1636.* San Francisco: Jossey-Bass, 1977.

Sadler, W. A., Jr., and Whimbey, A. "Teaching Cognitive Skills: An Objective for Higher Education." *National Forum,* 1980, *60*(4), 43–46.

Sanders, D. P. "Educational Inquiry as Developmental Research." *Educational Research,* 1981, *10,* 8–13.

Sarason, S. *The Creation of Settings and the Future Societies.* San Francisco: Jossey-Bass, 1972.

Schneider, C., Klemp, G. O., Jr., and Kastendiek, S. "The Balancing Act: Competencies of Effective Teachers and Mentors." *Innovation Abstracts,* 1983, *5*(4, entire issue).

Schor, J., and Fishman, S. *The Random House Guide to Writing.* New York: Random House, 1978.

Schwab, J. J. *Science, Curriculum, and Liberal Education.* Chicago: University of Chicago Press, 1978.

Sennett, R., and Cobb, J. *The Hidden Injuries of Class.* New York: Vintage, 1973.

Shaughnessy, M. *Errors and Expectations: A Guide for the Teacher of Basic Writing.* New York: Oxford University Press, 1977.

Shor, I. *Critical Teaching and Everyday Life.* Boston: South End Press, 1980.

Shulman, C. H. *Revamping Core Curricula.* AAHE-ERIC Higher Education *Research Currents.* Washington, D.C.: American Association for Higher Education, 1979.

Silverman, B., Franklin, R., and Kessler-Harris, A. *Liberal Arts and Worker Education for Democratic Participation*. Final Report on National Project IV to the Fund for the Improvement of Postsecondary Education. Hempstead, N.Y.: Hofstra University, 1981.

Simmons, J., and Mares, W. *Working Together*. New York: Knopf, 1983.

Sloan, D. "The Teaching of Ethics in the American Undergraduate Curriculum, 1876–1976." *Hastings Center Report*, December 1979, pp. 21–41.

Smith, V. B. "Views of Liberal Education: From the Periphery to the Center." Paper delivered at meeting of the National Conference on Liberal Education, New York City, June 1981.

Stack, H., and Hutton, C. M. *New Directions for Experiential Learning: Building New Alliances: Labor Unions and Higher Education*, no. 10. San Francisco: Jossey-Bass, 1980.

Taylor, W. "Technology, Values and Society: Some Reflections on the Quality and Character of Faculty Interaction." Stony Brook: Federated Learning Communities, State University of New York, n.d.

Tobias, S. *Overcoming Math Anxiety*. New York: Norton, 1978.

Toulmin, S., Rieke, R., and Janik, A. *An Introduction to Reasoning*. New York: Macmillan, 1979.

Tucker, A. L. *A Note on the Production of Doctorates and Law Degrees Among the Graduates at Talladega College*. Talladega, Ala.: Talladega College, 1978.

Watkins, B., and others. *"To Be Able to Look at It Fresh with New Eyes": An Evaluation of a Women's Studies Course*. Final Report on National Project IV to the Fund for the Improvement of Postsecondary Education. Evanston, Ill.: Program on Women, Northwestern University, 1981.

Weathersby, R. "Education for Adult Development: A Component of Qualitative Change." In E. Greenberg, K. O'Donnell, and W. Bergquist (Eds.), *New Directions for Higher Education: Educating Learners of All Ages*, no. 29. San Francisco: Jossey-Bass, 1980.

Weathersby, R. "Ego Development." In A. W. Chickering and

Associates, *The Modern American College: Responding to the New Realities of Diverse Students and a Changing Society.* San Francisco: Jossey-Bass, 1981.

Wee, D. *On General Education: Guidelines for Reform.* New Haven, Conn.: Society for Values in Higher Education, 1981.

Wegener, C. *Liberal Education and the Modern University.* Chicago: University of Chicago Press, 1978.

Whimbey, A., with Whimbey, L. S. *Intelligence Can Be Taught.* New York: Dutton, 1975.

Whitehead, A. N. *The Aims of Education.* New York: Mentor Books/New American Library, 1949. (Originally published 1929, Macmillan.)

Whitla, D. K. "Value Added: Measuring the Outcomes of Undergraduate Education." Unpublished report, Office of Instructional Research and Evaluation, Harvard University, 1977.

Winter, D. G., McClelland, D. C., and Stewart, A. J. *A New Case for the Liberal Arts: Assessing Institutional Goals and Student Development.* San Francisco: Jossey-Bass, 1981.

Wittig, S. "Politics and Practicalities." *GEM Newsletter* (Project on General Education Models), June 1981, no. 6.

Woditsch, G. A. "Developing Generic Skills: A Model for Competency-Based Education." CUE Project Occasional Paper Series No. 3. Bowling Green, Ohio: Bowling Green State University, 1977.

"Women's Studies Programs and Centers for Research on Women—1981." *Women's Studies Quarterly,* 1981, *9*(2), 25-35.

Zaltman, G., Duncan, R., and Holbek, J. *Innovations and Organizations.* New York: Wiley, 1973.

Zwerdling, D. *Workplace Democracy: A Guide to Workplace Ownership, Participation and Self-Management Experiments in the United States and Europe.* New York: Harper & Row, 1980.

Afterword

by David Riesman

This book has reported on a government-funded inquiry into fourteen undergraduate programs regarded as innovative—programs of almost extravagant diversity in terms of the types of students served, the sponsoring institutions, and the internal organization and aims of the projects. The document is a marked exception to a contemporary literature by beleaguered traditionalists and reformers alike, sometimes more despairing and sometimes more hortatory, concerning the triumph of academic departments and of subspecialization, the fragmentation of the curriculum, the absence of a learning and teaching community, and the dim prospects for liberal or general education in the coming years of occupational uncertainty and academic retrenchment. The volume does not, of course, remove despair. Its aims are more modest: it is enough that it is interesting and incrementally useful. It is a small but significant step to speak of *liberating* rather than *liberal* or *general* education. Both of the latter terms denote a fixed corpus in terms of content, characterized by wide though seldom universal agreement on what educated persons ought to have studied; and, if not that,

217

at least agreement on certain modes of inquiry and cognitive skills that every educated person should have mastered. Those terms also frequently imply education that is interdisciplinary rather than departmental and also frequently connote education for the long view, a prolegomenon to lifelong learning, rather than education for an immediate end in view, whether a job, a place in a selective graduate or professional school, or raised political consciousness for a cause, whether it be as general as civic and democratic alertness or as particular as gender, racial, ethnic, or class consciousness and militancy.

Correspondingly, to discuss *liberating* education rather than *liberal* education implies a very large shift in thinking about curriculum. *Liberal* always implies the liberal arts and sciences, a given legacy, although of course an enormously expanding one. Moreover, *liberal education* frequently connotes recruitment of faculty trained in the liberal arts traditions of Western culture.[1] Such a focus is not, as is sometimes charged, merely the preening of provincial and ethnocentric people of Western European descent or culture but also reflects the availability of cultivated scholars nourished by Western civilization, although it is obvious that many individuals of non-European background can contribute to the enhancement of some of the most traditional forms of liberal education while also broadening these beyond the American parish. However, such border-crossing individuals are as yet relatively rare. The continuity of what is often referred to as the liberal tradition has the advantages of cumulation. Individuals who have absorbed parts of that tradition can in turn respond to the elliptical poetry of T. S. Eliot or to Freud's metaphorical use of Greek dramatists' elaboration of ancient myths.

In contrast, there is no necessary continuity, no essentialist tradition in liberating education. This latter emphasis implies that the proper education is not what has already been defined as *liberal education* but is whatever is *liberating* in a particular context for a particular student body at a particular moment in time. I have long shared the view of many that the standard liberal arts are by no means necessarily nonvocational or liberating: they may be in fact efforts by faculty members to recruit disciples for their version of their particular discipline; they may be dogmatic, dehydrated, and deadening. Many vocational subjects can be taught in a liberating way, though I myself would find it more difficult to teach, for example, instrumentation (or elementary accounting) in a liberating way than to teach any one of the traditional liberal arts in a liberating way. It could only be liberating if it were what Donald Campbell refers to as a "novel narrowness," the embryonic area out of which a new specialty may develop.[2]

Larry M. Daloz contributes to this volume from his perspective as a mentor in the External Degree Program at Johnson State College in Vermont. Commenting on an earlier draft of this Afterword, he has written that liberating education must be individualized not only in terms of a particular student body but far beyond that in terms of a separate program for each student. Leaving cost aside, there are situations where teaching and learning are optimal in a tutorial setting, where the teacher is more like a coach, encouraging the student to perform at his or her best in a noncompetitive situation. But one advantage of a shared program, particularly in a residential setting, is the possibility of students' dormitory or dinner table conversations being animated by discussion of a common set of readings—conversations in which faculty members might also participate with profit to students and themselves.[3] When there is this potential for common intellectual nourishment, then individual tutorial on special projects or for the development of particular skills and crafts is also highly desirable. It is necessary to rely on the latter alone in the case of many external degree programs, which of course can be liberating in high measure but might be still more stimulating if shared.

Toward the aim of a common learning, Princeton and Yale in the 1970s put committees of eminent faculty to work trying to come up with a general education program on which all the faculty could agree. They had not learned the lesson that the present volume teaches: namely, that content is important but that no particular content is essential everywhere, and much traditional content on which most of us would agree as splendid and important should not be mandated anywhere. Gamson and

her coauthors give us a vivid account of the futility of arguing
whether one can be an educated person without having by
the time of one's baccalaureate engaged in formal study of
Aristotle, Shakespeare, or indeed any particular work that remains as a staple on the St. John's College list of Great Books.
Reading these passages, I was reminded of my gratitude that
neither my decayed-classical preparatory school nor my undergraduate English courses required me to read George Eliot,
Henry James, or Proust, whose discovery in adulthood has been
such a delight to me. Indeed, to think always of context means
raising the politically troublesome issue of insisting that anyone
who teaches required courses be an evocative or "liberating"
teacher to justify the risk of destroying rather than invoking potential enthusiasms among a captive audience.

Of the institutions whose efforts toward liberating education are reported or refracted in this volume, the only one that
embraces the whole undergraduate curriculum is the Core at
Saint Joseph's College in Rensselaer, Indiana. That program is
known to those who follow imaginative educational efforts outside the brand-name colleges and universities. I found its program as described in this book particularly exciting since it is a
rare example of a Catholic institution where the consequences
of Vatican II have not been further fragmentation of church-
related traditions but a structured renewal. The priests and
brothers of the Precious Blood Order are not an attenuated
memory at Saint Joseph's College. According to John Nichols,
there are some twenty priests and brothers of the order engaged
in teaching and administration at the college, where leadership
for the program has been provided by President-Father Charles
Banet. With religious and lay faculty cooperating, protecting
one another's emergence from the foxholes of their specialties,
they worked persistently and persuasively to decide what
themes from the Judeo-Christian and Greco-Roman traditions
were sufficiently seminal in the intellectual history of the West
to justify inclusion in the Core program. These judgments, however, were not simply canonical. Entering freshmen begin by
reading John Updike's *Rabbit, Run* in order to challenge over-
simple moralistic judgments either of literature or of conduct

and to be willing to see the hero of the novel as engaged in a quasi-Protestant religious quest—a rather shocking idea to some entering students from traditional Catholic backgrounds. This example illustrates the overriding importance of context, for to begin with *Rabbit, Run* in an Amherst freshman English class of generally sophisticated students largely from secular backgrounds would have quite different implications. Such students might find themselves somewhat disarmed by having to begin by reading Calvin's *Institutes* or the works of some early Christian mystics. In either case, a required program—and 45 out of 120 credit hours at Saint Joseph's College are preempted by the Core—signifies that faculty members must expose themselves to the hazards of discussing with students topics in the Core that are not among their own specialties. It does not trouble these faculty members that the largest plurality of their students are majoring in business administration. To them, any calling may possess a sense of vocation, and certainly business callings can and do.[4]

Talladega College also has a core curriculum, although here the religious tie (originally American Missionary Association [largely Congregational] and now United Church of Christ) is more legacy than presence. Roland Braithwaite, dean of the college, expresses (in colloquy with other contributors to this volume) his belief in the traditional goals of liberal education improving the competence and critical self-consciousness of students, along with a secularized sense of social responsibility, particularly, but by no means exclusively, for one's fellow blacks. It is consonant with the current Talladega outlook that a Talladega student responded to a Northwestern woman student who had had her consciousness raised by the program in women's studies by saying that women's studies "is only one subject. I think a liberal education means being exposed to a lot of different ideas and knowledge. It means being a jack of all trades. . . . I want to be able to talk to anyone about anything." Against a critical comment that this is the old cliché about being well rounded, Braithwaite defends the student by saying that college opens up a whole new world for previously provincial students, so that the remarks of the student just quoted express "a sense of himself as an educated person, as someone who lives in a wider world." In a letter commenting on an earlier draft, Braithwaite expresses his own preference for the original Chicago-style curriculum developed at Talladega in earlier decades. Its emphasis was on a core of fundamental knowledge, based on a belief in the possibility of a unified system of knowledge that intellectually hardy and venturesome faculty could acquire and help students to acquire. The student's comments reflect an overlapping but at the same time contrasting notion of liberal education as broad exposure to a variety of fields without a necessary core and without a belief in overarching synthesis. The main organizational characteristic of the latter emphasis is distribution requirements that demand such exposure of the students but not of the faculty. Raymond S. Franklin, instructor in the Institute of Applied Social Science sponsored by Hofstra and District 65 of the United Auto Workers, and also professor of economics and sociology at Queens College, regards traditional liberal education as obsolete, in part because he associates it with elitism, just as Bari Watkins, former director of the Northwestern University Program on Women, sees it as the preserve of educated people who are all "white, male, and upper class."

Two thirds of the students at Talladega College are women. However, Braithwaite expresses the continuing faith in traditional liberal education as also liberating for first-generation students in college, whether women or black or both. Students at Northwestern in the Core Curriculum program there would almost certainly read Shakespeare, and most of Hampshire's eclectic undergraduates are likely to have encountered Shakespeare in secondary school if not in their homes; Talladega wants to make sure that its students are given the same privilege while also being prepared for graduate school in medicine, law, and other fields. In fact, black students now to be found at Talladega and other leading predominantly black colleges are particularly allergic to educational experiments that are not highly visible on leading Ivy-type campuses. Their entry into the world of the college-educated and into postbaccalaureate possibilities is by certifiably nonexperimental transcripts.

Implicit in what I have just quoted and written is an echo

of conflicts over class and gender that spasmodically appear in the colloquies of participants in this volume and in some comments of Zelda Gamson. The term *empowerment* applied to students occurs occasionally and of course is a frequent term employed by educational reformers, who hope to increase students' sense of control. However, such terms are often applied too broadly, not to specific individuals in specific family, peer, and group contexts but to all students coming from the less privileged sectors of society. Sometimes the group thus exhorted is the elderly, for whom a particularly interesting program has been worked out by New York City Technical College; sometimes, as already indicated, it is women in general; sometimes it is blue- and white-collar employees. However, group membership is only one determinant of an individual's sense of control. Admirably, Zelda Gamson emphasizes the importance of having teachers understand who their students are in the most concrete ways: these particular students in this particular class in all their diversity.

Correspondingly, I do not believe one can tell by category who needs empowerment. I have observed classes in my own university where upper-class students have been subject to the tyranny of black students, many themselves from privileged backgrounds, parading as proletarians. I have seen devout students bullied by aggressive secularists of lower social origin. I do not think Zelda Gamson would disagree with the judgment that it is individual students who may need support against their fellows or against prevailing doctrine (including one's own), while other students may need to have what in that locale are hegemonic opinions challenged, not to deracinate them from their own views but to help them explore alternatives while suspending closure. Even in a setting that appears homogeneous from the outside, a teacher leading a discussion with as many as twenty articulate students must perform a complicated ballet in order to limit the development of oligopolies. Matters are very different where, as in some of the institutions included in this study, it takes the greatest effort to evoke any conversation at all. Here the effort to give students a greater sense of power is not too gross an overgeneralization.

Praise for the program at Talladega is coupled with a re-

mark in praise of W. E. B. Du Bois's search for a "talented
tenth" of blacks highly educated in the great reaches of Western
culture, as against a slighting remark toward Tuskegee Institute
and Booker T. Washington's desire for something that resembles
the land-grant model of an agricultural and artisan-mechanics'
institute. This judgment is common today among those who
consider themselves anti-elitist. However, Zelda Gamson makes
diversity a good in itself in higher education, both in terms of
the programs of individual students and of institutions. Diversity should have room for Tuskegee as it was and Talladega as it
was and seeks to remain without any need for either snobbery
on the part of the disciples of Du Bois or countersnobbery on
the part of those who see value in the broader relevance of
Booker T. Washington's combination of the expedient and the
future-oriented.

Talladega College and Saint Joseph's College in their very
different fashions maintain a sense of community among faculty—markedly so at Saint Joseph's College, where faculty
members, despite initial reluctance, were prepared to revise
their courses dramatically to create a new core curriculum in
which over 80 percent of faculty members teach. Zelda Gamson
notes that these faculty members teach a very heavy course
load, which is made still heavier by the comity required for cooperation.[5] On the whole, they do not resent presenting materials to their students that at first appear to the latter to have no
connection with their previous backgrounds or prospective careers. Pedagogy of this sort can work successfully where students are neither sullen nor insolent and where faculty are not
sarcastic but patient and invitational.

But there are other settings where the slogan of empowerment and the book's concern with liberation might miscarry for
some students. Raymond Franklin is surely sensible in his comment: "Just realizing that they can understand things they
didn't understand before is empowering for people who have
felt dumb or put down all their lives." And most of us would
also agree with Roland Braithwaite's metaphorical remark that
"the slaves have been freed." Nevertheless, certain kinds of empowerment of students can be damaging to them as individuals,

encouraging them in self-indulgence and perhaps litigiousness, and to groups whose education can be harmed when both teachers and curricula lose authority. I believe it is rarely the case that liberating education is advanced when, particularly in high schools, there are many settings where students have "rights" and many parental, societal, and juridical advocates on behalf of those rights. The belief of many teachers in an earlier era that, when children were reprimanded or punished in school, parents would support the teachers is not a nostalgic falsification; today, in contrast, teachers can be intimidated by parents who have more education and status than they do (reflecting the higher educational attainments in the country as a whole, and the relatively and in some cases absolutely declining academic qualifications of teachers), but less educated parents can also have power because of their membership in a locally influential cohort, with the all-American panoply of lawyer-advocates.[6] Similarly, in the selective colleges, students may not be consumers vis-à-vis the institution that they are eager to enter (although they will make tradeoffs vis-à-vis competitors in terms of requirements, financial aid beyond demonstrated need, and similar nonacademic considerations). But they may be consumers in terms of the traffic desired by departments in order to maintain their FTE, as well as in terms of individual faculty seeking to sustain or enhance their positions and sense of worth. While in general I believe that teachers still have power to wound students by sarcasm—even teachers who feel themselves to be almost weightless—I am sure that many of the participants in the collective Gamson enterprise have encountered students who can intimidate them by an arrogance coupled with forensic talent that is not merely defensive.

The difficulty with the widespread emphasis on empowerment is not that it is false but that it is a bit too overgeneralized. For example, the comment is made that "middle-class women until recently have been as limited in spheres outside the family as working-class women have been, perhaps more so." This is an overstatement, consonant with some feminist ideologies. The statement would have astonished Lillian Wald or Jane Addams, and certainly many of the emancipated women

of the middle class even in the South in the first decades of this
century. Even the aggressiveness of a Bella Abzug is not entirely
new in the metropolitan and ethnic settings of New York or
Chicago. Any of us faces the problem in our writing of how
much to qualify, and it is a question of degree, of the tone of a
work as distinct from its findings and recommendations. As already indicated with respect to students in the public schools,
individuals coming from previously disprivileged groups are not
necessarily helpless themselves. Black students (one of the
groups referred to) in the liberal white institutions that actively
recruit them have discovered the power that slogans carry, such
as accusations of institutional racism or charges of prejudice
against particular instructors or departments. In contrast, some
individual black students in the most selective institutions need
defense against the nearly all-powerful black peer group, which
runs a cocurriculum of activities, sometimes concentrates in
residential settings, and severely punishes those termed "oreos"
who seek to lead the integrated lives that they often had in their
home neighborhoods and preparatory schools.

Whatever the setting, many black students do experience
themselves as inadequate. This fact highlights the truly dramatic
changes in students that Talladega College has accomplished in
the past and is seeking currently. The Talladega College student
who notes that he has been led to "think about different subjects" by being required to read the *Wall Street Journal* has
learned something very important: namely, a form of observation made by James Tobin many years ago in a *Daedalus* issue
devoted to the Negro in America, where he commented that
Charles de Gaulle's views on the balance of payments might be
more important for the economic position of blacks in America
than studies focusing directly on interpretations of the Afro-
American experiences[7]—which is, of course, not to say that the
latter cannot also be valuable. The Talladega student given the
pseudonym "John" is a missionary for the Talladega College
program; now self-motivated, he is concerned with the fate of
his high school friends who dismiss the traditional curriculum of
Talladega College as not worthwhile.

Indeed, I cannot emphasize enough the importance of the

traditional liberal arts for nonelite students. Although I re-
marked at the outset that I do not think that particular content
is significant, that is an overstatement. When the University of
Massachusetts was established in Boston as a commuter college,
many of its faculty recruited in the late 1960s were devotees of
the New Left and the counterculture (contradictory as these
two complex movements were in some respects); they believed
in "relevant" education that would dismiss "whitey's bag" of
the standard liberal arts and focus on empowerment through
the use of contemporary materials. One faculty member recalls
a student of lower-middle-class origin saying to him at that
time: "They teach Shakespeare on the Amherst campus [that is,
the flagship campus]; why can't we have Shakespeare at the
Boston campus?" This is a poignant plea. As Diana Trilling re-
marked a great many years ago, concerning the education she
received at Radcliffe College, women at that time had to receive
an education quite as bad as that the men were getting in order
to believe they were having a superior education.[8] (One reader
misread the foregoing as implying that Shakespeare might be
bad educationally, but Diana Trilling's observation was geared
less to anemic content than to dehydrated teaching—which
might leave Shakespeare, or any other great writer, undamaged,
but not necessarily the student.)

    In contrast, Hampshire College quite properly can assume
that its highly educated students, who come generally from rea-
sonably cultivated upper-middle-class homes and schools, can
create their own version of a balanced academic ticket by adher-
ence to the three divisional stages of the Hampshire College program. The account of the teaching of the natural sciences at
Hampshire College in this volume, with its praise for the effort
from the outset to bring more women into the natural sciences
and across the barriers of math anxiety and quantitative reti-
cence, is properly approbatory. The scientists at Hampshire
have used legitimate devices, such as students' interests in the
environment, to lure them into the natural sciences; many come
to browse and stay to pursue careers. The diffident do not
"spoil" their grade records or GPAs by venturing into science
courses at Hampshire College; grades are replaced by system-

atic evaluations of student work, evaluations in which the students themselves cooperate. Some Hampshire students, socialized to associate grades with rigor, can establish their own academic sufficiency by taking courses regarded as difficult, hence rigorous, in the Five College Consortium (the University of Massachusetts, Amherst, Mount Holyoke, Smith, and Hampshire). For example, one student I knew who had transferred after his freshman year from Harvard to Hampshire reported that he had taken several philosophy courses at Mount Holyoke College in order to prove to himself that the work he was doing at Hampshire was indeed of high quality. He made the comment that one could appreciate neither Harvard nor Hampshire without experience of the other. Hampshire's determination to recruit more women into science than enter it at most selective colleges seems to be facilitated by the leadership and numerical predominance of women in the Natural Sciences Division, including the former dean, Susan Goldhor, and the present one, Nancy Lowry, who contributes to this volume's discourse.[9]

The Federated Learning Communities (FLC) at Stony Brook, discussed in Chapter Five and referred to throughout the volume, have the virtue of counting on the comparative advantage of certain faculty members secure enough to try something with which they will not be permanently stuck. The program has also pioneered the important invention of the Master Learner, a faculty member whose task it is to see as a participant what the students are learning and then to convey this information to faculty members so they can measure it against what they believe themselves to be teaching. In this way the Master Learner acts as a combination go-between and on-site evaluator. The Federated Learning Communities operate on a three-semester cycle for faculty and a two-semester cycle for students—perhaps preferable to a three-year one from the point of view of undergraduates properly seeking their own specializations.[10]

As Gamson recognizes, most faculty members in four-year colleges and universities think of themselves primarily as teachers and want to be rewarded and promoted as teachers rather than as scholars, creators, researchers. Most of the programs represented in the book have developed in institutions oriented primarily to baccalaureate degree or external credit students; the Federated Learning Communities at research-intensive Stony Brook are a marked exception.[11]

To the extent that there is a conflict between teaching and visible research, it would make itself felt for some faculty at Hampshire College, Saint Joseph's College, Talladega College; it was a factor in the innovative but now demolished program of a cluster college oriented to the liberal arts at Brooklyn College. However, these institutions and others embraced in the volume differ greatly among themselves, and except for Stony Brook differ also from research universities and the most highly selective liberal arts colleges in the degree to which peer and institutional support are forthcoming for exemplary teaching. It is well known that only a minority of faculty members publish anything of substance after completing their dissertations. Most prefer to be judged on their teaching, and to some extent on their community service—"community" being defined in both institutional and outreach terms.[12] Because of the individuated nature of teaching at Hampshire College, many faculty enjoy the opportunity to work with students as junior colleagues in scholarly enterprises of mutual interest. In some newly flourishing fields, faculty and students can regard themselves as happy pioneers. Thus, the Program on Women at Northwestern University may not have required a subordination of career ambitions to dedication to a nonestablished undergraduate program, thanks to the vogue of women's studies, the remarkable flourishing of scholarship dealing with women's history, women's perspectives in the United States and elsewhere, and contemporary problems of gender. The women's movements in the liberal universities such as Northwestern have provided a constituency for women faculty and a few feminist males in an academic setting where, as in the country as a whole, "teach or perish" is a far more imperative mandate than "publish or perish."[13] The external degree programs at Johnson State, Oklahoma, and Nebraska, and the joint labor union/Hofstra degree program, can make use of adjunct and other faculty who are not primarily seeking to make careers as scholar-researchers.

Much is said in the volume, and rightly so, about depart-

mental pressure on faculty members to avoid spending themselves on collaborative interdisciplinary teaching and about the
long-standing virtual taboo on faculty members making any effort to study problems of learning and teaching in order to become less awkward teachers themselves.[14] But there are other
handicaps to good teaching that the contributors to the volume
do not address. A number of state legislatures or other bodies
supervising the public sector mandate a certain number of contact hours or teaching hours for faculty. These mandates draw
support from the widespread resentment of many nonacademic
professionals and blue-collar workers against professors who
have nominally light schedules and long summer vacations.
Moreover, the backlash against the sometimes incendiary faculty of the late 1960s and the protests they supported, or at
least did not inhibit, has not spent its force. In addition, faculty members in state institutions are increasingly being sub-
jected to the standards of often-intrusive accountability designed in part to cut costs fairly by uniform contact hours and/
or student loads, as well as in the vain hope of monitoring faculty who do not do even a minimum amount of conscientious
teaching.[15] However, when it comes to such artful work as
teaching, more hours may in fact mean less intense and competent teaching. Sometimes even faculty members themselves fail
to recognize how exhausting it is to teach a somewhat diversi-
fied class when one is seeking to be liberating for every one of
its members and to encourage discussion that neither stifles the
shy (not to mention those who fear asking "stupid questions")
nor unleashes the assertive to spout conventional attacks on the
conventional wisdom. The planning required, so vividly illustrated in the efforts at Saint Joseph's College and in a different
way in the teaching of the natural sciences and mathematics at
Hampshire College, as well as in Hampshire's general program of
sequential, closely evaluated stages of a student's trajectory, is
itself time-consuming, frequently debilitating, and often unproductive.[16] Faculty engaged in such exercises cannot endure
doing a great deal of teaching if they are to develop themselves
as more competent teachers without losing touch with their specialties.

However, a large teaching load in terms of hours and in terms of number of students per class is in many cases not a serious hazard. For routinized faculty for whom teaching has become a "no sweat" affair, a tacit treaty is negotiated with the students that neither students nor teachers will seriously bother, let alone liberate, one another. How is an academic administration to provide lighter loads for some teachers who are working, one would hope collaboratively, to develop syllabi relevant to their own and their students' capacities and to engage in more hazardous—because untried—teaching? Just as colleges facing retrenchment find it easier to make across-the-board cuts rather than programmatic cuts based on qualitative judgments, so it is difficult for administrators, including department heads, to justify preferential treatment not based on seniority or academic status; that would be regarded as inegalitarian and unfair. At Saint Joseph's College and in some measure at Talladega College, one can count on a degree of commitment that is at least in part religious to overcome the anarchic individualism characteristic of many educated Americans. (At Johnson State College, as at Brooklyn College, a faculty union might inhibit any efforts at differential treatment of faculty in terms of the quality of their teaching. However, the faculty union of the State University of New York system that operates at Stony Brook seems not to have hampered the development of the Federated Learning Communities, for the union in collective bargaining deals with salaries and benefits but does not impose restrictive work rules as some unions have done.)[17]

The voices of students appear repeatedly on the pages of *Liberating Education*. They generally support the programs in which they have been enrolled. They do not seem to be decoys but were chosen in a somewhat random fashion. Perhaps because of the nature of the programs selected, and the voluntary nature of the great majority of them (Saint Joseph's and Talladega are the exceptions), the volume does not address the extent to which students are conservative concerning their education, however they may behave in terms of politics and styles of life. One gains no sense from the programs described here, or from the student voices, that new programs with their almost inevitable start-up difficulties may actually compete with established teachers who have learned how to court the student market in all the many varieties of showmanship that are widely encouraged today by declines in enrollment overall and a sometimes Hobbesian competition among institutions and within them for student customers. In my own limited observation, more innovative programs are destroyed by student indifference or active resistance than by direct faculty assault. To be sure, the two modes of resistance are related, not only by the indirect route of the market in which every faculty member is competing against all other faculty members (within the limits of systems of distribution that serve as partial tariff barriers) but also more directly as faculty members in high-status departments privately and sometimes publicly denigrate the supposedly and sometimes actually flaky innovators.

These comments are not meant as criticism of *Liberating Education*. The book is not intended as the last word on a subject that, as the authors note at the outset, has been the occasion of a veritable publishing industry in recent years. Indeed, Zelda Gamson urges more attention to questions of pedagogy, of learning as well as of teaching, of college climates and of "value added" by different sorts of academic milieu.

Much in this volume itself suggests further inquiry. A notable example is the comment of a philosopher of science in the Federated Learning Communities who referred to his early style of teaching as "The Inspired Presentation of Material"—a form of "intellectually responsible showing-off, teaching as if to say 'Look at me! Aren't I smart?' " Wherever egalitarianism is powerful, exceptional presentation of material is frowned on as being inappropriately elevated. One result is that students are not exposed to exhilarating displays of intellectual elegance but rather to garden-variety language not dramatically different from their artfully common-man argot.[18]

Another and related issue touched on in the volume is what one faculty member referred to as "academic strip mining," where the best students get all the attention and the rest are discarded. To be sure, no program dealt with in this volume faces an involuntary student body of different aptitudes, for example, differences symbolized by an SAT range from, let us say, 350 to 800. When there are such gaps, I am inclined to believe that there must be some tracking, despite the well-known objections to any form of classification, especially when accompanied by racial overtones. But even with a student body of relatively homogeneous ability and age, there will be large diversity in motivation and in aptitude for any particular class. To create conditions for discussion in which one neither bores the adept nor further inhibits the less competent is one of the most stressful and often unsuccessful efforts in which a faculty member can engage. Yet even when matters are not so desperate, there can be a fugitive element about good teaching and a kind of isolation even in discourse. A teacher in the Stony Brook program declares that "my experiences as a teacher had never been quite what I wanted them to be, but I was at a loss when it came to understanding why. It seemed to me that those moments when I had come closest to absolute confidence and command in front of the class were haunted by a kind of loneliness, even when my audience was with me all the way." The "kind of communal conversation" she sought was "something that I felt helpless to make happen."

Throughout the book and in her conclusion, Gamson emphasizes the need for dedicated teachers to succor one another in their loneliness and hazard. A number of the faculty members who contributed to the book either as coauthors or in colloquy and quotation express the desire for more community in the joint enterprise of teaching and learning. However, participation in the federally sponsored programs described in the book was voluntary, and the faculty contributors to the project are far from typical. With great variations in terms of subspecialty, size of institution, and faculty preference, natural scientists and some social scientists are used to collaborative research and are not in principle allergic to cooperation in teaching. But in the traditional humanities and the social sciences closest to the humanities, such as anthropology, individual work is the rule and collective research may be frowned on as lacking the personal voice of the teacher of literature or art history.[19] In their pro tem nature, the Federated Learning Communities do seem to achieve an admirable degree of collegiality. As already indicated, such a sense of community helped make the Saint Joseph's College program feasible and continues to carry it and be in turn strengthened by it. The volunteer faculty in the former Brooklyn College program had a strong sense of shared and even defiant marginality.[20]

Yet it is at this point that our systems of selection, evaluation, and promotion of faculty seem to me deeply flawed: for example, the recruitment of faculty on a one-by-one basis, rather than as members of collaborative teams.[21] The prevailing model of work in the sociology of science is individualistic, as in the studies of eminence and visibility by Robert K. Merton, Harriet Zuckerman, Stephen and Jonathan Cole, and others. There are fewer studies of the productivity of cohorts, though some evidence suggests that catalytic individuals make a great difference in the productivity of a research group. I am not aware of research analyzing the impact of a destructive individual on the productivity of a colleague group, whether as scholars or as teachers. However, this is a phenomenon I have observed in selective colleges and universities and in law schools over four decades of teaching. Few teachers have the hardihood to face a class with an untried mode of teaching—which in all likelihood will fail—in the face of anticipated contempt from a coruscating and sadistic colleague. Nevertheless, any attempt to assess directly whether candidates have the personal qualities of mentors or what might be thought of as antimentors in recruitment, retention, or promotion faces large obstacles. I have already referred to the traditional individualism of faculty members, notably in the humanities—an outlook that is highly resistant to taking account of any excursions into group dynamics outside the purely academic in assessing a prospective colleague. And where such assessments are made, they come under widespread attack as reflecting "the old boy network," in which one recruits to a department people of one's own sort with whom one feels comfortable and who hold no views threatening to the schools of thought prevailing in the department. Indeed, much affirmative action is directed against such antique legacies

as the old boy network, but it can also be an obstacle to an effort to build a department in terms of overall quality. I am
using "affirmative action" here to include action taken on behalf of those who can present themselves as members of political minorities, so that one or two radical activists, for example,
might demolish an experimental program of teaching Great
Books by allegations that it is a way of avoiding conflict and
supporting the evilly established order of things, academic and
social. Moreover, teachers who are venturing to teach outside
the trenches dug by the disciplines are vulnerable in comparison
with those teachers, sometimes also activists and sometimes
not, who are firmly embedded in their disciplines. The latter
may even increase their influence when they are sadistic toward
a minority of students, especially those who do not belong to
a visible minority; their very contempt can make them attrac-
tive; they appear unafraid and forceful. They appeal to the students' own contempt and subtly flatter the students who are in
the majority. Student evaluations of such teachers are uniform-
ly high, whereas evaluations of less departmentalized faculty
members are often mixed.

Undergraduate programs could do a better job of evaluating teaching than currently prevails in most settings. Students'
assessments of their teachers should not be weighted equally.
St. John's College in Annapolis and Santa Fe asks seniors to
comment on the relative effectiveness of their teachers in a setting in which discussion is preferred to minilectures. Moreover,
teaching at St. John's College is by pairs of teachers, and the
program is entirely fixed, so that faculty can evaluate each other on the basis of direct observation.[22] Carleton College follows
the excellent practice of asking recent graduates as well as
undergraduates to evaluate teachers who are up for renewal or
promotion to tenure. This is the work of the dean, who asks the
faculty member in question to provide him with a list of some
particularly able students and some less able ones; the dean then
supplements this list by use of the registrar's class lists. The ver-
dict of students who have graduated cannot easily be manipu-
lated by faculty seduction or peer pressure, and it has the added

advantage of tending to deflate the amiable raconteur or enter-
tainer who has left the graduate no legacy of skill or knowledge.[23]
The Carleton example makes plain that assessment of teaching
must be a hand-crafted process if it is to make qualitative dis-
tinctions and not be swayed by numbers or temporary allergies
or enthusiasms.

Made-to-order evaluations are hard and often controversial. To go further and ask what a faculty member contributes
to his or her colleagues and to take scrupulous account of this
contribution in recruitment and retention is even more demanding. There are a number of settings in which one would
not wish to give students only sympathetic teachers or faculty
only sympathetic colleagues. Overaggressive and overconfident
students may benefit from encountering faculty who are not
pleased by their attempts to dominate and turn a cold eye.
Here as elsewhere, everything depends on context: students are
not likely to be crushed by those fellow students and faculty
members whose attitudes toward them are anything but wel-
coming, provided that they have some support from other influential faculty members or respected adults, even sometimes
parents. In terms of relations among faculty members, how are
we to distinguish the wish for a comfortable coddling of our
often fragile self-esteem from salutary and eventually stimulating criticism and the latter, in turn, from that kind of brilliant
destructiveness that recognizes and targets the vulnerabilities
most of us, having been children once, cannot escape? I believe
that such judgments can only be made by people who are not
afraid of judgments, that is, by Americans who do not believe
that everything must be decided by a committee to assure
equity and justice. Indeed, one may want to subordinate equity
and justice to other values, including the overall effectiveness of
a program for teaching and learning. How, in an egalitarian society, can we defend this even to ourselves? And if we can defend
it, as I am prepared to defend it, how can we accomplish it in a
fashion that does not seem capricious to ourselves, while recognizing that it will appear elitist and arbitrary to most?

It is one of the values of the collaborative effort represented in this volume that it provokes such questions.

Notes

1. For a scholarly discussion of the development of contrasting rhetorical and analytical traditions from classic times through medieval times to the present, see Bruce Kimball, *Orators and Philosophers: A History of Liberal Education* (New York: Teachers College Press, forthcoming).

2. See Donald Campbell, contribution to a symposium in *Syracuse Scholar*, 1979-80, *6* (1), 208.

3. See the discussion of community in John P. Nichols, "Saint Joseph's College: A Case Study in Collegiate Community," *The NICM Journal* (National Institute for Campus Ministries), Spring/Summer 1983, *8* (2-3), 25-34. See also Alston Chase, *Group Memory* (Boston: Little, Brown, 1980).

4. I regret that no Protestant church-related college was included in the congeries of institutions, for here a sense of community has often remained more potent—though not necessarily with imaginative consequences—than in the once-Catholic colleges, where most of the religious have "kicked the habit."

5. Some faculty members not yet involved in the Core would like to be but cannot spare the time because their specialties are overloaded with students, and Saint Joseph's College, largely tuition-dependent, cannot afford to free them to participate in the philosophical and programmatic concerns of the Core.

6. Of course, the power of students to frustrate and defeat teachers is not new. Willard Waller observed it in his classic book, *The Sociology of Teaching* (New York: Wiley, 1932). However, the power of students to intimidate teachers, in alliance with parents, partly reflects the American forms of the widespread revolt against authority. See, for example, Gerald Grant, "The Education of Character and the Character of Education," *Daedalus,* Summer 1981, *10* (3), 135-150.

7. James Tobin, "The Negro American," *Daedalus,* Fall 1965, *94,* 878-898.

8. See Diana Trilling, *We Must March, My Darlings: The Critical Decade* (New York: Harcourt Brace Jovanovich, 1977). William Neumann, an advanced graduate student at Syracuse

University, has observed that criticism of Harvard-style education can only be afforded by those relatively privileged individuals, such as Diana Trilling, who have experienced it; they can
afford to see its limitations. Neumann recalls his own experience as a Peace Corps Volunteer in Central and East Africa and
his initial effort to dissuade "unspoiled" Africans from their
passionate hunger for the "cargo cult" of industrialization and
its consumer wizardry. Recognizing that his views were seen by
the Africans he dealt with as condescending or even some kind
of imperialist effort to keep them "down on the farm," and recognizing also that most Americans did not share the critical out-
looks of most volunteers, Neumann learned to avoid overprais-
ing indigenous values and derogating standard American ones.
For further discussion of this theme, plainly applicable to cultural clashes within the United States, see Lawrence Fuchs,
*"Those Peculiar Americans": The Peace Corps and the Ameri-
can National Character* (New York: Meredith Press, 1967).

        9. I am indebted to Nancy Lowry and to President Adele
Simmons for clarifying comments on the draft of this Afterword.

        10. Some years ago I suggested to a hard-working Com-
mittee on Undergraduate Education at Massachusetts Institute
of Technology that the cross-disciplinary courses they were
seeking should be taught by senior faculty not allowed to be
away from their research for more than three years. Frank
Press, who chaired the committee, responded that a scientist
could not be away from his or her research for as long as three
years without losing touch completely in the more rapidly
moving areas; two years was the maximum before one became
obsolete. A program such as the one I suggested would have to
take account of the different half-lives of different scientific
and scholarly careers and their phasing. (Incidentally, the tenure rules of the American Association of University Professors
are themselves unduly abstract in not doing this. A mathema-
tician can establish talent in two or three years, whereas serious
and probing work in history and similar fields may require a
lead time considerably longer than six years.)

        11. Some of the Boston-area faculty members who are

teaching adults in the Radcliffe Seminars may be scholars, but in the seminar program they are primarily moonlighters teaching on a part-time voluntary basis.

12. See Martin Trow (Ed.), *Teachers and Students: Aspects of American Higher Education* (New York: McGraw-Hill, 1975); also, numerous publications by E. C. Ladd, Jr., and S. M. Lipset, including *The Divided Academy: Professors and Politics* (New York: McGraw-Hill, 1975).

13. Under the guidance of a liberal provost who cares deeply about the quality of undergraduate education, Northwestern University faculty must satisfy both canons. Bari Watkins, who headed the Program on Women at Northwestern during the life of the Gamson and associates project, is now dean at Rollins College in Florida.

14. At church-related colleges, notably at Saint Joseph's College in Indiana, this taboo can be overcome by the emphasis on community, on serving others and on sharing with them. At Saint Joseph's College in particular, Catholic theological teaching and the philosophical training common to priests in many orders allow discourse concerning teaching and learning to appear grounded in powerful intellectual traditions rather than floating on vaporous clouds of psychological jargon. At major research universities such as Stony Brook, discussion of teaching and learning is associated with the denigrated tasks of schools of education; faculty are of course supposed to know how to teach simply by having been students themselves and perhaps serving as teaching assistants rather than the preferred posts of research assistants during their graduate student careers. James B. McKenna, director of the Federated Learning Communities, who has taken the place of Patrick Hill (now academic vice-president/provost at Evergreen State College), has written me: "I have been impressed by the major contribution FLC makes to faculty development at a place where it is virtually 'taboo' to talk about the need for anything called faculty development. I think we succeed because we have never openly confronted the taboo. At the same time, we pay the price of being inhibited in advertising what we accomplish for faculty in terms of improved teaching and research abilities. To drama-

tize what FLC does for faculty is to suggest that there are things that indeed need to be done, which in turn will invite a backlash effect, determined to deny that any need exists at all. So I am not quite sure how far to go in emphasizing how much the faculty members who participate in FLC benefit from the experience...." The Harvard Graduate School of Business Administration makes very large efforts to prepare neophyte faculty members as teachers by the case method, under the guidance of experienced practitioners of the art. See C. Roland Christensen, *Teaching by the Case Method* (Cambridge, Mass.: Harvard Business School Press, 1982).

To be sure, research-oriented institutions sometimes seek to recognize outstanding teachers by prizes or awards for "best teacher of the year"; for the most scholarly faculty, such an award may be a mixed blessing. President John Silber at Boston University initiated some University Professorships granted to faculty members considered to be outstanding teachers, who did not necessarily have a record of scholarly publishing. To pay outstanding teachers, particularly those who act as tacit or overt mentors to other teachers, a great deal more in research-oriented colleges and universities, either in salary or in terms of teaching loads reduced in formal terms of credit hours, would excite the same envies and antagonisms as merit pay in precollegiate education. See, for interesting analogies, Sherwin Rosen, "The Economics of Superstars," *The American Scholar,* Autumn 1983, *52* (4), 449–461.

15. As faculty in state institutions resort increasingly to collective bargaining, contact hours and student loads may become part of the collective bargaining agreement, reducing still further individual decisions concerning the appropriate levels of effort that a group of colleagues will accept and, it is hoped, approve.

16. Nancy Lowry, dean of the School of Natural Science at Hampshire College, contends in a letter that for her colleagues their labor-intensive teaching is more rewarding than unproductive. In such settings, as in all settings, there is considerable variation among teachers in the extent to which they are easily or rarely discomfited, wounded, or challenged by student

indifference and the extent to which they are anxious about what students are learning and what they are presenting—all the varieties of energy, experience, character, and temperament that differentiate teachers' lives under seemingly equitable conditions.

17. For a brief discussion concerning the impact of the faculty union on an innovative program in music at Florida State University, see David Riesman, "Opportunities and Vicissitudes of a Curriculum of Attainments Program: A Case Study of the Florida State University, 1973-1977," in Gerald Grant and others, *On Competence: A Critical Analysis of Competence-Based Reforms in Higher Education* (San Francisco: Jossey-Bass, 1979).

18. In some selective liberal arts colleges, the taboo against showing off is so powerful that students fare badly when they must make a presentation of self in coming before a regional Rhodes Scholarship Committee or when they go for a job interview or an interview for admission to a favorite professional school. In such colleges even today, any noticeable elegance of dress and demeanor would mark one down as a prig or a preppie.

19. When I was at the University of Chicago, two sociologically minded historians who worked together and published jointly were regarded with some distaste by many of their colleagues, who viewed any departure from the norm of work by individual scholars as a concession to American corporate vulgarity.

20. I write here on the basis of the Gamson and associates volume and also on the basis of interviews with a former leading faculty member in the program. Nancy Lowry in a letter declares that the science program at Hampshire College develops high morale in part because of the admirable effort of bringing women undergraduates into science and into comfort with quantitative work.

21. There are two kinds of exceptions. One is the recruitment of a small research team, particularly in the natural sciences, where research is the priority and teaching is secondary. The other is the increasing willingness and indeed requirement

of finding positions for both members of a two-career family, who are on rare occasions placed in the same department, though this is certainly not the preferred mode, even now.

22. St. John's College, which has no faculty ranks, does elevate the most highly regarded and senior teachers to the status of Archons, that is, mentors for their fellow teachers. See Gerald Grant and David Riesman, "The Telic Reforms: St. John's and the Great Books," *The Perpetual Dream: Reform and Experiment in the American College* (Chicago: University of Chicago Press, 1978, pp. 40-77).

23. For details, see David Riesman, "Can We Maintain Quality Graduate Education in a Period of Retrenchment?" Second David D. Henry Lecture, University of Illinois at Chicago Circle, April 29, 1975.

Index